MY NEW
Mediterranean
COOKBOOK

ALSO BY JEANNETTE SEAVER

JEANNETTE'S SECRETS OF EVERYDAY GOOD COOKING
SOUPS
THE (ALMOST) NO CHOLESTEROL GOURMET COOKBOOK

MY NEW
Mediterranean
COOKBOOK

Eat Better, Live Longer by Following the
Mediterranean Diet

Jeannette Seaver

Illustrations by Nathalie Seaver

Arcade Publishing
New York

FIRST EDITION

Library of Congress Cataloging-in-Publication Data

Seaver, Jeannette.
  My new Mediterranean cookbook : eat better, live longer by following the Mediterranean diet / by Jeannete Seaver. — 1st ed.
      p. cm.
  ISBN 1-55970-723-2
1. Cookery, Mediterranean. I. Title.

TX725.M35S42 2004
641.59'1822—dc22   2004009483

Published in the United States by Arcade Publishing, Inc., New York

Distributed by Time Warner Book Group

Visit our Web site at www.arcadepub.com

10 9 8 7 6 5 4 3 2 1

Designed by Charles Rue Woods

PRINTED IN CANADA

To Dick, who has been my supreme inspiration culinarily, editorially,
and in all aspects of my life. And to Nathalie, my delicious illustrator;
Alexander, Nicholas, Bill, Christine, and Michelle,
who by their high standards, love of food, and positive input
have also contributed to make this book better.
And to my darling Jack, Brendan, Maggie, and Kelly,
whose keen palates have also been an important barometer for me.

Contents

xv INTRODUCTION

FIRST COURSES

Seafood

2 Basket of Young Fresh Vegetables with an
   Anchovy Cream *(Anchoiade)*
4 Shrimp and White Beans in a Rosemary and
   Thyme Vinaigrette, with Lemon and
   Shallot Gremolata
5 Quenelles of Pike or Shrimp
9 Chicory with Two Salmons, Shrimp, and
   Mussels
10 Tunisian Briks with Salmon, Capers, and Egg
12 Taramasalata
12 Scallop Kabob with Beet Hummus
14 Terrine of Monkfish with Green Sauce
16 Tuna Tartare with a *Différence*
17 Antipasto of Red Peppers and Anchovies

Soups

18 Gazpacho
19 Chilled Cream of Green Pea Soup
20 White Gazpacho with Almonds and Grapes
21 Beet Gazpacho
22 Cappuccino of Squash and Porcini
23 Gwen's Caviar Soup
24 Cream of Sorrel Soup
25 Provençal Garlic and Sage Consommé
   with a Float of Poached Egg
26 Jill's Cold Zucchini Soup with Chutney
28 Leek and Potato Soup
29 Tomato Soup with Puff Pastry
30 Cream of Watercress Soup, Cold, with Caviar
31 Cream of Yellow Pepper Soup, Cold
32 Egyptian Green Herb Soup
32 Cold Greek Cucumber Soup
33 Cream of Artichokes, Cold
34 Cream of Chervil, Cold
34 Fennel Soup with Goat-Cheese Toasts
35 Cream of Parsnip Soup with Truffles, Hot

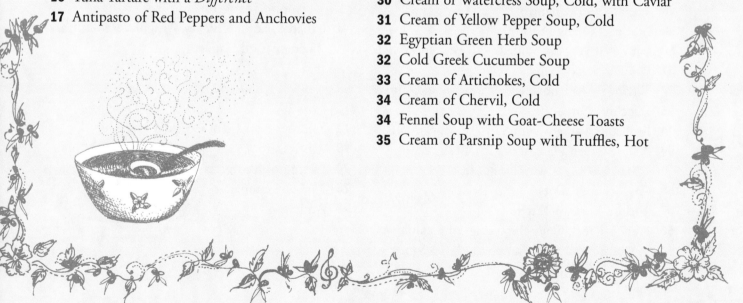

Vegetables

36 Slowly Roasted Tomatoes
37 Eggplant Caviar
38 Provençal Gâteau of Vegetables and Eggs
39 Greek Purée of Lima Beans with Garlic and
    Olive Oil
40 Cucumber in Yogurt
40 Gâteau of Eggplant
42 Ragout of Artichokes
43 Ragout of Baby Carrot, Green Peas, Snap Peas,
    Leek, and Tiny Potato
44 Artichoke Hearts Braised in White Wine
45 Baked, Stuffed Artichokes
46 Black-Olive Tart
47 Dandelion Salad with New Potatoes and
    Bacon
48 Red Beet and Leek Mimosa
49 Radish Vinaigrette
49 Tomato with Cilantro
50 Beet and Orange Salad
50 Baby Bell Peppers Stuffed with Feta and Olives
51 Pita Crackers
52 Terrine of Artichoke with Tarragon and Chives
53 Zucchini Carpaccio
54 Broiled Asparagus with Shiitake Mushrooms
54 A Very Green Plate of French Green Beans
    and Asparagus with Fresh Herbs
56 Carpaccio of Beets
57 Turkish Tomato Tartare
58 French-Greek Cold Dumplings of Cauliflower
    Mousse in a Feta Cheese and Herb Sauce

59 Pear, Arugula, Blue Cheese, and Walnut
    Vinaigrette
60 Terrine of Ratatouille
61 Endive, Toasted Walnuts, and Roquefort Salad
62 Beet Tartare
63 Chicory with Warm Goat Cheese and Bacon
64 Stuffed Zucchini Blossoms with Red-Pepper
    Coulis
66 Little Round Zucchini Stuffed with a Tomato-
    Basil Granita
67 Sicilian Salad of Lemon and Artichoke
68 Middle Eastern Salad of Tomato, Black Olives,
    Cucumber, and Feta Cheese
68 Radishes Served Mickey's Way
70 Oranges and Black-Olive Salad, Moroccan
    Style
70 Fennel Salad with Roasted Walnuts in a
    Lemon Vinaigrette
71 Italian Salad of Chicory, Arugula, Radicchio,
    Lemon, and Capers

Meat

72 Mickey's Mousse of Chicken Livers
73 Rillettes
74 Gâteau of Marinated Chicken in Aspic
75 Pâté de Campagne
78 Antipasto

MAIN COURSES

Seafood

79 Shrimp, Spanish Style, on a Griddle

80 Shrimp in a Piperade Sauce, Basque Style

81 Spaghetti with Clams

81 Nathalie's Salmon on a Bed of Smoked-Eggplant
    Caviar with a Julienne of Cucumber

84 Halibut in a Crown of Stuffed and Baked
    Vegetables

86 Gratin of Fresh Cod with Spinach and
    Anchovies

87 Broiled Trout

88 Stuffed Squid

90 Trout with Sorrel

91 Salmon and Olive Tart

92 Fillets of Salmon, à la Bourguignonne

93 Gratin of Cod with Leek, Olives,
    and Truffle (optional)

94 Gigot of Monkfish

95 Salmon with Onion Confit, Spanish Style

96 Fillets of Skate in an Oyster Emulsion,
    on a Bed of Spinach

97 Grilled Snapper with Chili and Garlic

98 Salmon in Cabbage Purses on a Bed of
    Roasted Vegetables

99 Tiger Shrimp with Feta and Tomato

100 Spanish Tiger Shrimp with Cream, Lemon,
    Chili, and Pappardelle

101 Angel Hair with Trout Caviar

102 Le Grand Aioli

103 Grilled Sea Bass with Fennel and Herbs

104 Bouillabaisse

108 Cod Purée with Garlic and Truffles

Meatless

110 Leek Tart

111 Galette of Potatoes and Wild Mushrooms

112 Roast Portobello Mushrooms with Gremolata

112 Soupe au Pistou

114 Eggplant Roulades

116 Eggplant Cutlets Milanese with a Yogurt Sauce

118 Morel and Truffle Tart

119 Lemon and Artichoke Risotto

Meat

120 Moroccan Lamb Meat Balls with Prunes and Almonds

122 Chicken Tagine with Preserved Lemons and Olives

123 Greek Pork Loin in a Dried Figs Sauce

124 Chicken Bouillabaisse

126 Cassoulet

130 Marinated Grilled Rabbit in a Mustard Sauce

131 Broiled Duck Breasts with Grilled Peaches

132 Roast Leg of Lamb Provençal with Pastis-Pernod Flambé

133 Roast Chicken with 40 Caramelized Garlic Cloves

134 Roast Chicken with 50 Garlic Cloves

134 Roast Chicken in "Mourning Clothes"—with Truffle

135 Roast Squab with Olives

136 Moussaka

137 Moussaka of Artichoke and Veal

138 Greek Roasted Lamb Stuffed with Baby Spinach, Dill, and Feta Cheese

140 Beggar's Purses of Stuffed Chicken

141 Grand Pot-au-Feu with Warm Marrow Brioches

144 Rack of Lamb

145 Couscous of Lamb and Chicken

146 Harissa

148 Molded Egyptian Baked Rice Stuffed with Chicken and Mushrooms with a Turkish Walnut Sauce

150 Roasted Cornish Game Hens with Fresh Figs

151 Lamb Stew, Avignon Style

152 Turkish Lamb Dumplings with a Yogurt Sauce

154 Stuffed Crown Roast of Pork

156 Broiled Chicken with Rosemary and Lemon

156 Polenta Squares with Sautéed Swiss Chard, Broccoli Rabe, and Pancetta

158 Daube of Venison

160 An Italian Slow-Roasted Pork Shoulder

162 Individual Beef Wellingtons

164 Duck Confit

165 Pork Tonnato

166 Coq au Vin

Vegetables

167 Braised Endives

168 Zucchini Alfredo Topped with Onion Rings

169 Spinach, Mediterranean Style

170 Zucchini Cakes, Greek Style

171 Roasted Mediterranean Vegetables

172 Broccoli with a Zing

172 Casserole of Zucchini and Tomatoes

173 Carrots Provençal

174 Swiss Chard Cakes

175 The Fabulous *Purée Blanche* (Mashed Celeriac, Turnip, Garlic, Onion, and Potato)

176 Roasted Radicchio

177 Purée of White Beans with Anchovies

178 Tomato Tart

178 Gratin of Swiss Chard and Asparagus

179 Braised Fennel

180 Casserole of Red Peppers Stuffed with Anchovies

181 Casserole of Eggplant, Tomato, and Chickpeas, Tunisian Style

182 Eggplant Fritters

183 Mushroom Flan

184 Spinach Dumplings

185 Cèpes, Mushroom, and Potato Ragout

Salads

186 Baby Spinach Salad with Croutons

187 Chicory Salad

187 Nathalie's Mint and Dill Salad with Mesclun

188 Arugula with Orange Slices and Red Onion, in a Lemon Vinaigrette

188 Boston Lettuce with Lemon Vinaigrette and Chives

189 Endive Salad

189 Endive, Watercress, and Beet Salad

190 Watercress Salad

190 Chicory Salad with Roasted Shallots and Walnuts

DESSERTS

raspberry tart

192 Roasted Peaches with Verbena

193 Bananas Flambées

193 Broiled Pineapple Slices with Brown Sugar

194 Chocolate and Strawberry Napoleon

195 Apricot Crumble

196 Cantaloupe with Beaume de Venise or Any
    Other Dessert Wine of Your Choice

197 Raspberry Tart with Vanilla Custard

198 Rhubarb and Strawberry Soup with White
    Peaches

198 Tarte Tropézienne

200 Almond Tart with Strawberries

201 Apricot Tart

202 Amazing Lemon Macaroon Torte

203 Blueberry Crumble

204 Sinful, Flourless, Almond Chocolate Cake

206 Watermelon, Cantaloupe, and Honeydew
    with Ginger

206 Floating Islands

208 Cold Little Grapefruit Soufflés

209 Cherry *Clafoutis*

210 Apple Tart

211 Strawberry Soup with Raspberries

212 Panna Cotta with Sliced Peaches and
    Blackberry Coulis

213 Orange Slices in a Red Wine

214 Plum Tatin

215 Lemon Cake with Amaretto Cream and
    Strawberries and Raspberries

216 Poached Pears in Wine Sauce
    with Pear Wafers Dipped in Chocolate

217 Napoleon of Almond Wafers with Raspberries

218 Raspberry Tart

219 Plum Compote and Plum Sorbet

220 Lemon Tart

222 Grapefruit Sorbet

222 Almond Lace Cookies

223 Rhubarb Tart

224 Vacherin of Meringue with Raspberries

225 Cold Lime Soufflés

226 Fruit Salad

226 Bleu, Blanc, Rouge Tart

227 Sour Cherry Compote

228 Gratin of Baked Raspberries

228 Platter of Sliced Fresh Fruit with a Chocolate
Sauce

229 Gratin of Peaches

230 "Petits Pots" of Chocolate-Mocha Mousse

230 Broiled Fresh Figs with Honey

231 An Italian Pear Tart

232 Grape *Clafoutis* (Custard with Grapes)

232 Plum Compote with a Meringue Topping

233 Apples in a Hood

234 Blackberry Tart

235 Soufflé Omelette with Grand Marnier

236 Poached Peaches with Lemon Verbena

236 Dacquoise

239 MENUS

245 INDEX

Introduction

That gastronomy has long been considered not only an art but a supreme art, one pleasing to all the senses, has long been known. For centuries, however, that art was restricted to the happy few—royalty and aristocrats whose cooks outdid themselves to please their demanding masters. In France, there are stories of kings who arrested, or even murdered, aristocrats whose cuisines dared rival, or even excel, the royal table.

Since the late eighteenth century, however, an irreversible gastronomic democratization has taken place. Today, everyone has the possibility of cooking well. Firmly established culinary institutes have sprouted everywhere; and a plethora of cookbooks, food magazines, television food channels, newspaper columns devoted to food and wine, and the thousands of new restaurants that open their doors each year the world over, all are a growing confirmation that eating well is definitely one of today's high priorities.

Although a successful career as an artist per se may not be given to everyone, in each of us lies that little creative element—often hidden and just waiting to be tapped. Planning, preparing, and serving attractive and succulent food—also an act of giving—helps fulfill that creative side of us. For me, cooking represents both a means of tapping into my imagination and indulging those around me. What I find difficult to understand is hearing people declare, as if proudly, "I don't cook!" or, "I don't have time to cook!"—often citing work as a deterrent. I work full-time, yet I have found that with a little planning, cooking, and cooking well, is easier than you think.

The impulse for this book came from two sources: first, I have lived and cooked "Mediterranean" for many years, and this is my personal selection of favorite recipes— which I hope explains the "My" in the title. Second, recent medical studies have further confirmed the important health and life-enhancing aspects of the Mediterranean diet, which only reinforced my desire to put this collection together.

This cookbook emanates essentially from two sources. First, since my most recent cookbook, *The (Almost) No Cholesterol Gourmet Cookbook,* whenever I served a course my guests particularly enjoyed, they would inevitably ask: "Is that in your cookbook?" Nine times out of ten the answer was "no," and as time went on I began to make notes of those dishes that had elicited more than faint praise and toss those recipes in a box marked "special."

Second, since the publication of my first cookbook, *Jeannette's Secrets of Everyday Good Cooking,* more than twenty-five years ago, I have spent a great deal of time in our house in Provence and traveled extensively through the entire Mediterranean basin, tasting and enjoying their specialties and, increasingly, recreating them at home. Soon, my "special" box became overwhelmingly "Mediterranean" oriented. Sifting through the mounting pile, some finger-smeared and yellowed with age, I separated them into two batches, "Mediterranean" and "Other." The "Mediterranean" pile, it turned out was almost three times the "Other." So I began looking through the former to cull my favorites. Despite their distinct cultural identities, I have found that all these sun-drenched coastal regions and countries—from southern France, Spain, Italy, Sicily, Greece, Turkey, Tunisia, Morocco, Israel, and the Middle East—share many common points in their cuisines, namely fish, fresh fruit and vegetables, legumes, wonderfully aromatic herbs that grow in such abundance, and, happily, wine with meals.

In Provence itself, known as France's orchard, in spring and summer the air is heavy with the scent of its seasonal fruit, the perfume of the ubiquitous lavender, and its rich variety of wild herbs—thyme, rosemary, sage, basil—which overwhelm you as you stroll through the redolent streets and markets.

In whatever Mediterranean city, town, or village I happen to be, as I wander through the fragrant rows of fresh produce, basket in hand, I invariably find myself smiling, and have an instant desire to buy and prepare virtually everything I see: the beautiful fish fresh from the sea; the baskets of olives, each cured in different spices; the fabulous white asparagus, the plump bright red tomatoes; the thin *haricots verts,* tender French beans that I have repeatedly brought back to the States and tried to grow here, with limited success; the sinfully seductive, ever-expanding variety of cheeses; the mountains of melons, strawberries, raspberries, and peaches—both white and yellow—whose perfume fills the air. This daily feast for the senses constantly turns my head and, I am sure, would that even of the most novice cook. Invariably, I purchase far more than I need. Who can resist the explosion of color and fragrance in this blessed part of the world? Part of the reason, I'm sure, is that wandering through local outdoor markets, where the farmers not only vocalize their fare, but often take time to give you a recipe or two is so much more colorful, personal, and seductive than buying food in impersonal supermarkets, so often stocked with foodstuff picked or plucked days if not weeks before, and transported for thousands of miles to their destinations. One need only recall those winter peaches that look so enticing in their crates—but whose flesh is as rock-hard as it is tasteless—or those out-of-season pinkish monstrosities that parade as strawberries but taste like sawdust if they taste at all.

One of the virtues—and glories—of Mediterranean food is that it is seasonal and invariably *fresh*. I have been dockside early morning in half a dozen Mediterranean countries and witnessed the fishermen arrive with their silver catch glistening in the sun. You know that within hours of the catch it will be served on the tables of the region, whether in homes or in restaurants. I will never forget one evening at the Miramar, one of the terrace restaurants directly in the old port in Marseilles, watching two fishermen, their heavy boots squishing with every step, carrying a huge pot half-filled with sea water and swarming with fish—their catch of the afternoon—heading directly for the kitchen. Forty-five minutes later, one of the best bouillabaisses ever arrived steaming at our table.

If I were asked for the second most important ingredient of the Mediterranean cuisines—freshness being the first—I would say without hesitation: *enjoyment*. Wherever I have traveled through this part of the world, I have always been struck by the postcard — perhaps clichéd—image of people sitting convivially on sun-drenched restaurant terraces, indulging heartily and unhurriedly in the local food and wine, laughing, gesticulating, and talking animatedly, which to me is a colorful confirmation of that ebullient, ongoing celebration—a contagious sense of gastronomic entitlement that seems to permeate the entire Mediterranean region.

Lunch that starts at 12:30 or 1 P.M. and ends at 4 P.M. is not uncommon. (One has only to spend some time in Spain to know that dinner often starts at 10 P.M. and ends well after midnight.) "How do these people manage to get any work done?" foreigners often ask. "How is it, given the lengthy lunches and dinners, that most Europeans aren't obese?" The fact is, most Mediterraneans are far trimmer than their northerly neighbors, and far, far thinner than their American counterparts. One answer may be: Leisurely is better than rushed. Despite its encroachment, American-style fast food is anathema to most people in the region. Another answer is that meals may be lengthy but portions tend to be smaller, and, too, wine in moderation, especially red, seems to have a definite therapeutic effect.

There is, of course, another reason to eat as the Mediterraneans do: your health. Over the past three decades or so, various studies have shown that people of the Mediterranean basin tend to be to be healthier and live longer than the rest of the Western world. They also have fewer heart attacks and a far lower incidence of cancer.

Since there are sixteen countries that border the Mediterranean, each with its own culture and cuisine, economy, and varying agriculture, there is obviously no one "Mediterranean diet." But they all share some basic characteristics:

- olive oil (rather than butter) as a primary fat source
- high intake of fruits, vegetables, bread, potatoes, legumes, unrefined, wholegrain foods, nuts, and seeds
- moderate consumption of cheese and yogurt
- fish at least twice a week
- moderate amounts of poultry
- little consumption of red meat (and that mostly lamb)
- eggs two to four times a week
- wine with meals, again in moderation

As I have said, what I have tried to do here is share with the reader recipes I have culled in the course of my travels around the Mediterranean basin. (Since I was born and raised in France and, over the past two decades, spent a great deal of time in my house in the Vaucluse region of Provence, the reader may find a disproportionate number of southern French recipes in this book, but all, or virtually all, are consistent with the broad outlines of the health-oriented Mediterranean diet.)

Most of the elements that make up the Mediterranean diet are readily available in America at most major supermarkets or your local grocer. That in itself is a comment on how extraordinarily American culinary tastes have broadened and become sophisticated over the past few decades.

The recipes in this book focus on ingredients that go into making up the dishes that people in the Mediterranean region savor daily. I have also tried to emphasize the gourmet rather than the mundane—I didn't feel the world needed one more recipe for tomato and mozzarella though I often enjoy it very much. In all cases, despite the gourmet aspect of some of the recipes, I have endeavored, as I have in all my earlier cookbooks, to make the preparations as simple and easy as possible. Most—if you discount the time it takes an ingredient to marinate, refrigerate, or simmer—can be made in a reasonably short time. I believe all will prove rewarding, both in the making and in the eating.

"The discovery of a new dish does more for human happiness than the discovery of a star," noted Brillat-Savarin, the legendary nineteenth-century French writer—the first to write about food. A poetic statement and a slight exaggeration, no doubt, but not that far from the mark if one loves food as much as I and so many of my friends do. Unquestionably, I derive great pleasure in probing each day a little more the seemingly endless variety of Mediterranean cuisine.

A study conducted by a research team led by Dr. Dimitros Trichopoulos, a professor at the Harvard School of Public Health, and published in late June 2003, came up with some extraordinary new statistics confirming and further pinpointing the positive results of "eating Mediterranean." Over four years, some 22,000 adults, ranging in age from 20 to 86, adhered—to varying degrees—to the Mediterranean diet. Working on a ten-point scale that gauged adherence to the "diet," researchers found that even an increase of two points on that scale led to a 25 percent reduction in over-all death rates! Breaking things down further, the study determined that following a Mediterranean culinary regime led to a 33 percent reduction in coronary heart disease and a 24 percent reduction in death from cancer. Remarking on these "substantial and impressive" statistics, Dr. Trichopoulos noted: "It shows you what diet can accomplish." Taken as a whole, the Mediterranean way of eating works for the people of the region . . . and it should work for you.

Despite all the meticulous and lengthy studies, however, no one to this day has been able to determine *which* Mediterranean ingredients are responsible for the astonishing results. Is it the olive oil? The olives? The garlic? The fish? The cheeses? The fresh fruit and vegetables? The yogurt? The wine? What we do know is that all the ingredients mentioned above contribute to some degree not only by themselves but in combination. Generally speaking, however, we can say that the prevalence of garlic and onions in Mediterranean cuisine is one factor, for both foods have long been touted as healthy for the heart. The emphasis on fresh fruit and vegetables is also key. Tomatoes, for instance, are rich in both vitamin A and C, also contain lycopene, an active antioxidant that reduces the risk of prostate and breast cancers. And fresh tomatoes contain more lycopene than the hothouse variety.

Fish? Mediterraneans eat some form of fish, which is rich in unsaturated fats and reported to reduce both heart disease and strokes, at least two or three times a week—and so should you. This said, a word to the wise on tuna, an excellent, high-protein source of the omega-3 fatty acids, which are believed to reduce heart disease. Recent government advisories about mercury levels in albacore tuna have caused many to avoid that most popular fish. Although these advisories should not be ignored, they should not be exaggerated as they were especially aimed at children, pregnant women, and women who want children—and even those categories were advised to eat albacore tuna—not all fish—no more than twice a week, very much in keeping with the guidelines of the Mediterranean diet. I maintain that fish should remain part of any healthy diet.

And then the matter of wine. Vintner friends of mine—wine merchants as well—rejoiced when, a few years ago, statistics indicated that wine, in moderation, is good for your health. Red wine especially: it apparently lowers the incidence of both heart attacks and strokes, and, one study suggests, sharpens the synapses in older people. Here again, moderation is the key.

In this book, following a basic tenet of the Mediterranean diet, I use olive oil where butter or some other saturated fat might be called for in Western cooking. Olive oil, rich in vitamin E, is not only a staple of the Mediterranean region but also, as a monounsaturated lipid (fat), does not raise cholesterol levels the way saturated fats do. Still, "fat is fat" and an excess of fat under whatever name can lead to weight increase, an obvious deterrent to good health. "Watch your portion size," notes Samantha Heller, a senior clinical nutritionist at New York Medical Center in New York City. "Even if you eat healthy food you still have to watch out for how *much* you eat."

I want to add, however, that though health is very important—and indeed a key element here—this is not a diet book. It merely and basically reflects what I have enjoyed, eaten, and cooked through the years. I have attempted to make each of these recipes succulent and temptingly delicious as I could, for since my first cookbook I have believed and maintained that eating, and eating well, is one of life's greatest gifts.

Another key factor—one that has been a guiding light in my life—needs to be mentioned. At the risk of proselytizing, I cannot overstate the importance of approaching each meal, however modest, as a daily, pleasurable ceremony. The simple act of sitting down to dinner—formally or not—with a candle or two, facing your partner or surrounded by members of family as you offer the bounties of your kitchen, elevates what would otherwise be an uninteresting, functional activity to a bonding moment. Most people do make an extra effort when they entertain, both culinarily and in the presentation. My point—and one my husband and I have unfailingly practiced over many decades virtually every day of our lives (we have undoubtedly kept the candle industry afloat with our taper consumption through the years)—is to apply the same special effort, the same celebratory thrust and joy on a daily basis, with those who share your life, making the mundane special. To me, it's a way of paying homage to a relationship, of momentarily chasing away nagging concerns, of developing as well as satisfying one's palate. Even when our children were small, we generally joined forces at dinner to exchange thoughts and ideas, discuss the day's problems, large and small. As the children grew older, we invited them to be present when we had guests, even (especially) important ones—mostly writers and artists. Now, years later, our children tell us how important those moments of food and talk were to them.

With a modicum of planning, you should be able to participate fully in and enjoy your own dinner party. Most of my recipes can be prepared largely in advance, thus keeping you from disappearing for any length of time before dinner—leaving guests behind with a touch of guilt "for all the work you're doing alone in the kitchen." "Avoid being confined to stove duties while everyone else is having fun in the living-room," has been my life-long culinary motto, and should be your Number-One-Rule-of-Entertaining as well! I guarantee you'll find that advance preparation is easy to organize and will be your best friend in preparing a dinner party.

Finally, I wish you happy reading, but most of all happy eating!

MY NEW
Mediterranean
COOKBOOK

FIRST COURSES

Through the ages, meals of virtually every cuisine — no matter its ethnic origin — have begun with a first course that the French call entrée (entry), for it actually opens the way to what is to follow. The Italians often have two "first courses," antipasto, *primi piatti*, usually some pasta, and sometimes even *secondo piatti* prior to serving their main course. In Spain, they have *tapas*. The Middle-Eastern/Arab cuisine features its famous *mezes* — a quantity of small platters offering a variety of salads and fish preparations.

The great chefs who have made their mark throughout the history of gastronomy prided themselves in creating dishes so elaborate and so substantial it defies today's perception of eating. The privileged class, whose personal cooks constantly attempted to out-create their peers, and who heartily indulged in multi-course feasts, didn't have to work and went straight to take their siesta after each meal.

Times have changed, and so have culinary approaches to menus. Today's increasing sensitivity to health awareness has made the new food gurus trim down yesteryear's feasts. If first courses are still very much here today, they are, however, far lighter and served in more modest quantities than in the past.

I do feel that a savory, light first course should stimulate the taste buds, whet the appetite, and act as a friendly, tasty prelude to any good meal.

In this section of the book I offer four categories of first courses: seafood, soups, vegetables, and meat. In keeping with the principles of the Mediterranean diet, I have limited the number of meat first courses, and emphasized the soups and vegetable recipes. There is also a fair selection of seafood offerings, all of which can serve as lunches or main courses, as directed.

SEAFOOD FIRST COURSES

Basket of Young Fresh Vegetables with an Anchovy Cream (*Anchoïade*)

This colorful palette of fresh, new vegetables, presented in a basket and served with a delicious anchovy cream — the *anchoiade* — is among Provence's most popular and traditional first courses. The combination of vegetable crunch and the bite of anchovy cream is a perfect opener to any meal.

In America, raw vegetables with a dip are most often offered at cocktail time, but in Provence the anchoiade receives its well-deserved recognition by being formally presented at the table in some attractive arrangement, often on a tray of bark from the olive tree, celebrating the rich Provençal summer harvest. You may choose any number of fresh vegetables to suit your preference. This colorful still life is as pretty as it is appetizing, and will quickly reinforce conviviality around the table. The following recipe is one I have often served, but from which you may vary according to the availability of local vegetables.

FOR THE BASKET

> 4 young carrots, peeled, washed, and left whole with a little stem showing
> 1 celery heart, split in four lengthwise
> 2–3 tomatoes, quartered
> 1 green pepper, washed, seeded, white membrane removed, cut into large sticks
> 1 yellow pepper, washed, seeded, white membrane removed, cut into large pieces
> 1 fennel bulb, trimmed and quartered
> a few white mushrooms
> part of 1 cauliflower, cut up in florets and blanched 2 minutes
> handful French green beans, blanched 2 minutes

Arrange your vegetables artistically in a basket and place on a large platter.

MY ANCHOIADE

Traditionally, the anchoiade is served warm, and kept warm in a small chafing dish at the table. My anchoiade, however, can be enjoyed cold; I find it easier to serve. I have also added a touch of cream cheese, which does not feature in the original Provençal anchoiade recipe, but renders the sauce smoother and, frankly, more delicious. It also has the virtue of taking away some of the saltiness of the anchovies. I prepare it ahead, and keep it refrigerated until shortly before serving.

> 2 jars anchovy fillets (in oil)
> 3 garlic cloves
> 1 tablespoon capers
> 3 ounces cream cheese
> ⅓ cup olive oil

Mash all ingredients to form a thick purée. (I used to do this in a mortar; today, the blender or food processor has proven a faster and more efficient substitute.) You can obviously play with the proportions of ingredients to suit your taste. You might prefer more or less garlic, fewer capers, or more oil to make the sauce more liquid.

Transfer anchoiade to a small crock. Either set anchoiade in the center of the basket of vegetables, or to the side, and serve. SERVES 6–8.

Shrimp and White Beans in a Rosemary and Thyme Vinaigrette, with Lemon and Shallot Gremolata

Both Italy and France share this tasty, simple-to-prepare first course, which also makes a lovely lunch. The gremolata — lemon zest, shallots, and finely chopped parsley — offers an additional aromatic flavor to the salad.

1 cup dried white beans
1 small onion, finely chopped
1 carrot, peeled and sliced
1 leafy celery stalk, peeled, washed, and diced
1 bay leaf
pepper and salt
20 large shrimp
1 shallot, finely chopped
1 cup flat parsley leaves, finely chopped
1 teaspoon finely chopped thyme
½ teaspoon finely chopped rosemary
6 tablespoons olive oil
2 tablespoons balsamic vinegar
watercress sprigs

In a bowl, cover beans with water and let stand overnight. Discard water, and add fresh water, together with onion, carrot, celery, bay leaf, pepper, and salt. Bring to a boil, reduce heat, cover, and cook 40 minutes, until beans are tender but not too soft. If beans are not sufficiently cooked, continue cooking a few more minutes. Drain.

In a saucepan, cover shrimp with water. Bring to a boil and cook 2 minutes. Drain. Remove tails, shells, and devein. Set aside.

In the serving bowl, mix shallot, parsley, thyme, rosemary, olive oil, vinegar, pepper, and salt. Add beans and shrimp and toss. Place some watercress on each plate, and top with one or two tablespoons of beans/shrimp. SERVES 4–6.

FOR THE GREMOLATA
> grated zest of 3 lemons
> 2 shallots, finely chopped
> 1 bunch flat parsley, finely chopped

In a small bowl, combine lemon zest, shallot, and parsley. Sprinkle on salad and serve.

You'll likely have some leftover. Don't worry: it keeps well for up to a week in the refrigerator. SERVES 4–6.

Quenelles of Pike or Shrimp

These extremely elegant quenelles, considered one of French gastronomy's finest and enjoyed throughout the land, are not only reserved to fancy restaurants. These refined dumplings — for want of a better translation — are absolutely doable in your kitchen. Many years ago, when I first attempted to make quenelles — and succeeded — I felt triumphant. What I realized then was that we home chefs, too, could produce the "finest" in our kitchens if only we overcame our initial hesitation.

I have since served quenelles often over the years, and once again I must reassure you: they are not that difficult to prepare! They do demand a little extra preparation time, but if you do it in stages, in the interstices of your schedule, making quenelles will appear easy and certainly rewarding. Make them when you have a quiet moment, a day or two before your dinner. Both the quenelles and the Nantua sauce — the classic sauce made of lobster or fish stock that accompanies quenelles — (see page 7) can be kept refrigerated a few days until final assembling.

From time to time, I alternate and make shrimp quenelles — the recipe is the same, just substitute roughly the same amount of shrimp for the pike. I find, however, that the original recipe with pike has a more subtle taste than that of shrimp, which tends to dominate in flavor.

Tip: Quenelles are served with equal frequency as a main course, or entrée.

There are five stages — or acts — in making quenelles: the panade, the fish mousse, combining the last two into quenelles and poaching them, the Nantua sauce, and the final baking.

ACT ONE

THE PANADE
  1½ cups milk
  2 tablespoons butter
  pinch of salt
  ¾ cup all-purpose flour, sifted
  1 egg

In a small saucepan, heat milk, butter, and salt. Bring to a boil. Turn heat off, and quickly stir flour into milk mixture. Turn heat back on, and stir in egg for 5 seconds. This is called *panade* — the first step to making quenelles. It should look like a doughy batter that is a little solid. Transfer to bowl. Cover and chill 1 hour.

ACT TWO

THE FISH MOUSSE
  12 ounces pike fillets, skinned and cut into pieces, or 12 ounces
      shrimp, deveined
  14 tablespoons butter, melted and cooled
  4 whole eggs
  3 egg whites
  ½ cup heavy cream
  ½ teaspoon nutmeg
  pepper and salt

In the food processor, purée pike or shrimp. Add cooled butter and process until smooth. Blend in the whole eggs, one at a time, then, the additional egg whites. With the processor running, add cream, nutmeg, pepper, and salt. Remove panade from refrigerator and add to processor. Continue puréeing for another minute, until ingredients are well combined. Transfer mixture to large bowl, cover, and refrigerate several hours (or overnight). This is the light dough that will become quenelles.

ACT THREE

MAKING THE QUENELLES

Fill a wide rimmed pan with water and 1 teaspoon salt. Bring to a boil and reduce immediately to simmer.

Remove quenelle dough from refrigerator, and with the help of 2 spoons, form into 4 oblong-shaped quenelles. Roll them in flour and plunge into simmering water. The quenelles will rise to the surface within minutes; continue cooking in simmering water 15 minutes, until they look more solid and hold well together when you touch them — you can check consistency when you turn them over in the water.

Butter 4 individual ovenproof dishes. With a slotted spoon, remove quenelles, drain well, and place 1 quenelle on each prepared dish. Cover with plastic wrap and refrigerate.

ACT FOUR

MAKING THE NANTUA SAUCE

Ever wondered what that sauce was all about when you saw it on restaurant menus? It is the classic, specific sauce used with seafood and is made of strong fish or lobster stock and cream.

2 tablespoons butter
1 shallot, minced
2 tablespoons flour
2 cups half-and-half
1 cup strong fish or lobster stock
4 tablespoons Cognac
pinch of cayenne pepper
pepper and salt

In a small saucepan, heat butter and sauté shallot until light brown. Stir in flour. Gradually pour in half-and-half and stock, stirring all the while until sauce becomes thick and creamy. Add Cognac, cayenne, pepper, and salt. Set aside.

Tip: All preceding "acts" can be made ahead, and kept refrigerated until you're ready to make the quenelles, or you can make the quenelles and refrigerate until you stick them in the oven.

ACT FIVE

THE FINAL BAKING
  prepared quenelles
  3 tablespoons butter, melted
  Nantua sauce

Preheat oven to 350°.
  Remove dishes with quenelles from refrigerator. Drizzle a little melted butter over each quenelle. Bake 12 minutes, until the quenelles swell a little. Remove dishes from oven.
  Pre-heat broiler.
  Pour sauce to cover generously each dish. Place dishes under broiler and broil a few seconds until top bubbles and becomes golden. Serve.

Tip: I often skip the last minute broiling, and simply put the dishes with the sauce back in the oven for a few minutes until top bubbles, and serve.

Note: You will have more quenelles than needed for 4. They freeze well.

Chicory with Two Salmons, Shrimp, and Mussels

Easy and handy (especially when you happen to have some previously baked or poached salmon leftover in your refrigerator), this meal-opener is particularly tasty and light. If you don't have leftover salmon, simply buy half a pound fresh salmon. Squeeze some lemon juice on it, wrap fish in foil, and bake 10 minutes in a 350° oven. Cool. Set aside for later.

> 12 mussels, scrubbed
> ½ glass white wine
> salt and pepper
> 12 shrimp
> 1 small shallot, minced
> 1 tablespoon Dijon mustard
> juice of 1 lemon
> 4 tablespoons olive oil
> 1 head of chicory, discard dark leaves and retain only white and
>   yellow part, washed and dried
> 2 tablespoons pine nuts, toasted
> 1 cup cooked salmon, cut into small pieces

In a kettle, put mussels with ½ glass white wine. Cover and cook 5-10 minutes, shaking the kettle until mussels open. Cool. Discard shells and liquid. Reserve mussels.

In a small pan, bring ¼ cup water to a boil and ½ teaspoon salt, and cook shrimp 3 minutes. Turn off heat. Transfer shrimp into a bowl of ice water. Drain. Peel, devein.

In a small bowl, combine shallot, mustard, lemon juice, olive oil, pepper, and salt. Distribute chicory among four plates and sprinkle dressing over chicory. Top chicory with pieces of salmon, and the mussels, shrimp, and pine nuts. Pour a few drops of vinaigrette over seafood and fish and serve.

Tip: If you are cooking salmon fresh, do it while mussels are opening in the kettle — they'll be ready at the same time. SERVES 4–6.

Tunisian Briks with Salmon, Capers, and Egg

From Tunisia, *brik* is a crisp "cushion" of light pastry — filo dough — stuffed with different fillings: crabmeat, shrimp, tuna, salmon, anchovies, ham, even an egg; capers, and herbs, and then fried or baked. I found it just as tasty baked. In the fried version, however, nothing is more pleasantly surprising than that first bite of crisp dough followed by the taste of warm capers and flakes of salmon or shrimp, and all of a sudden, a sunny-side-up egg peeks through it all. The egg cooks while the brik fries, and makes this dish particularly seductive. For me, Tunisian brik ranks among the most delectable first courses of the Mediterranean region.

The only slightly negative consideration in cooking this Tunisian delicacy, in my view, is that it demands to be cooked at the very last minute, which, for me, limits the offering to only four or, at most, six guests. Even after preparing most of the briks ahead, i.e., filling the pastries, covering them with a damp cloth, and keeping them refrigerated until frying time, you will need to absent yourself from your guests and stand by the stove minding the frying — 1–2 minutes for each side of each brik. Since only a few can be fried at a time, you'll have to drain the first batch, and repeat until all briks are cooked while your guests are having fun without you. So the baked version often replaces the fried one.

Tip: Briks can be baked successfully in an oven preheated to 450° for 10 minutes, until puffed and golden brown. If you decide to include an egg with your choice of filling for the brik, you can no longer include a raw egg, as it would become hard during the baking. Instead, scramble 2 eggs ahead, let them cool, and divide the scrambled eggs into 4 filo packages with the rest of the filling.

> 4 sheets of filo dough
> egg white for brushing
> 6 ounces salmon, divided in 4 pieces
> 4 anchovy filets
> 2 tablespoons capers
> 4 eggs for the frying version, or 2 scrambled eggs divided in 4 for
>   the baked version
> pepper and salt
> oil for frying, such as peanut or corn oil

Remove 1 filo dough sheet at a time from the package, keeping remaining sheets covered with plastic wrap and a damp cloth. Fold up bottom third of sheet over the middle third; fold top portion over all. You now have a rectangular ribbon of dough. Brush with olive oil.

Divide salmon into four equal portions. Place one fourth in center of filo rectangle, place an anchovy filet over salmon, sprinkle with one fourth of the capers, and break one egg over salmon and capers. (Be careful that the egg doesn't run outside the dough.) Sprinkle with pepper and salt and quickly fold dough from both ends over filling. Seal by pinching with wet fingers. Proceed with the other filo sheets and filling in similar fashion.

Spread salad leaves of your choice on 4 plates.

FOR THE FRIED VERSION:

In a wide kettle, with as wide a rim as you can find — the quantity of briks you'll be able to fry at a time will depend on the width of your kettle — heat the oil. When oil is hot but not smoking, fry briks about 1 minute per side — no more, otherwise your egg will become hard. When one side of brik is golden brown, with the help of a spatula and a fork, turn brik over to the other side. Cook 1 more minute (or less). Drain on paper towels. Sprinkle salt over brik. Continue frying remaining briks in the same way. Put each brik on its bed of salad on a plate and serve immediately. SERVES 4.

Taramasalata

This delicate and soft Greek purée of carp roe is always a winner. *Tarama* — the carp roe — can be found in specialty food stores, and of course in Greek food stores. The milk-soaked bread acts as a binding and neutralizing agent, and it also takes some of the roe's salt away. While already prepared taramasalata can be found in fancy food shops, I recommend, if possible, making it from scratch. It requires very little time, and the result is far superior.

1 (5-ounce) jar carp roe
juice of 1 lemon, plus 1 lemon, cut into wedges
1 cup olive oil, or more if needed
6 slices white sandwich bread or baguette, soaked in milk and
      squeezed
1 small onion, minced
3 ounces cream cheese
pepper and salt
½ cup black Kalamata olives
several slices of pita bread, warmed in the oven

In the food processor, purée carp roe, lemon juice, olive oil, bread, onion, cream cheese, pepper, and salt. Taste; it might require more lemon juice and more olive oil. Be careful with salting; the roe is naturally salted. Your taramasalata should look like a light pink cream. Transfer to serving platter. Garnish with lemon wedges and black olives. Serve with pita bread. SERVES 8–10.

Scallop Kabob with Beet Hummus

This Greek first course, with contrasting flavors and colors, makes an original, colorful opener for any meal.

FOR THE KABOB
8 sea scallops, muscle removed, cut in half
juice of 2 lemons

¼ pound prosciutto di Parma, very thinly sliced
a few sprigs mint
¼ cup olive oil

FOR THE BEET HUMMUS
2 small beets or 1 (7-ounce) can sliced beets, drained
2 slices white bread, soaked in water and squeezed dry
1 garlic clove, minced
juice of 1 lemon
1 bunch cilantro, chopped
½ cup olive oil or more if needed
2 tablespoons tahini (sesame-seed paste, available in specialty shops)
1 teaspoon ground cumin
pepper and salt

Tip: I recommend making the beet hummus first. It should be ready in a serving bowl by the time scallops broil. Scallops take only 5 minutes to cook.

Preheat oven to 350°. Wash and wrap beets in aluminum foil and bake 40 minutes. Cool a little, peel, and slice. In the food processor, purée beets, bread, garlic, lemon juice, cilantro, ½ cup olive oil, tahini, cumin, pepper, and salt. It should become a thick purée, not liquid like a sauce. If you find it too thick, add 1 or 2 tablespoons olive oil and a few drops water until desired consistency. Taste and adjust seasoning. Transfer to serving bowl. Set aside.

Preheat broiler or outside grill. Rinse scallops, pat dry, and place in a bowl. Pour half the lemon juice over scallops. Remove from bowl, and wrap each scallop in a piece of prosciutto. Slip some mint in between scallop and prosciutto.

Thread scallops onto skewers, either on a large skewer or on several smaller ones, place in broiler pan, and drizzle with remaining lemon juice. Brush with olive oil. Place under broiler or over grill and cook 5 minutes, turning skewers and brushing with more olive oil as needed. Serve with beet hummus. SERVES 4.

Terrine of Monkfish with Green Sauce

A slice of this elegant and light terrine is a perfect first course for any meal. The firm consistency of the monkfish gives the illusion of crab or even lobster meat.

Tip: You can, and probably should, make the terrine a day ahead of serving. It yields far more than needed to serve four people, but you can use it for subsequent meals. Covered, it can be kept in the refrigerator for several days.

> salt
> 1½ pounds monkfish filets
> 2 pounds ripe tomatoes, peeled, seeded, and cut into small pieces
> 6 eggs, lightly beaten
> a few sprigs fresh tarragon, stems removed, finely chopped
> pepper
> olive oil for greasing the terrine and parchment paper

Preheat oven to 350°.

In a kettle of simmering salted water, poach fish 5 minutes, until half-cooked. Drain. Cool. Cut fish in 1-inch chunks. Set aside.

In a bowl, gently whisk tomatoes and eggs. Incorporate fish pieces, tarragon, salt, and pepper.

Oil bottom and sides of terrine and fill with fish mixture. Set terrine in a baking dish filled with an inch of water; cover with oiled parchment paper. Bake 45 minutes. Let cool completely. Refrigerate overnight. Meanwhile, make the green sauce.

GREEN SAUCE

There are an infinite variety of green sauces from one Mediterranean country to another and from chef to chef. Some have spinach; others don't. Some feature mainly herbs. Here is one of my favorites. Light and tangy, it goes especially well with the monkfish terrine. Served together, the pinkness of the terrine with the green sauce makes an attractive presentation.

½ (10-ounce) package frozen chopped spinach
3 anchovies
1 garlic clove, minced
juice of 1 lemon
1 cup fresh dill, finely chopped
1 cup water or vegetable stock
½ cup flat parsley, chopped
5 tablespoons olive oil
1 tablespoon capers
pepper and salt

In a kettle, bring 1 cup water to a boil. Cook spinach 3 minutes. Drain in a colander and squeeze all liquid out of spinach by pressing with a fork.

In the food processor, purée all ingredients, reserving 1 teaspoon dill for later. (If you find your green sauce too thick, feel free to add a little water.) Transfer to serving bowl. Top with the reserved dill.

To serve: Remove terrine from refrigerator and run a knife along all sides to loosen it. Place serving platter on top of terrine, flip, and unmold. Refrigerate for at least 4 hours (overnight is better). Bring to the table, slice, and serve 1 or 2 thin slices with some green sauce on the side. SERVES 4–6.

Tuna Tartare with a *Différence*

Because of my predilection for tuna tartare, I often prepare it, and order it frequently in restaurants both here and abroad. When I first sampled this one, at Jean-Georges' restaurant in New York, I found it such a cut above the others that it inspired me — and I am indebted to that wonderful chef — to try it in my own kitchen.

1 avocado, pitted and peeled
juice of ½ lime
1 tablespoon olive oil
pinch of ground cumin
pepper and salt
1 pound fresh tuna — the *very* best quality there is — preferably
    yellow tuna for sushi
¼ small red onion, very finely chopped
2 tablespoons fresh lemon juice
1 teaspoon Worcestershire sauce
pepper and salt

FOR THE GARNISH
10 red radishes, washed and sliced lengthwise
4–5 slices of thin whole wheat bread, cut into triangles, and
    toasted

In a bowl, mash avocado, lime juice, olive oil, cumin, pepper, and salt. Set aside.

With a sharp knife, chop tuna finely. (*Do not* be tempted to use the food processor. Your fish might well turn into soup!) Chopping the tuna is extremely easy, and that process gives you the right consistency for the tartar.

In a bowl, with the help of a fork, mix tuna, onion, lemon juice, and Worcestershire sauce. Adjust seasoning to your taste. Onto the center of individual plates, spread a little mashed avocado. Form tuna patties. Place a tuna patty over the avocado, cover patty with slices of radish, and serve surrounded with pieces of toast.

Make sure the portions are small. Remember, it's only a first act. SERVES 4.

Antipasto of Red Peppers and Anchovies

A familiar feature throughout Italy and Italian restaurants as well as in the south of France, roasted red peppers taste particularly good with anchovies and capers.

> 2 red peppers
> 2 yellow peppers
> 1 small shallot, minced
> freshly ground black pepper
> salt
> 6 ounces good Italian anchovies in oil
> 2 tablespoons capers
> ½ cup fresh basil, chopped
> ½ cup olive oil
> 1 cup black olives

Over a grill, or the flame of the stove, char peppers on all sides. Keep charred peppers sealed in a paper bag 20 minutes.

Under running water, peel charred skin off peppers. Remove white membrane and seeds. Cut peppers into large pieces and place the pieces on a shallow serving platter. Sprinkle peppers with shallot, black pepper, and salt. Top with anchovies, capers, basil, and olive oil. Dot with black olives. SERVES 4–6.

SOUPS FIRST COURSES

Gazpacho

Practically unknown in America until not all that many years ago, this wonderful Spanish cold soup has penetrated American cuisine today to such an extent one can find it in hundreds, if not thousands, of specialty food shops and delis throughout the land. Though store-bought gazpacho is fine, I nonetheless prefer my own fresh variety. Gazpacho is healthy, refreshing, and delectable, and should not be restricted to summer fare. It is a welcome meal opener all year around.

4 tomatoes, peeled and cubed
2 green peppers, washed, seeded, white membrane removed, and
    diced
1 cucumber, peeled and cubed
1 onion, minced
half a baguette, soaked in water until soft, and squeezed a little
    (if you don't have a baguette handy, any bread will do)
juice of 1 lemon
4 cups chicken stock
½ cup olive oil
⅓ cup wine vinegar
1 teaspoon Tabasco sauce
pepper and salt

FOR THE GARNISH
>
> 1 green pepper, washed, seeded, membrane removed, and diced
> 1 tomato, diced
> ½ cucumber, peeled and diced
> bread croutons from 3 slices of French baguette sautéed in
>   olive oil

In the blender, in several batches, purée vegetables, soaked bread, lemon juice, stock, oil, vinegar, and Tabasco. Pour into soup terrine, and with a wooden spoon, mix well. Season with pepper and salt. Cover. Refrigerate overnight if possible — it will bind the various flavors well.

Serve accompanied by several little serving bowls of garnish. SERVES 4–6.

Tip: The gazpacho keeps well for a couple days in the refrigerator.

Chilled Cream of Green Pea Soup

The easiest soup you could ever make, this pea soup distinguishes itself — in the Mediterranean basin — from mother's old favorite by the addition of yogurt and plenty of mint. It also has the virtue of requiring virtually no preparation time.

> 1 (1-pound) package frozen small green peas
> 3 cups chicken stock
> 2 cups plain yogurt
> 1 cup tightly packed fresh mint leaves
> pepper and salt
> 6 scallions, finely chopped

Purée all ingredients except scallions in the blender. Refrigerate. Serve topped with scallions. SERVES 4–6.

White Gazpacho with Almonds and Grapes

With a different taste, this is a slightly more elaborate variation of the more often served red gazpacho. I think you'll find it equally appealing and refreshing.

2 yellow peppers
10 tablespoons olive oil
croutons made from 6 slices bread, cubed
½ teaspoon minced garlic, plus 2 garlic cloves, minced
2 yellow tomatoes, skin removed, cut into small pieces
1 onion, finely chopped
1 turnip, peeled and cut into small pieces
1 seedless cucumber, peeled and cubed
juice of 1 lemon
½ baguette, soaked in water and squeezed
6 cups chicken stock
1 cup slivered almonds
½ cup white vinegar
1 teaspoon chopped fresh tarragon
1 teaspoon Tabasco sauce
pepper and salt
1 cup white seedless grapes, cut in half
½ cup finely chopped chives

Over a grill or the flame of the stove, char peppers on all sides. Keep charred peppers sealed in a paper bag 20 minutes.

Under running water, peel charred skin off peppers. Remove white membrane and seeds, and cut peppers into small pieces. Set aside.

In a skillet, heat 2 tablespoons olive oil and fry croutons until light brown. Turn heat off, and sprinkle croutons with ½ teaspoon minced garlic. Toss, put in a bowl, and set aside.

Reserve ½ cup chopped yellow peppers. Place remainder in a blender and purée with remaining garlic, tomatoes, onion, turnip, cucumber, lemon juice, baguette, stock, ½ cup almonds, vinegar, remaining olive oil, tarragon, Tabasco, pepper, and salt.

Transfer contents of blender into soup terrine. Mix well. If it seems too thick, add a little stock or water. Check seasoning. Chill in the refrigerator at least 4 hours, but preferably overnight. As with the more traditional gazpacho, it will season well. In the toaster-oven, toast remaining almonds. Serve gazpacho topped with reserved yellow peppers, grapes, chives, toasted almonds, and croutons. SERVES 6–8.

Beet Gazpacho

This beet variation on the traditional theme may appear at first glance like cold borscht — it isn't. It doesn't have dill, which is the typical herb for borscht, and has all the gazpacho characteristics from the flavor viewpoint.

2 small beets, baked, peeled, and sliced
1 small red onion, peeled and coarsely chopped
1 green pepper, seeded, white membrane removed
1 cucumber, peeled, seeded, and sliced
juice of 1 lemon
½ baguette, soaked in water and squeezed
4 cups stock (or water)
1 cup cilantro leaves, chopped, plus more to sprinkle on top
½ cup olive oil
½ cup wine vinegar
½ teaspoon Tabasco sauce
pepper and salt
1 hard-boiled egg, chopped "mimosa" style
1 cup bread croutons, fried in olive oil

In the blender, purée all ingredients except extra cilantro, the egg, and croutons. (You will have to do it in batches.) Combine in a soup terrine. Check seasoning and add whatever you think is needed: more pepper, more lemon juice, Tabasco, etc. Refrigerate at least 4 hours (again, overnight is better). Remove from refrigerator, sprinkle with the extra cilantro, the chopped egg, and croutons. SERVES 4–6.

Cappuccino of Squash and Porcini

With its aroma of porcini and truffle cream, this remarkably flavorful soup arrives at the table bubbling in its squash shell, looking oh so elegant, and giving an autumnal air to the dinner. You mustn't limit it, however, to autumn. It makes a festive and unusual opener any time of the year — provided you can find squash.

4 small acorn squash, washed and left whole
1 cup boiling water
½ cup dried porcini
2 tablespoons olive oil
1 medium onion, finely chopped
½ teaspoon grated nutmeg
pinch of curry powder
3 cups chicken stock
2 teaspoons white-truffle cream, or paste, from a tube
pepper and salt
½ cup heavy cream, whipped

Preheat oven to 350°.

Bake directly on oven rack for 50 minutes. Cool 10 minutes. Cut off tops with a sharp knife and reserve. Scoop out insides, discarding threads and seeds, and leaving shells padded with some pulp. Chop coarsely squash meat.

In a small bowl, pour boiling water over porcini and let stand 30 minutes. Drain and reserve liquid. Chop reconstituted porcini.

In a skillet, heat olive oil, and cook onion until light brown. Add chopped squash, nutmeg, half the porcini, and a pinch of curry powder, and continue cooking over low heat another 5 minutes. Turn off heat.

In a blender purée chicken stock, squash/porcini, 1 teaspoon truffle cream, the pepper, and salt. If you find it too thick, add some stock to desired consistency. Transfer to kettle, and keep simmering.

In a small bowl, fold remaining porcini and teaspoonful of truffle cream, and a few drops reserved porcini liquid into the whipped cream.

Ladle hot soup into acorn squash shell, top with a dollop of porcini-flavored cream, and serve with squash top on the side. SERVES 4.

Gwen's Caviar Soup

The trick here, as my friend Gwen Clark, a longtime resident of Provence, once warned me, is to add just enough garlic and curry to give the soup flavor. In as much as adding substance to the flavor, garlic and curry should remain discreet, she said, never intrusive. One should enjoy the "mysterious" flavor without being able to recognize specifically the ingredients. The point, of course, is not to overwhelm the caviar. If your garlic cloves are large, use only one, and adjust final seasoning. The soup must remain indescribable, delicate, and surprising.

> 2 cups plain yogurt
> 2 cups chicken stock
> 2 garlic cloves, minced
> 1 teaspoon curry powder
> pepper and salt
> 1 cup sour cream
> 4 ounces caviar (or black lumpfish roe as substitute)
> ½ cup finely chopped chives

Mix half the yogurt, all the stock, garlic, curry, pepper, and salt in a blender for 2 minutes. Pour into a soup terrine. With a hand whisk, stir in remaining yogurt and the sour cream. Refrigerate 2 hours. Ladle soup into individual soup plates, and top it with a spoonful of caviar or black lumpfish roe. Sprinkle with chives. Serve chilled. SERVES 4.

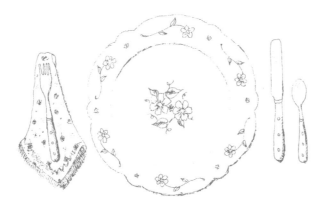

Cream of Sorrel Soup

Sorrel, like spinach, has many virtues — such as vitamin A and iron. Its lemony, tangy flavor gives a nice "kick" to the soup.

⅓ cup olive oil
1 leek, well washed, trimmed of its dark green leaves, and sliced
1 medium onion, minced
6 cups fresh sorrel, washed and coarsely chopped
2 potatoes, cut into small pieces
3 cups chicken stock
2 egg yolks
½ cup heavy cream or nonfat yogurt

In a kettle, heat olive oil. Sauté leek with onion until wilted but not brown. Add sorrel and potatoes and continue cooking 5 minutes. Add stock and 2 cups water, cover and cook another 15 minutes. Turn off heat. Cool. Purée in the blender. Transfer to soup terrine.

In a small bowl, whisk yolks and heavy cream (or yogurt). Pour into soup. (This step makes the sorrel soup silky and delicious, but is, of course, optional. For those with cholesterol issues, you may — no, should — skip this last step.)

Refrigerate 3 or more hours. Serve chilled, garnished with chives. (The soup is also good warm.) SERVES 4–6.

Tip: Nonfat yogurt could (almost) do the trick as well instead of the egg yolk and cream liaison.

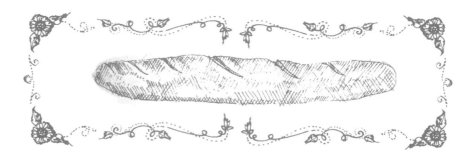

Provençal Garlic and Sage Consommé with a Float of Poached Egg

This is again one of Provence's traditional and elegant offerings. The original recipe calls for serving the consommé with boiled garlic. I prefer to slightly caramelize it. Don't be put off at the thought of so much garlic: it merely flavors the broth. With cooking, garlic loses its pungency and the usual aftertaste.

This soup is easy to prepare — especially if you already have a good consommé stored in your refrigerator (which you always should).

Like any good consommé, this soup is a light meal opener.

salt
15 garlic cloves, peeled
12 sage leaves
5 cups strong beef or chicken consommé
1 teaspoon saffron
pepper
olive oil
4 eggs

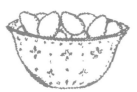

FOR THE GARNISH (OPTIONAL)
1 carrot, cut into very thin strips
1 slice of beef fillet, cut into thin strips (or any leftover meat is fine)
some rose petals, cut into thread-thin strips

In a saucepan, bring 2 cups salted water to a boil and cook garlic 20 minutes. With a slotted spoon, remove garlic and set aside. Add sage to same hot salted water, cover, and let infuse 20 minutes. Discard sage and add saffron and pepper.

In another saucepan, heat a few drops of olive oil and sauté boiled garlic a few minutes, until it turns light brown. Turn off heat and set aside. Bring consommé to a simmering boil.

Poach the eggs in an egg poacher.

Ladle consommé into individual soup plates and add a poached egg and 3 caramelized garlic cloves to each. Sprinkle carrot, meat strips, and rose petal strips around egg. SERVES 4.

Jill's Cold Zucchini Soup with Chutney

Jill Jakes, a former judge who currently raises sheep and a dear friend whom we visited far from the Mediterranean, when zucchini was plentiful — surprised us with this simple, exotic soup which I decided would have been right at home in any part of the Mediterranean world where zucchini abounds. Good cold, the soup can be enjoyed hot as well.

½ cup olive oil
1 large onion, finely chopped
3 medium zucchini, washed, not peeled, and cubed
2 garlic cloves, minced
1 teaspoon ground cumin
½ teaspoon curry powder
4 cups chicken stock
pepper and salt
1 bunch parsley, finely chopped
1 small bunch cilantro, chopped
1 cup yogurt
chutney, recipe follows

In a kettle, heat olive oil and sauté onion until light brown. Add zucchini, garlic, cumin, and curry. Cook 5 minutes over medium heat. Stir in stock. Season with pepper and salt. Cover and continue cooking 10 minutes. Add parsley and cilantro. Remove from heat. Let cool. Purée contents of kettle in a blender. Transfer to bowl, stir in ¾ cup yogurt, adjust seasoning, cover, and refrigerate until cold.

Ladle soup into each soup plate, top with a spoonful of yogurt and a dollop of chutney. SERVES 4–6.

CHUTNEY

There are countless wonderful chutney recipes, as well as a rich variety of ready-made chutney of all kinds in most stores. Still, I enjoy making my own and have often prepared this easy and simple apple/mango chutney. (If you are pressed for time, you may of course opt to buy, without guilt, your favorite kind.)

⅓ cup olive oil
1 large onion, finely chopped
2 green apples, peeled, cored, and diced
2 mangos, peeled and cut into chunks
½ cup golden raisins
½ cup white cider vinegar
1 tablespoon dry mustard
1 tablespoon brown sugar
1 tablespoon peeled and grated fresh ginger
1 garlic clove, minced
1 teaspoon curry powder
½ teaspoon cayenne pepper
½ teaspoon coriander seeds
½ teaspoon ground cumin

In a saucepan, heat the olive oil and sauté onion until translucent. Add apples, mangos, and garlic; stir in raisins, vinegar, mustard, sugar, ginger, curry, cayenne. In a frying pan, sauté coriander and cumin a few seconds. Grind in the coffee grinder (which should be well cleaned before grinding coffee) and add to saucepan. Cook over low heat 10 minutes. Let cool, and adjust seasoning to taste. Pour in a serving bowl, cover, and refrigerate until cold.

Leek and Potato Soup

La soupe aux poireaux et pommes de terre is made virtually in every home — rich or poor — all year long, whether in the north or south of France. I personally consider it our national soup. It's very easy to make, its ingredients are available year around, and it's most accessible for any budget — all of which probably explain its popularity.

Growing up in Paris, I remember the aroma from the leeks that often greeted me as it emanated from the concierge's loge at the entrances of various buildings and permeated the whole place. For me, whenever I make leek and potato soup (and I often do) its aroma brings me back home to my childhood for a moment. It's my *Madeleine*.

Served steaming hot, the soup is most soothing, and served iced, with a touch of cream and some chopped chives, it changes identity to become the elegant vichyssoise.

> 1 large leek, well washed and sliced (white and green)
> 2 baking potatoes, washed, peeled, and sliced
> 5 cups stock (or water)
> pepper and salt

Make sure all sand has been removed from the leek. In a kettle, cover leek and potatoes with stock or water, pepper, and salt. Bring to a boil, reduce heat, cover, and cook 15 minutes. Cool. Purée in blender. Put back in kettle and bring to a boil. Transfer to soup terrine and serve. (My mother used to put a teaspoon of butter on top as she served the soup — it makes it smoother.) SERVES 4.

Tip: You may skip puréeing the soup. Simply dice the vegetables finely before cooking and serve the soup as is. (I prefer it puréed.)

Tomato Soup with Puff Pastry

This soup, with its golden dome of puff pastry, sets an elegant tone for any meal.

2 tablespoons olive oil
2 large onions, finely chopped
2 celery stalks, peeled and finely minced
1 carrot, peeled and finely minced
6 tomatoes, quartered
1 garlic clove, minced
1 bay leaf
1 teaspoon herbes de Provence
6 cups chicken broth
½ teaspoon rosemary, finely chopped
2 sheets of packaged frozen puff pastry
1 egg, beaten with 1 tablespoon water (egg wash)

In a kettle, heat olive oil and sauté onion until translucent. Add celery and carrot. Continue stirring 10 minutes. Add tomatoes, garlic, bay leaf, herbes de Provence, and rosemary. Reduce heat and cook 20 minutes. Turn off heat. Discard bay leaf. Let soup cool and transfer content of kettle to blender. Purée.

Defrost pastry sheets as package label directs.

Preheat oven to 400°.

Ladle soup into individual ovenproof bowls. Place on a rimmed baking sheet.

Roll puff-pastry sheets to about ⅛-inch thickness. Cut out 6 pastry rounds to match circumference of soup bowls. Brush with egg wash. Place pastry rounds with egg-wash side down over bowls, making sure to seal tightly around the rim. Brush top of pastry rounds with egg wash as well. Bake 20 minutes. SERVES 4.

Tip: Adding puff-pastry tops to bowls of simple beef or chicken consommé will dress them up with the same elegance.

Cream of Watercress Soup, Cold, with Caviar

Watercress grows in abundance in bogs and along great many rivers in spring and summer in Europe, and very much in Provence. In the United States, watercress is available year-round, which makes the preparation of this soup possible from January to December.

Often, as I was growing up, my mother would plant a small clump of watercress at the side of our plate with the main course — before the actual salad course. To assuage my increasing exasperation, my mother used to tell me that watercress had an astringent quality that would help balance the main course's richness. It was good for me, she insisted. As a result, an early aversion to watercress developed that was to last for many years. Now I've learned to love it.

With its mild tanginess, watercress soup is excellent in and of itself. Now and then I indulge — watercress lends itself superbly to the combination of flavors — by adding a spoonful of caviar with a dollop of crème fraîche which elevates it to a whole new level. Caviar is of course optional.

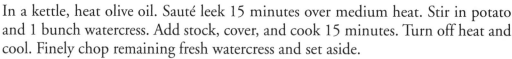

¼ cup olive oil
1 leek, washed, trimmed, and sliced
1 large potato, peeled and diced
1½ bunches watercress, not trimmed, washed and dried
5 cups chicken stock
pepper and salt
½ cup crème fraîche
2 ounces caviar

In a kettle, heat olive oil. Sauté leek 15 minutes over medium heat. Stir in potato and 1 bunch watercress. Add stock, cover, and cook 15 minutes. Turn off heat and cool. Finely chop remaining fresh watercress and set aside.

In the blender, purée cooked vegetables until creamy. Transfer to serving bowl. Refrigerate.

If you find the soup too thick, add a little stock or water. Sprinkle remaining watercress into the soup. Serve chilled with a dollop of crème fraîche and a tablespoon of caviar. SERVES 4.

Cream of Yellow Pepper Soup, Cold

The delicate flavor of roasted peppers and their bright yellow color make this first course aesthetically pleasing and culinarily satisfying.

4 large yellow peppers, seeded, white membrane removed
4 cups chicken stock
1 teaspoon saffron
1 tablespoon olive oil
1 onion, finely chopped
3 garlic cloves, minced
2 celery stalks, peeled and diced
½ cup white wine
½ teaspoon ground cumin
pepper and salt
½ cup heavy cream
½ cup fresh cilantro leaves, finely chopped
½ cup chives, finely chopped
1 cup plain yogurt for garnish

Over a grill, or the flame of the stove, char peppers on all sides. Keep charred peppers sealed in a paper bag 20 minutes.

Under running water, peel charred skin off peppers. Remove white membrane and seeds, cut peppers into small pieces. Set aside.

In a kettle, bring stock to a boil. Sprinkle with saffron, turn heat off, cover, and let infuse 10 minutes.

In a skillet, heat olive oil and cook onion until translucent. Add peppers, garlic, and celery. Cook 20 minutes stirring frequently. Stir in wine, cumin, pepper, and salt. Add to kettle of stock. Bring to a boil, reduce heat to simmer, and cook 10 minutes. Cool.

In the blender, purée contents of kettle. Return to kettle and stir in cream. Heat through and sprinkle with cilantro and chives. Serve with a dollop of yogurt. SERVES 4.

Egyptian Green Herb Soup

The original Egyptian recipe, a light brothy soup is made with a green flavoring called *milookhia* — a spinach-like herb — but since it's not always available, I have approximated the soup by substituting a little cooked and fresh spinach and fresh cilantro.

> 5 cups chicken stock
> 2 garlic cloves, minced
> ½ cup cooked and squeezed dry spinach
> 2 tablespoons finely shredded raw spinach
> ½ cup fresh parsley leaves, finely chopped
> ½ cup fresh cilantro leaves, finely chopped
> 2 tablespoons coriander seeds, toasted and ground
> 1 tablespoon chopped fresh thyme leaves (no stems)
> 1 tablespoon tomato paste
> pepper and salt

In a kettle, heat up stock, and stir in garlic, cooked and uncooked spinach, parsley, cilantro, coriander, thyme, tomato paste, pepper, and salt. Bring to a boil. Turn off heat. SERVES 4.

Cold Greek Cucumber Soup

Each country throughout the Mediterranean basin offers some variation of this refreshing soup. In the following recipe, I have combined a touch of Moroccan and Iranian flavors to the original Greek soup by adding raisins and cilantro.

> 3 garlic cloves, minced
> 2 seedless cucumbers, peeled, and cut into chunks
> 1 pint plain yogurt
> 1 cup mint, finely chopped
> 2 cups chicken stock
> pepper and salt

1 red chili
1 tablespoon olive oil
1 tablespoon tomato paste
1 bunch radishes, washed, stemmed, and sliced
½ cup raisins, finely chopped
½ cup fresh cilantro, finely chopped

In the blender, purée garlic, cucumber, yogurt, and mint. Add stock, pepper, and salt. Transfer to serving bowl. Refrigerate.

In a small bowl, mash hot chili with olive oil and tomato paste.

At serving time, remove from refrigerator, sprinkle soup with radishes, raisins, cilantro, and small dots of hot chili mixture. SERVES 4.

Cream of Artichokes, Cold

I make this wonderfully fragrant meal opener when artichokes are plentiful, big, and in season.

salt
juice of 1 lemon
5–6 large artichokes
5 cups chicken stock
1 bunch flat parsley, finely chopped
½ cup heavy cream, whipped
pepper

In a kettle with 2 quarts water, salt, and half the lemon juice, cook artichokes 40 minutes. Drain. Remove leaves and chokes. (Save leaves for serving later with a vinaigrette.) Dice artichoke hearts and place in a blender. Add stock and remaining lemon juice and purée. Transfer to soup terrine. Refrigerate 4 hours.

Fold parsley into whipped cream with a little pepper and salt, and transfer to small serving bowl.

Bring soup terrine to the table, ladle soup into plates, and top each plate with a dollop of parsley/whipped cream. SERVES 4.

Cream of Chervil, Cold

Chervil, a delicate and fragrant herb resembling flat parsley but with a more subtle perfume, is available in fine produce shops. This cream of chervil recipe comes from the south of France and makes a remarkable meal opener, both in winter and summer.

salt
5 bunches chervil, washed, stems cut off but kept
3 egg yolks
½ cup heavy cream or yogurt
pepper

In a kettle, bring 4 cups water and 1 tablespoon salt to a boil. Put chervil stems in the boiling water and cook 10 minutes. Put 4 bunches chervil leaves (reserve 1 bunch for later) in a heat-safe bowl, and pour liquid and stems from kettle over leaves. Cover and cool completely. Refrigerate overnight. This will infuse, and become a kind of chervil tea. The next day, strain the chervil tea and discard stems and leaves. Return strained liquid to kettle. Bring to a boil. Turn heat off.

In a bowl, whisk yolks and cream or yogurt until blended. Gradually whisk hot liquid into yolk/cream. Keep whisking. Return to kettle, bring to scalding point while whisking. *Do not boil.* (The yolks will curdle if you boil them.) Turn heat off. Whisk until cool; season with pepper and salt. Refrigerate 4 hours or more. Remove from refrigerator, divide into 4 soup plates, and sprinkle with reserved fresh chervil leaves. Serves 4.

Fennel Soup with Goat-Cheese Toasts

Easy-to-make, this light Italian soup is pleasantly different in fragrance and presentation. Although I usually discard the leaves when I make fennel salads or even when I braise fennel, for this recipe, they are kept, chopped, and incorporated.

3 fennel bulbs, trimmed of their outer layers, with their leaves
    finely chopped
5 cups chicken stock
pepper and salt

4–5 tablespoons goat cheese
4 slices French bread, toasted
¼ cup olive oil
⅓ cup grated Parmigiano-Reggiano cheese

Quarter fennel and slice finely. In a kettle, bring stock to a boil, reduce heat and cook fennel 20 minutes. Add chopped up leaves, pepper, and salt.

Spread goat cheese on each toast.

Bring kettle to the table. Drizzle olive oil in the soup, float goat cheese-toasts on top of soup. Sprinkle with Parmigiano-Reggiano cheese. SERVES 4.

Cream of Parsnip Soup with Truffles, Hot

Parsnip is a pale and not particularly attractive looking root vegetable. I used to walk right past parsnips in markets. Cooking parsnips isn't necessarily on most people's mind, I realize. A mistake, I've recently learned. Nothing is more exquisite than your first spoonful of this velvety soup. When cooked, this dull root vegetable takes on an unexpected personality, and is transformed into an astonishingly fragrant and sweet creamy soup. The optional addition of truffle shavings, of course, elevates it into a rare treat.

2 parsnips, peeled, washed, and sliced
1 potato, peeled and sliced
1 slice white bread
2 cups chicken stock
1 teaspoon sugar
pepper and salt
1 black truffle, finely sliced

In a kettle, combine parsnips, potato, bread, 3 cups water, stock, sugar, pepper, and salt. Bring to a boil, reduce heat, and cook 15 minutes. Cool. Purée in a blender. Return to kettle.

Bring soup kettle to the table, ladle soup into soup plates, and sprinkle truffle shavings on top. SERVES 4.

Note: The bread absorbs any possible bitterness the parsnip might have.

VEGETABLE FIRST COURSES

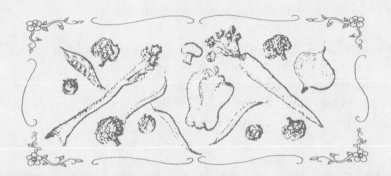

Slowly Roasted Tomatoes

Roasting tomatoes a long time at low temperature gives them an intense and incredibly delicious flavor — a kind of essence of tomato. That process is called *confire,* and these are *tomates confites*. The two or three hours baking tend to make them shrink. As a first course, I allow two tomatoes per person. If you make a larger quantity, that's fine. Tomates confites keep well if covered with plastic wrap in the refrigerator for up to a good two weeks.

If you wish to serve them warm, they can be warmed up (15 minutes) in the oven before serving. After cooking, roasted tomatoes should be allowed to cool for three to four hours. (Served cold, they offer a very tasty entrée.)

⅓ cup olive oil
8 tomatoes
3 garlic cloves, slivered
½ cup basil leaves, chopped
pepper and salt
a few arugula leaves
a few Boston lettuce leaves
more basil

Preheat oven to 350°.

Brush baking dish with some of the olive oil. Place tomatoes side by side in the dish, and bake 15 minutes. Remove baking dish from oven, and with a knife, peel tomatoes (the skin will come right off). With your knife, make slits on top of tomatoes. Into each slit, insert slivers of garlic and some of the chopped basil. Sprinkle with pepper and salt. Place tomatoes back into baking dish. Trickle ½ teaspoon olive oil over each tomato top. Reduce heat to 200°.

Bake 2, even 3, hours. The tomatoes will reduce in size, and appear a trifle wrinkled and sad, but don't let that worry you: That's the way they should look. Let cool.

Top with remaining chopped basil and more freshly ground pepper. Trickle a few drops of olive oil over each tomato. Serve 2 tomatoes on a bed of greens — arugula, lettuce, and basil — per person. SERVES 4.

Eggplant Caviar

Each Mediterranean cuisine has its version of eggplant purée. In Turkey, Lebanon, and other parts of the Middle East, it is called *baba ganoush;* in France, *caviar d'aubergine.* I prefer my version, a combination of the French and Rumanian recipes (a Rumanian friend in Paris gave me her recipe many years ago), which has no garlic — just onion — and is exquisitely smoky and smooth.

> 1 large eggplant
> 1 onion, chopped
> juice of 1 lemon
> 1 cup cilantro leaves
> ⅔ cup olive oil
> 1 tablespoon ground cumin
> pepper and salt
> lemon wedges
> pita bread, warmed

On an outside grill or directly over the flame of the gas stove, grill the eggplant on all sides. It will ooze some juice, shrink, and look rather pitiful — don't worry, that's as it should be. Under running cold water, peel charred skin off. In the food processor, purée eggplant, onion, lemon juice, cilantro, olive oil, cumin, pepper, and salt. Transfer purée to serving platter. If you're going to serve it that same day, it is not necessary to refrigerate the eggplant caviar — just cover with plastic wrap. Serve with lemon wedges and warm pita bread. SERVES 4.

Provençal Gâteau of Vegetables and Eggs

This traditional Provençal first course, called *crespeau,* represents several different small vegetable omelets prepared separately, piled together in a small tower, and served cold.

Though simple to prepare, by virtue of having to make several omelets, this recipe takes more time than most other first courses, but I think you'll find it well worth the effort. The result is festive, unusual, and certainly delicious. This dish is quite filling, and inevitably yields more than four servings — probably six or even eight. You'll be able to keep it covered in the refrigerator several days.

Tip: You'll need several bowls ready on your counter. The number of bowls is optional and varies according to your choice of vegetables.

The more contrasting the vegetables, the more colorful the result. Here is a combination of six vegetables I have enjoyed for my "cake." Again: you may reduce the number of vegetables if you wish.

10 eggs
2 large onions, minced, sautéed in olive oil and puréed
2 artichoke hearts, sautéed in olive oil and puréed
1 red pepper, skin charred, peeled, cleaned, and puréed
1 medium eggplant, peeled, cubed, sautéed, and puréed
tapenade (in food processor, purée 3 anchovies, 2 garlic
    cloves, ½ cup black pitted olives, ⅓ cup olive oil,
    1 tablespoon capers)
2 bunches parsley, finely chopped
pepper and salt
olive oil
6 tablespoons fresh thyme leaves, chopped

Beat 2 eggs in each of 5 bowls and whisk 1 purée into each with some pepper and salt. Into the first bowl, incorporate 1 cup chopped parsley, pepper, and salt.

When all your bowls of puréed vegetables are incorporated, begin making the omelets. Heat a frying pan with a few drops olive oil. Over low to medium heat, cook your omelets, one after the other, making sure they are smooth, equal in size, and flat on top. Sprinkle with thyme. Slide each omelet, one on top of the other, on a serving platter according to your choice of color, pressing lightly before adding the next omelet. Cover the *crespeau* with plastic wrap and refrigerate until serving time. It will look like a layered cake.

Remove gateau from refrigerator. Carve into small wedges, sprinkle with remaining parsley, and serve.

Note: You can also opt to make fewer omelets if you wish — or more — but to give the desired effect, 4 or 5 vegetables seems about right to me. SERVES 6–8.

Greek Purée of Lima Beans with Garlic and Olive Oil

Greece and the Middle-Eastern countries excel in the preparation of vegetables and legumes with olive oil, lemon juice, garlic, and various spices. In almost every Middle-Eastern country, as you enter a restaurant — or someone's home at meal-time — a familiar sight is a tray laden with many small bowls, each filled with a different salad or marinated vegetable surprise. The idea is to enjoy a spoonful of each before the main course. Inevitably, one of those bowls will be this purée. While I prefer fresh lima beans, in this case, to save preparation time and at no detriment to quality, I often skip cooking the lima beans from scratch, substituting canned or frozen baby lima beans.

      1½ cups cooked lima beans
      4 garlic cloves, minced
      juice of 1 lemon
      ½ cup olive oil
      1 teaspoon finely chopped fresh thyme
      pepper and salt

In a food processor, purée all ingredients. Check seasoning, and adjust to taste. It may need more olive oil, more thyme, more salt, or lemon juice, etc., according to your palate. Cover and set aside in a serving bowl.

You will doubtless have more than you need for four. Remember however, this is a first act, and people will eat no more than a tablespoonful, especially if you serve several other bowls of marinated or prepared vegetables like eggplant caviar or other salads. It keeps well a few days refrigerated, and will provide another round of first courses for another meal or lunch fare. SERVES 6–8.

Cucumber in Yogurt

This simple Greek dish is refreshing and can be prepared in a matter of minutes. It can be served immediately, but I prefer it chilled. If you can, use the Greek-style yogurt — it's creamier.

> 1 seedless cucumber, peeled and cubed
> 1 garlic clove, minced
> 8 ounces plain Greek-style yogurt
> 1 cup fresh mint leaves, finely chopped
> ½ cup flat parsley leaves, finely chopped
> pepper and salt

In a serving bowl, mix all ingredients, cover, and refrigerate a few hours until serving. SERVES 4–6.

Gâteau of Eggplant

This remarkable *gâteau* — or cake — made of eggplant and served with red-pepper coulis comes out of the traditional Provençal gastronomy and is called *papeton* there. This attractive and unusual dish will surprise your guests, since at first glance it could be mistaken for a dessert. In fact, as it arrives at the table, papeton looks for all the world like a chocolate cake.

While it is a wonderful first act to any dinner, it also makes a delicious luncheon when served with a green salad.

Start by preparing the coulis.

FOR THE RED-PEPPER COULIS
2 red peppers
½ cup olive oil

1 small onion, finely chopped
1 tablespoon balsamic vinegar
pepper and salt

Char peppers on all sides over the grill, or directly on the stove flame. Keep in a paper bag 20 minutes. Under running water, peel peppers. Seed and remove white membrane. Chop peppers coarsely.

In a skillet, heat a little of the olive oil and sauté onion until light brown. Purée onion in blender with roasted peppers, remaining oil, the vinegar, pepper, and salt. Pour coulis into a serving bowl. Set aside.

FOR THE EGGPLANT GÂTEAU
1 large eggplant or 2 medium ones
2 onions, finely chopped
½ cup olive oil, plus extra for oiling mold and eggplant peels
2 garlic cloves, minced
1 tablespoon herbes de Provence
pepper and salt
4 eggs, lightly beaten

Peel eggplant lengthwise to obtain long strips of skin. Set aside for later use. Dice eggplant meat. In a skillet, sauté onions in ½ cup olive oil until translucent. Add eggplant meat, season with garlic, herbes de Provence, pepper, and salt, and cook 20 minutes, until mixture is soft. Let cool and add beaten eggs to eggplant mixture.

Preheat oven to 350°.

Lightly oil a charlotte mold or a deep cake mold. (A not too tall soufflé dish will also do.) Line mold with eggplant peels — light side up, dark side down. It is imperative that they hang over edges of mold. Pour eggplant mixture inside mold, fold peels over eggplant mixture, and close tightly like a package. Lightly oil top of peels and place mold in a baking dish. Pour enough hot water into the baking dish to come 1 inch up sides of mold. Bake 40 minutes. Cool.

To unmold: Place a serving platter on top of mold, flip, and unmold gâteau onto your serving platter. Bring to the table.

To the chorus of "oohs" and "aahs" that invariably greet its arrival, slice eggplant gâteau ceremoniously with a serrated knife as you would a cake, and place a small wedge on each plate. Cover with coulis. SERVES 4–6.

Ragout of Artichokes

As mentioned earlier, artichokes are common to many Mediterranean cuisines, so there are several versions of this vegetarian stew. This one is especially attractive if you can find very small artichokes.

> 12 baby artichokes, outer leaves removed, choke scrapped off, cut in half
> juice of 1 lemon
> salt
> ½ cup or more olive oil
> 2 onions, finely chopped
> 8–10 very small russet potatoes, scrubbed but not peeled
> 5 garlic cloves, minced
> 2 carrots, peeled and sliced
> 1 bunch parsley, washed and finely chopped
> pepper
> 1 cup white wine
> 1 cup small fresh or frozen green peas
> 2 tablespoons herbes de Provence

Pour a little of the lemon juice over each artichoke half.

In a kettle, cook artichokes in salted water 30 minutes. Drain.

In a skillet, heat ½ cup olive oil and sauté onions until light brown. Add cooked artichoke halves, remaining lemon juice, potatoes, garlic, carrots, parsley, pepper, herbes de Provence, and salt. Cover with water. Add wine. Cover skillet and simmer 20 more minutes over low heat. Stir in peas and continue cooking 2 minutes. SERVES 4.

Tip: If you can't find baby artichokes, use four regular size ones, remove leaves, scrape choke, quarter the hearts, and proceed as with baby artichokes.

Ragout of Baby Carrot, Green Peas, Snap Peas, Leek, and Tiny Potato

These fresh baby vegetables, bubbling in their light sauce and served in individual crocks, bring a bit of spring to the table. First of all, they are delicious, but more importantly, fresh vegetables with their respective properties of different vitamins are also very healthy.

Presenting the ragout in individual ovenproof dishes gives it a special touch.

> 2 tablespoons olive oil
> 2 leeks, white portion only, washed and sliced
> 8 long, thin, baby carrots, peeled, with a little of their stems showing
> 8 small potatoes, whole
> ½ pound snap peas, trimmed
> 1 cup fresh or frozen green peas
> 1 cup vegetable stock
> pepper and salt
> 1 tablespoon butter (optional)
> 1 cup parsley leaves, finely chopped

In a kettle, heat olive oil and sauté leeks until translucent. Cook 5 minutes. Add carrots and potatoes, cook over low heat another 15 minutes. Stir in snap peas and peas. Pour in stock, cover, and simmer 5 minutes. Add pepper and salt. At the time of serving, I like to add 1 tablespoon butter to the sauce, which makes it more silky, but this is optional, of course. Sprinkle with parsley. Transfer to individual crocks. SERVES 4.

Artichoke Hearts Braised in White Wine

One of southern France's many traditional specialties is braised artichokes — its Provençal name is *Artichauds en Barigoule* — and is often served as a first course rather than as a side dish.

For this recipe, one can, without guilt, use frozen artichoke hearts, though I have found that they are not always available in American stores. Most often, the available artichoke hearts on the market are the marinated variety in jars.

As with so many regional dishes, each corner of southern France, and virtually every home, claims its "real and authentic" recipe. There are therefore many barigoules, and I have made several. Here's one I especially like.

> 4 tablespoons olive oil, plus extra for oiling baking dish
> juice of ½ lemon
> 4 large artichokes (or 8 small ones), outer leaves and choke
>   removed (as before, save leaves for future vinaigrette)
> 4 garlic cloves, minced
> 1 bunch parsley, washed and finely chopped
> 2 tablespoons fresh thyme
> pepper and salt
> 2 cups white wine

Preheat oven to 300°. Lightly oil a baking dish.

Pour lemon juice over artichoke hearts and immerse in a bowl of cold water. In a small bowl, mix garlic, parsley, thyme, pepper, and salt. Remove artichokes from water, drain, and dry. Cover each artichoke heart with the garlic/parsley mixture and 1 tablespoon olive oil (½ tablespoon if using small artichokes). Place in lightly oiled baking dish. Pour wine over and bake for 1½ hours. The wine should have evaporated, and the artichokes should be caramelized. SERVES 4.

Baked, Stuffed Artichokes

I love making these. The kitchen is permeated with the wonderful Provençal aroma, and everyone, it seems, enjoys eating stuffed artichokes. It is, however, a rather substantial first course, so I recommend following it with a light main course.

juice of 1 lemon
salt
4 globe artichokes
4 tablespoons olive oil, plus extra for oiling dishes
1½ cups breadcrumbs
4 garlic cloves, minced
1 cup flat parsley leaves, finely chopped
1 tablespoon herbes de Provence
pepper

In a kettle, bring 2 quarts water, half the lemon juice, and 1 teaspoon salt to a boil. Cook artichokes 30–35 minutes (until a leaf can easily come off; you may need a few more minutes). Drain. Cool 1 hour.

In a skillet, heat olive oil and sauté breadcrumbs 5 minutes or so, until breadcrumbs become blond. Stir in garlic, parsley, herbes de Provence, pepper, and salt.

When artichokes are cool enough to handle, with scissors cut off sharp edge of leaves, and gently push artichoke leaves apart a little. With a spoon, scrape and discard choke.

Preheat oven to 350°. Lightly oil 4 small ovenproof dishes.

With a spoon, stuff breadcrumb mixture in between each leaf and on top of the hearts. Close artichokes. Place artichokes on individual oiled ovenproof dishes and drizzle remaining lemon juice and olive oil. Cover with foil.

Bake 20 minutes.

Remove from oven, remove foil, and bring to table. Serves 4.

Black-Olive Tart

Olives abound in the Mediterranean and are part of many — if not all — of those countries' cuisines. This striking-looking tart, with its black-olive topping, is as satisfying as it is mouthwatering.

FOR THE PIECRUST

This piecrust is my mother's recipe, which I introduced more than twenty-five years ago in my first cookbook, *Jeannette's Secrets of Everyday Cooking*. It is miraculously easy and foolproof. Time and again I've tried other piecrusts, some excellent, some okay, but inevitably, I find myself returning to this one. I call it my "old reliable."

It takes no more than three minutes to prepare — no more, I promise! (I know, because *I had to* time a precise three-minute demonstration for my television appearances, and I never ran over.)

MY MOTHER'S FOOLPROOF PIECRUST RECIPE
12 tablespoons unsalted butter
4 ounces cream cheese
1½ cups all-purpose flour

Preheat oven to 350°.

In a food processor, combine the ingredients and pulse until dough comes together and becomes almost smooth. Cover with plastic wrap and refrigerate for an hour. Remove from refrigerator, roll out onto a floured board, and line an 8-inch pie mold. Prick with a fork, and bake 20 minutes. Remove from oven.

FOR THE FILLING
2 cups black olives, pitted and halved
1 tablespoon olive oil, plus extra for trickling over filling
1 head Boston lettuce, leaves separated, washed, dried, and
    chopped
pepper and salt
juice of ½ lemon
8 ounces goat cheese, separated into chunks
1 teaspoon herbes de Provence

In a saucepan, bring 2 cups water to a boil. Drop olives into water and cook 10 minutes. Drain.

In a skillet, heat 1 tablespoon olive oil and cook lettuce over medium heat for a few minutes, until wilted and liquid has evaporated. Season with pepper and salt and lemon juice. Remove from heat and, with a fork, mix in goat cheese. Spread lettuce and goat cheese mixture onto baked pie crust. Top with pitted olives, cut side down. Sprinkle with herbes de Provence. Trickle a few drops of olive oil over top. Bake 20 minutes, and serve.

Can be enjoyed cold or hot. I prefer the latter. SERVES 4–6.

Dandelion Salad with New Potatoes and Bacon

Dandelions grow wild everywhere and are often dismissed as lawn nuisances. Mediterraneans, however, take full advantage of this weed, serving it as a coveted salad. Young, tender dandelion is a very flavorful green. (Get only young ones, otherwise they tend to be a trifle tough and bitter.)

> 8–10 ounces small dandelions
> 4–6 baby new potatoes, scrubbed and whole
> 2 tablespoons olive oil
> 8 slices bacon, cut into small pieces
> 2 shallots, minced
> 3 tablespoons red wine vinegar
> pepper and salt

Discard outer leaves of dandelions. Cut off roots. Wash leaves in several changes of water as they tend to be very sandy. Dry well and transfer to salad bowl.

In a small kettle, cook potatoes in water 12 minutes. Drain.

In a frying pan, heat 1 tablespoon olive oil and sauté bacon until crisp. Try to ignore your nutritionist who will raise his or her arms in horror with the next step: Pour bacon fat and bacon pieces on top of dandelion. You may omit the bacon fat — but that would be too bad — and simply add olive oil.

In same frying pan, adding remaining tablespoon olive oil and cook shallots until light brown. Pour in vinegar — it will bubble, toss in potatoes, and cook 1 minute. Transfer to salad bowl. Add pepper and salt. Toss. SERVES 4–6.

Red Beet and Leek Mimosa

Emanating from the old traditional French *cuisine bourgeoise,* the combination of these two root vegetables — a lovely contrast in both color and texture — served with a vinaigrette, is as easy to prepare as it is satisfying to eat.

FOR THE VINAIGRETTE
2 tablespoons balsamic vinegar
1 tablespoon Dijon mustard
6 tablespoons olive oil
pepper and salt

salt
4 leeks, well washed, white part only
2 beets, cooked, peeled, and sliced
½ cup finely chopped parsley
2 hard-boiled eggs, finely chopped
½ cup finely chopped chives

Mix vinaigrette ingredients in a small bowl. Set aside. In a kettle, filled with 1 quart salted water, cook leeks 15 minutes. Drain well. Cool. Cut leeks in quarters, lengthwise.

On each individual plate, place 1 or 2 pieces of leek, spreading them like a fan. Pour some vinaigrette over leeks, add 2 or 3 beet slices, and trickle more vinaigrette on top. Continue in same fashion, ending with a beet slice. Pour remaining vinaigrette on top and sprinkle with parsley, chopped egg (egg mimosa), and chives. SERVES 4.

Radish Vinaigrette

Westerners are accustomed to eating radishes dipped in a bit of salt, as appetizers. Radish served with vinaigrette, however, is typically Middle Eastern. The first time I was served this radish salad was in an Arab restaurant in East Jerusalem. After my first taste, I remember thinking: "What a great idea! Radishes as salad!"

1 bunch (or more, depending of their size) radishes, washed, stems removed, and sliced
1 small shallot, minced
3 tablespoons olive oil
1 tablespoon wine vinegar
pepper and salt

In a bowl, mix all ingredients, cover, and refrigerate. Serves 4.

Tomato with Cilantro

Cilantro gives a special Middle-Eastern kick to the tomatoes, and offers a welcome variation from the usual basil and parsley topping.

4 ripe tomatoes, peeled and cubed
1 small red onion, finely chopped
1 bunch cilantro, finely chopped
3 tablespoons olive oil
1 large tablespoon balsamic vinegar
pepper and salt

In a bowl, toss ingredients. Serves 4.

Beet and Orange Salad

With its striking color combination, this simple salad, both sweet and tart, is a light and refreshing first course, especially recommended if the main course that follows is hearty. If you're short of time, and can't cook fresh beets, the canned variety — sliced — will for once do just fine.

> 2 beets, cooked 50 minutes in the oven, peeled, and sliced, or 2
>   small cans sliced beets, drained
> 2 navel oranges, peeled, pith and pits removed, and sliced
> ⅓ cup olive oil
> 2 tablespoons lemon juice
> pepper and salt

If you are using canned sliced beets, keep the juice for another use. (A soup? A sauce?) In a bowl, combine beets, oranges, and dressing made from oil, lemon juice, pepper, and salt. Toss. Serve.

This Middle Eastern tradition of serving several salads for the first course opens a meal with a joyful note and triggers instant conviviality. Portions remain small and should merely whet the appetite for what is to follow. SERVES 4–6.

Baby Bell Peppers Stuffed with Feta and Olives

This colorful recipe of small peppers, both crunchy and with a creamy stuffing, is Greek, but appears in slightly different forms in other countries of the Mediterranean basin.

> 8–10 baby red, yellow, and green peppers
> ½ onion, minced
> 1 cup crumbled feta cheese
> ½ cup black olives, pitted and chopped
> ⅓ cup sour cream
> 1 teaspoon finely chopped fresh thyme
> ¼ cup olive oil

Wash peppers, and remove seeds and membrane, keeping peppers whole. Dry. Set aside.

In the food processor, purée onion, feta cheese, olives, sour cream, and thyme. With a spoon, stuff each pepper with feta mixture. Place on serving platter. Drizzle with olive oil. SERVES 4–6.

Pita Crackers

These Middle Eastern crackers are delicious in themselves, but also make a perfect accompaniment for all the previous salads. Whenever I make the crackers, I store them in a jar, and think I'll have a nice supply for a few days or even weeks. They are so tasty, however, they tend to disappear so fast that I often find myself having to replenish my supply far more quickly than anticipated.

I suggest making these crackers on an afternoon when you are relaxed at home. The herbs and garlic will fill the house with Mediterranean aromas. Making two batches will (hopefully) provide you with a plentiful stock. Stored in a closed jar or tin, they keep well for weeks.

2 garlic cloves, minced
½ olive oil
1 tablespoon ground cumin
1 tablespoon rosemary leaves
4 pita breads
coarse salt

Preheat oven to 350°.

In a food processor, purée garlic, olive oil, cumin, and rosemary.

Cut pita into little triangles, place on a baking sheet, brush with garlic mixture, and sprinkle with coarse salt. Bake 15 minutes. The triangles should be crisp and golden. Cool. Serve with the first course.

Note: Before cutting triangles, I often separate each pita into two with a serrated knife to obtain thinner crackers.

Terrine of Artichoke with Tarragon and Chives

When artichokes are in season and plentiful, one can be extravagant and indulge in creating this elegant terrine. The result is well worth the effort.

Tip: Prepared and refrigerated a good twenty-four hours before serving, the terrine will benefit both in taste as well as in firmness.

        salt
        6 large globe artichokes
        juice of 1 lemon
        pepper
        4 eggs
        2 yolks
        2 cups heavy cream
        2 tablespoons finely chopped fresh tarragon
        1 bunch chives, finely chopped
        olive oil for oiling pan

Preheat oven to 375°.

In a kettle, bring 3 quarts salted water to a boil. Cook artichokes with half the lemon juice 35 minutes. (You'll know your artichokes are cooked when you can pull a leaf off easily.) Drain. Remove all leaves (save leaves to eat later with a vinaigrette) and scrape off choke. Thinly slice artichoke hearts. Sprinkle with remaining lemon juice, some pepper, and salt. Set aside.

In a bowl, whisk eggs, yolks, 1½ cups cream, 1 tablespoon tarragon, half the chives, and a little pepper and salt.

Oil an oblong loaf pan. Arrange artichoke slices in pan. Sprinkle some tarragon, and some of the remaining chives over artichokes. (Save a little for decoration, later.) Pour egg mixture over artichokes. Place filled terrine in a roasting pan and add enough hot water to pan to come 1 or 2 inches up the sides of the terrine. Bake 40 minutes. Remove from oven and cool. Cover and refrigerate overnight.

Whip remaining cream in an iced bowl. Set aside in the refrigerator.

Remove terrine from refrigerator, and run a knife along sides to loosen from pan. Place a serving platter on top of terrine. Flip over and remove loaf pan by lifting it carefully off the terrine. Sprinkle with some remaining tarragon and chives.

Slice terrine. Serve a slice topped with a small dollop of whipped cream sprinkled with more tarragon and chives. SERVES 4–6.

Zucchini Carpaccio

I defy you to find an easier to prepare, fresher, and more satisfying first course. The uncooked zucchini's crunchiness, combined with shaved Parmigiano-Reggiano cheese and lemon, offer a nice opener for any meal.

Unlike most of my recipes that I recommend preparing well ahead, this one is preferably made just before serving. In order to keep the zucchini's crispness, I recommend having all the ingredients for this carpaccio ready, slicing and assembling them only at the last minute.

Tip: This also makes an excellent luncheon main course.

>   juice of 1 lemon
>   1 small shallot, minced
>   3 tablespoons olive oil
>   pepper and salt
>   1 bunch arugula, washed and leaves left whole
>   1 green zucchini, washed — not peeled — trimmed, and cut into
>   thin slices, diagonally
>   1 yellow summer squash, washed — not peeled — trimmed, and
>   cut into thin slices diagonally
>   ½ cup pine nuts, toasted
>   4 ounces fresh Parmigiano-Reggiano cheese, shaved

In a small bowl, make your vinaigrette with lemon juice, shallot, olive oil, pepper, and salt.

Divide arugula among serving plates. Top each arugula base with zucchini and summer squash slices. Pour one-fourth of your vinaigrette onto each plate. Sprinkle with pine nuts. Cover with cheese shavings. SERVES 4.

Broiled Asparagus with Shiitake Mushrooms

Asparagus always make an elegant starter. I like them so much, in fact, I prefer serving them solo as a first course rather than a side dish with a main course, where they always strike me as a second citizen. The addition of a few mushrooms gives this dish a whole other dimension.

⅓ cup olive oil, plus extra for oiling baking sheet
1 pound asparagus, trimmed 2 inches from their tips
8 shiitake mushrooms, wiped clean, stems discarded, and sliced
juice of ½ lemon
½ teaspoon freshly grated nutmeg
½ cup Parmigiano-Reggiano cheese, grated
1 tablespoon breadcrumbs
pepper and salt
½ cup parsley leaves, finely chopped

Preheat oven to 475°.

On an oiled baking sheet, spread asparagus interspersed with mushrooms. Sprinkle a little olive oil and lemon juice. Cook in the oven 2 minutes. Remove from oven. Turn on the broiler, and wait a few seconds for it to be fully red hot.

Sprinkle nutmeg, cheese, breadcrumbs, pepper, and a little salt over asparagus and mushrooms. Trickle on a few more drops of oil. Place baking sheet under broiler for 1-2 minutes, until cheese has melted and a light crust has formed. Remove from broiler.

With tongs, apportion asparagus and mushrooms onto each plate, and sprinkle with parsley. SERVES 4.

A Very Green Plate of French Green Beans and Asparagus with Fresh Herbs

Green beans and asparagus are, more often than not, featured as side vegetables, accompanying a roast. Here they arrive by themselves, in all their simple splendor.

Note: Don't be deterred by the number of ingredients; you can produce this succulent starter in under half an hour.

½ pound French green beans, trimmed and left whole
½ pound asparagus, trimmed, tips only
½ cup finely chopped chives
½ cup fresh tarragon leaves, finely chopped
½ cup flat parsley leaves, finely chopped
¼ cup fresh basil leaves, finely chopped
1 bunch arugula, washed and trimmed with leaves left whole

FOR THE MAYONNAISE
1 egg
juice of ½ lemon
⅔ cup olive oil
pepper and salt
1 fennel bulb, quartered and sliced
1 cup black olives, pitted and minced

In a blender, mix egg with lemon juice. With machine running, gradually drizzle in olive oil, add pepper and salt, and blend until mixture thickens to mayonnaise consistency. Turn blender off, and check seasoning. Transfer mayonnaise to a bowl, add fennel and olives, mix well, and set aside.

Steam green beans 3 minutes. Immerse in a bowl of iced water for 20 minutes. Drain and dry. Steam asparagus tips 2 minutes. Drain.

FOR YOUR LEMON VINAIGRETTE
5 tablespoons olive oil
2 tablespoons lemon juice
pepper and salt

Mix vinaigrette ingredients in a small bowl.

In a large bowl, mix green beans, asparagus, and all but 1 tablespoon of the chives, tarragon, parsley, basil, and vinaigrette.

On each plate, spread a few leaves arugula, trickle with some of the remaining lemon vinaigrette, then place one-fourth of the green-bean mixture on top of arugula. Top with a small mound of olive-fennel-mayonnaise mixture. Sprinkle with remaining fresh basil, tarragon, and parsley. SERVES 4–6.

Carpaccio of Beets

This bright-red beet carpaccio looks like the original beef version created in 1950 in Venice by the founder of Harry's Bar, Giuseppe Cipriani. The story goes that one day, one of Giuseppe's prestigious and ravishing clients, the Contessa Moncenigo, arrived at Harry's Bar in a state of great agitation. She informed him that her doctor had just forbidden her to touch any pasta or cooked meat, and begged for something to appease her hunger. Rushing to his kitchen, he put his creative mind quickly to work, and a platter of paper-thin cut slices of raw beef displayed like a fan emerged. Sprinkling some capers, olive oil, and shaved Parmigiano-Reggiano cheese on it, he presented the platter to the contessa.

"What do you call this attractive dish, she asked?" It so happened that that week banners announcing the painter Carpaccio's current exhibit were hanging all over Venice. Suddenly inspired, Giuseppe named his creation: carpaccio. And thus it has remained.

Reminiscent of the original in looks, this beet carpaccio claims its own pretty presentation. The addition of green avocado purée enhances both the taste and look.

2 large beets, cooked, peeled, and cut into paper-thin slices
1 ripe avocado
juice of 1 lemon
½ teaspoon ground cumin
pepper and salt
4 tablespoons olive oil
1 small red onion, finely chopped
2 tablespoons capers
3 ounces of Parmigiano-Reggiano cheese, shaved

Preheat oven to 350°.

Bake beets 45 minutes. Cool and peel. If you happen to have a mandoline, I recommend using it to obtain paper-thin slices. Otherwise, cut as finely as you can with a sharp knife.

In the food processor, purée avocado with half the lemon juice, the cumin, pepper, and salt.

Arrange beet slices neatly in a circle — like petals of flowers — on each plate. Divide avocado purée in four, and place a little mound of it in the center of each "flower." In a small bowl, mix olive oil, remaining lemon juice, some pepper, and salt and pour dressing over beet slices. Sprinkle with onions and capers. Cover with cheese shavings. SERVES 4.

Turkish Tomato Tartare

Turkish cuisine offers countless varieties of finely chopped and puréed vegetables as first courses. Each is surprisingly fresh and tempting. I delighted in all of them. This tartare version — the Turks call it salad — is particularly good when tomatoes are in season.

> 4 ripe tomatoes, skinned and quartered with little of the juice squeezed out by pressing with a fork
> 2 onions, finely chopped
> 1 green pepper, seeds, and white membrane removed, and cut into small pieces
> 1 small cucumber, peeled and cubed
> 1 garlic clove, minced
> ½ cup parsley leaves, finely chopped
> 1 tablespoon olive oil
> 1 tablespoon wine vinegar
> ½ teaspoon paprika
> ¼ teaspoon cayenne pepper

> FOR THE GARNISH
> 1 lemon, sliced
> ½ cucumber, peeled and sliced thickly
> 1 cup black olives, pitted

With a sharp knife, chop vegetables finely.

Put chopped vegetables in a colander over a bowl and let excess liquid drain out for 15 minutes. When all liquid has drained, transfer vegetables to serving bowl. Season with garlic, parsley, olive oil, vinegar, paprika, and cayenne pepper, and mix well. Refrigerate 2 hours. Serve crowned with lemon slices, thick cucumber slices, and black olives. SERVES 4–6.

French-Greek Cold Dumplings of Cauliflower Mousse in a Feta Cheese and Herb Sauce

The ingredients for this extremely airy and elegant first course will yield more than what is required for four people. You'll be able to save a fair amount for another lunch or dinner, since it keeps well in the refrigerator for at least a week. As you'll see, this requires advance preparation — a day ahead of serving.

salt
juice of 3 lemons
1 cauliflower, trimmed and separated in florets
1 cup chicken stock
½ teaspoon curry powder
1½ tablespoons unflavored gelatin
½ teaspoon Tabasco sauce
pepper
¾ cup heavy cream

In a kettle, bring 2 quarts salted water and the lemon juice to a boil. Drop in cauliflower, reduce heat, cover and cook 20 minutes. Drain, and cool. Refrigerate a few hours.

In a food processor, purée cauliflower.

In a saucepan, bring stock and curry powder to a boil. Reduce heat, and simmer 15 minutes, until it reduces by half. Soften gelatin in a tablespoon cold water. Add and stir into stock reduction, along with Tabasco, pepper, and salt. Incorporate purée of cauliflower. Cool. In a cold bowl, whip heavy cream and fold into cauliflower mixture.

Refrigerate overnight.

FOR THE SAUCE
2 tablespoons olive oil
1 shallot, minced
½ cup fresh dill, finely chopped
5 ounces feta cheese
1 cup chicken or vegetable stock
½ cup chervil, leaves pulled off the stems

In a saucepan, heat olive oil and sauté shallot until light brown. Stir in dill. Pour into blender, add feta cheese and stock, and purée. Cool, cover, and refrigerate.

The next day, remove cauliflower mousse from refrigerator.

With the help of 2 spoons, shape little oblong shapes of mousse. Spread a thin layer of feta sauce on each plate. Arrange these oblong shapes like "petals" in a crown, on the sauce. Sprinkle with chervil. SERVES 6–8.

Pear, Arugula, Blue Cheese, and Walnut Vinaigrette

The marriage of sweet and sharp contrasting flavors works particularly well in this combination salad.

> a few drops lemon juice
> 2 pears, quartered, peeled, and cored
> 1 big bunch arugula, stems removed, washed, and dried
> 4 ounces blue cheese, cut into small chunks
> 1 cup walnuts, toasted
> 1 tablespoon sherry vinegar
> 3 tablespoons olive oil
> pepper and salt

Sprinkle lemon juice over pear to prevent discoloration. Divide arugula among the plates. Add pear quarters and blue cheese and top with walnuts. Make vinaigrette in a cup, with olive oil, vinegar, pepper, and salt, and sprinkle over each salad plate. SERVES 4.

Terrine of Ratatouille

The French verb *touiller* means: to mix. Stewed and mixed summer vegetables are a staple of southern France gastronomy. Ratatouille, I am glad to report, has now seriously entered American cuisine. It is often served cold, alone as an appetizer, or hot, as a side dish with either fish or meat. Each French restaurant or Mediterranean household has its own recipe for ratatouille, but basically it always includes tomatoes, zucchini, eggplants, onion, garlic, and green peppers cooked in olive oil with herbes de Provence.

This attractive variation on a theme — the theme here being ratatouille — is easy and great fun to make as well as to present at the table. Taking the extra step of encasing the ratatouille in cooked eggplant slices, baking it, and enveloping it in a white-wine jelly gives it a special touch.

⅓ cup olive oil, plus extra for oiling pan
2 onions, peeled and chopped
6 tomatoes, cut into chunks
4 regular chubby eggplants, peeled and chopped
2 green peppers, seeded, white membrane removed, cut into chunks
1 zucchini, cut into chunks
4 garlic cloves, minced
1 cup basil leaves, plus extra for oiling pan
1 tablespoon fresh thyme, plus sprigs for garnish
3 tablespoons tomato paste
pepper and salt
4 long eggplants, cut lengthwise into slices
5 eggs, lightly beaten
2 tablespoons unflavored gelatin
⅔ cup white wine

In a kettle, heat all but 1 tablespoon olive oil and sauté onions until translucent. Add tomatoes, chopped eggplant, green peppers, and zucchini. Cook 15 minutes. Add garlic, basil, thyme, tomato paste, pepper, and salt. Stir, reduce heat, cover and cook 30 minutes. Turn heat off, cool and set aside.

In a frying pan, heat 1 tablespoon olive oil and fry long eggplant slices 2 minutes on both sides. Set aside.

Preheat oven to 300°.

Add eggs to ratatouille, stir well to combine. Oil a loaf pan and line with fried eggplant slices, allowing the slices to overhang. Fill the loaf pan lined with eggplant slices with the ratatouille/egg mixture. Fold eggplant slices over ratatouille. Place loaf pan in baking pan and add enough hot water to roasting pan to come 1 inch up the sides of the loaf pan. Bake ratatouille 1 hour.

Soften gelatin in a little wine in a small saucepan, and stir in remaining wine. Bring gelatin mixture to a boil. Turn heat off.

Remove terrine/loaf pan from oven, and pour gelatin over terrine. Cool 30 minutes, and refrigerate overnight.

Run a knife along the edges, unmold terrine onto a serving platter, and decorate with basil leaves and fresh sprigs of thyme. Slice terrine at the table. Serves 8-plus.

Endive, Toasted Walnuts, and Roquefort Salad

Endives, generally known as Belgian — or French — belong to the chicory family and are commonplace and available everywhere. Crunchy and delicate, they offer a refreshing starter to any meal.

> 3 endives, sliced
> 1¾ cups walnuts, toasted
> 6 ounces Roquefort cheese, crumbled
> juice of 1 lemon
> 3 tablespoons olive oil
> 1 teaspoon Dijon mustard
> ½ teaspoon sesame oil
> pepper and salt

Combine all ingredients. Serves 4.

Beet Tartare

Undoubtedly, you will have noted my predilection for tartare in any shape or form. Over the past several years I have experimented and discovered a multitude of vegetables, as well as fish, that can be successfully made into a tartare. After tasting this particular beet tartare at the New York restaurant Jean-George's, I liked it so much that I attempted to replicate it the following day. (I can't say I replicated it integrally, for I neither asked nor was given the recipe. But trusting my sense of taste and experience, I believe I was able to decipher the ingredients.) I am grateful to the creative chef for opening my imagination, as well as my palate, to this oh-so-delectable first course.

Again, I recommend preparing this dish a day ahead of time, and refrigerating it until serving.

2 large beets, washed, baked in the oven 45 minutes, tops cut off, peeled, and cut into thick pieces
1 small onion, peeled and quartered
juice of 1 lemon
1 cup parsley leaves, finely chopped, plus a whole sprig for garnish
⅓ cup olive oil
1 tablespoon Dijon mustard
½ teaspoon Worcestershire sauce
1 tablespoon capers
pepper and salt
4 slices whole wheat bread, toasted and cut into triangles

With a sharp knife, chop beets finely and place in a bowl.

In a food processor, mince onion with lemon juice and parsley. Add olive oil, mustard, and Worcestershire sauce and process until blended. Combine contents of processor with chopped beets. Stir in capers, pepper, and salt.

Adjust seasoning to taste. Refrigerate several hours. Decorate with a sprig of parsley and toasted triangles. SERVES 4.

Chicory with Warm Goat Cheese and Bacon

Goats abound in many countries of the Mediterranean, and each village or region takes pride in its own local production. Every market features tables with crates of appetizing goat cheeses. They come in various shapes and sizes: intense, creamy, less creamy, covered with ashes or different spices and herbs, soft, or very fresh, which I especially recommend for preparing this dish. In my region, one of the standard meal openers is the crisp and very simple to make *frisée au chèvre chaud* — chicory and goat-cheese salad. Why *frisée* — chicory — you might ask? Because its crunchiness nicely complements the richness of the cheese. Easy and quick to prepare, it brings a nice touch to any menu.

>1 head chicory, yellow part only
>1 small garlic clove, minced
>juice of ½ lemon
>1 tablespoon Dijon mustard
>pepper and salt
>5 tablespoons olive oil
>½ cup breadcrumbs
>½ teaspoon finely chopped fresh thyme
>4 small goat cheeses, cut in half, crosswise
>3 slices bacon, fried and crumbled (optional)

Discard green part of chicory head. Immerse yellow part in cold water 30 minutes. Dry. In a small bowl (or bottom of salad bowl) make the dressing by combining garlic, lemon juice, mustard, pepper, and salt. Whisk in 3 tablespoons olive oil. On a plate, mix breadcrumbs with thyme. Coat goat cheese halves on both sides with crumb mixture.

In a frying pan, heat remaining 2 tablespoons olive oil. Over medium-to-low flame, sauté coated cheeses until crisp and golden. With a spatula and a fork, turn over and cook goat cheeses until second side is also golden and crisp. Pour dressing over chicory. Toss well. Divide chicory among plates, topping each with two crisp cheese halves. Sprinkle bacon on top of each. SERVES 4.

Stuffed Zucchini Blossoms with Red-Pepper Coulis

There is always something irresistible, almost magical, about seeing the platter of golden, crisp, stuffed flowers arriving at the table.

Tip: The blossoms are very fragile, and are best prepared as soon after purchase as possible. After 24 hours they wilt and lose their crispiness, even if refrigerated.

FOR THE RED-PEPPER COULIS

Because of its delicacy, and the fact that once in the hot oil, the fritters cook quickly, everything else needs to be ready, thus it is essential to prepare the coulis ahead.

> 3 red peppers
> 1 small onion, finely chopped
> ⅓ cup olive oil
> 3 tablespoons balsamic vinegar
> pepper and salt

Char peppers over the grill or directly on the stove flame. After a few minutes, they should look black and burnt on all sides. Let burned peppers rest in a closed paper bag for half an hour. Under running water, peel charred skin off the peppers. (You'll see how easy it is.) Remove white membrane and seeds.

In a skillet, heat a little of the olive oil and sauté onion until light brown.

In a blender, purée peppers and cooked onion with the remaining oil, vinegar, pepper, and salt. Set aside.

FOR THE BLOSSOM STUFFING
> 2 tablespoons olive oil
> 1 very small zucchini, washed, not peeled, cut into small cubes
> (cubed, it should fill a cup)
> 2 garlic cloves, minced
> 1 small, soft goat cheese
> ½ cup basil leaves, finely chopped
> ½ cup breadcrumbs
> pepper and salt
> 12 zucchini blossoms

In a skillet, heat olive oil and sauté cubed zucchini until light brown (about 8 minutes).

In a bowl, mix cooked zucchini with garlic, goat cheese, basil, breadcrumbs, pepper, and salt. With a teaspoon, carefully insert stuffing into each flower. Close petals gently over stuffing with your fingers.

FOR THE BATTER
　　1 cup all-purpose flour
　　1 tablespoon olive oil
　　1 egg, separated
　　1 teaspoon baking powder

In a large bowl, mix flour, oil, ½ cup water, and the egg yolk. Stir in baking powder. Beat egg white until stiff, and fold into mixture. Gently put stuffed blossoms in batter, turning them to insure that each blossom is well coated.

FRYING THE BLOSSOMS
　　2 quarts peanut oil for frying

In a deep kettle, heat peanut oil until it's very hot. (To check proper temperature, I drop a little batter into oil. If the batter sizzles and rises to the surface, the oil is ready.)

With a spoon, carefully lower each blossom into the hot oil. After a minute, as soon as they become golden, with the help of a fork and a spatula, turn each blossom over and fry until golden crisp on other side. Drain on paper towels. Season with salt and pepper. Serve. Spread some coulis of peppers on each plate, place 2 or 3 blossoms on top, and serve hot. SERVES 4–6.

Tip: If you do not wish to make fritters with the zucchini blossoms, you may opt to place the stuffed blossoms — without batter — in an ovenproof dish. Trickle a few drops olive oil on each, and bake 15 minutes in a preheated 350° oven. I think you'll like the result, but I guarantee you'll like the fritter variety infinitely more.

Little Round Zucchini Stuffed with a Tomato-Basil Granita

This very elegant first course was a discovery for us some years ago in a restaurant in Provence. It is relatively easy to prepare, although as you'll see, the sorbet needs time in your freezer, so you should prepare a day ahead. The result is as much a pleasure to the eyes as it is to the palate.

Because these round zucchini are not always available, I often substitute with regular zucchini and simply cut them into chunks roughly the size of the little round ones.

> 4 round zucchini (or 2 small zucchini)
> 2 ripe tomatoes, peeled and finely chopped
> 1 cup fresh basil leaves, chopped, plus extra for garnish
> ½ cup olive oil, plus extra for trickling over zucchini
> ½ cup fresh lemon juice, plus extra for vinaigrette
> salt
> pepper

With a sharp knife, cut off tops of zucchini and level bottoms by taking a thin slice off — they will stand on the plate better. Scoop out insides of zucchini. (Reserve this zucchini meat for a later recipe.)

In a kettle, place zucchini side by side, cover with water, and cook 3 minutes over medium heat. Drain. Cool. Dry shells with paper towels.

If you are using a regular zucchini, chop into 3-inch chunks. Scoop out insides, partially leaving some space as lining. Proceed as with small round ones.

FOR THE TOMATO-BASIL GRANITA

In a food processor, purée tomatoes, basil, ¼ cup olive oil, ½ cup lemon juice, 2 tablespoons salt, and pepper. If you don't have an ice-cream maker, pour mixture into a metal bowl and freeze 4 hours. Remove, stir with a spoon, and return to freezer for several more hours. Stir and whisk from time to time to obtain a smooth sorbet.

FOR THE VINAIGRETTE

Combine lemon juice, olive oil, salt, and a little pepper. Season zucchinis inside and out with lemon vinaigrette.

Remove sorbet bowl from freezer, and scoop out 2 tablespoons — more if needed — to fill seasoned zucchini. Garnish with a few basil leaves, and a trickle of olive oil. Place zucchini tops back on and serve. SERVES 4.

Sicilian Salad of Lemon and Artichoke

Lemon in any form or incarnation is one of my gastronomic favorites. As are artichokes. When I first tasted this Sicilian combination, I was immediately seduced and have made it one of my pet first-course choices. Because it is rather substantial, when offering it as first course, I suggest limiting servings to small portions. (What's left will keep a few days in the refrigerator.)

salt
4 lemons, washed and whole
4 artichokes
1 cup almonds, toasted
½ cup olive oil
3 tablespoons finely chopped fresh thyme
2 tablespoons honey
pepper

In a kettle, bring 3 cups salted water to a boil. Cook 3 lemons 20 minutes. (Following the advice of the chefs of The River Café, a very good London restaurant, I turn the lid upside down to ensure that the lemons are well submerged, and cook better.) Drain. Cool.

Add artichokes to another kettle with enough boiling salted water to cover, and cook 35 minutes. Drain. Remove and discard leaves and chokes. (Leaves can be enjoyed at a later date with a vinaigrette or mayonnaise.) Cut artichoke hearts in half (if small) or in quarters (if large).

Cut cooled lemons in half. Scoop out and discard pulp, retaining only the skin. Cut soft skin into quarters.

In a bowl, combine lemon quarters with artichokes and almonds. Mix olive oil with juice of fourth lemon, thyme, honey, pepper, and salt. Combine, toss, and serve. SERVES 4.

Middle Eastern Salad of Tomato, Black Olives, Cucumber, and Feta Cheese

I can't think of a more Middle Eastern staple than this red-green-black-and-white salad. When traveling through Turkey, I found it was a daily, almost automatic, feature — for breakfast (yes, breakfast), lunch, or dinner. Before we had even ordered, we were always routinely presented a platter of this salad — or some variation. Needless to say, it was always welcome.

4 anchovy fillets
3 tomatoes, peeled, and cut into wedges
1 green bell pepper, seeded, white membrane removed, cut into chunks
1 cucumber, peeled and diced
1 red onion, peeled and sliced
1 garlic clove, minced
1 cup feta cheese, cut into cubes
½ cup black olives, pitted and cut in half
½ cup basil leaves, finely chopped
½ cup parsley leaves, finely chopped
3 tablespoons olive oil
1 tablespoon red wine vinegar
1 teaspoon chopped fresh thyme leaves
pepper and salt

In a bowl, mix all ingredients. Toss well and apportion to each plate. Serve small portions. SERVES 4–6.

Radishes Served Mickey's Way

In France, radishes are traditionally served with some butter and salt. Why butter? Because some people find that radishes can be a bit too sharp; the butter neutralizes and enhances their flavor.

My mother, whose nickname was Mickey, served them with two different herbed butters. She would wait for the butter to be soft, divide it into two bowls, mix fresh thyme in one and chives in the other. Each batch would then go on some parchment paper that she would roll like a fat cigar and refrigerate. When it came time to serve, the rolls of herbed butter would come out of the refrigerator and the parchment paper was removed. She would then cut the small "cigars" into slices, arrange the herbed butter slices in the center of a serving platter, and surround them with pink radishes and a bowl of salt. We would literally "butter" each radish with a small knife, dip it in salt, and always enjoy them tremendously before proceeding to the main course. She turned a rather ordinary little vegetable into a fun first course.

Since then, I have elaborated by adding different seasonings, spices, and herbs like basil and garlic, or mashed black olives and garlic, to the butter rolls. Whatever butter is left over becomes an elegant spread for French bread. (It also keeps well in the refrigerator.) This recipe calls for two bunches of radishes.

FOR THE THYME BUTTER
  4 tablespoons unsalted butter, softened
  1 tablespoon fresh thyme, finely chopped

FOR THE CHIVE BUTTER
  4 tablespoons unsalted butter, softened
  2 tablespoons finely chopped chives

FOR THE BASIL-GARLIC BUTTER
  4 tablespoons unsalted butter, softened
  ⅓ cup basil leaves, finely chopped
  1 garlic clove, minced

FOR THE BLACK-OLIVE—GARLIC BUTTER
  4 tablespoons unsalted butter, softened
  ⅓ cup black olives, pitted and mashed finely
  1 garlic clove, minced
  radishes

  small bowl of salt

In a food processor, purée each batch of butter and flavoring(s) separately, and transfer each mixture to a piece of plastic wrap. Roll into a cigar shape. Refrigerate 2 hours. Remove from refrigerator, remove plastic wrap, and slice. On a serving platter, place herbed-butter slices and surround with radishes and a small bowl of salt. SERVES 6–8.

Oranges and Black-Olive Salad, Moroccan Style

I first tasted this striking combination of salty black olives and perfumed sweet orange slices in a spicy vinaigrette at a Moroccan friend's house in Paris. I liked it so much that I have since adopted it as a fun — and exotically different — first course for many of my dinners.

> 4 navel oranges, peeled, white membrane and pits carefully
>   removed, cut into slices
> 1 medium red onion, peeled and thinly sliced
> 1 garlic clove, minced
> 1 cup black olives, pitted and finely chopped
> 2 tablespoons olive oil
> 1 tablespoon sherry vinegar
> 1 teaspoon ground cumin
> ½ teaspoon ground cinnamon
> pepper and salt

In a serving bowl, mix and toss all ingredients. Refrigerate. SERVES 4–6.

Fennel Salad with Roasted Walnuts in a Lemon Vinaigrette

The Italian name for this bulb vegetable is *finocchio*. With its slightly licorice flavor, it always makes for a welcome and crunchy preliminary course that takes only minutes to prepare. Especially popular in Italy, this salad has spread to various neighbors throughout the Mediterranean.

> 2 fennel bulbs, washed and trimmed
> juice of 1 lemon
> ½ cup walnuts, chopped coarsely and toasted
> ½ cup olive oil
> pepper and salt

Cut fennel lengthwise in quarters, then slice crosswise. In a bowl, combine all ingredients and toss. SERVES 4–6.

Italian Salad of Chicory, Arugula, Radicchio, Lemon, and Capers

With its sharp bite, this salad may not be to everyone's taste. If you happen to have a predilection for lemon, as I do, I think you will appreciate its tart and tangy flavor. Serve it either as a first course, or as a welcome accompaniment to cold meat or fish.

> 3 large lemons, peeled, seeded, all pith scraped off, and very finely sliced
> salt
> olive oil
> 1 bunch fresh thyme, leaves picked from stems and finely chopped
> 1 small jalapeño pepper, seeded, and finely chopped
> ½ cup capers
> pepper
> 1 head radicchio, leaves separated, washed, and dried
> 1 head chicory (use only the yellow center leaves), washed and dried
> 1 bunch arugula, leaves only, washed and dried
> juice of 2 eating oranges

Lay lemon slices on a plate, and sprinkle with salt and 1 tablespoon olive oil.

In a small bowl, combine thyme, jalapeño pepper, capers, 3 tablespoons olive oil, and salt, and pour over lemon slices.

On a platter, arrange radicchio, chicory, arugula leaves. In a small bowl, mix orange juice with equal amount olive oil, pepper, and salt. Pour over greens. Slide lemon slices and capers with their dressing on top of greens. SERVES 4.

MEAT FIRST COURSES

Mickey's Mousse of Chicken Livers

Despite the fact that there are dozens of charcuteries per neighborhood in France, my mother, Mickey, was famous for her mousse, which she made often to the delight of all of us — family and friends. I have since compared her mousse to the best pâtés of Dordogne and none compares. I suggest making this ahead, so it has plenty of time to set in the refrigerator.

1 pound chicken or duck livers
16 tablespoons butter
4 tablespoons duck or chicken fat (available in most markets)
1 garlic clove, minced
⅓ cup Cognac
½ teaspoon sweet paprika
½ teaspoon ground thyme
pinch of dried tarragon, crumbled
pepper and salt
1 (8-ounce) package cream cheese
2 slices French bread, soaked in milk, squeezed dry
½ cup parsley leaves, finely chopped
cornichons
6-8 slices white sandwich bread, toasted and cut into triangles.

With a knife, remove sinews from livers. In a small pan, heat butter and duck or chicken fat (chicken or duck fat adds to the flavor). Sauté livers 5 minutes. Add garlic, Cognac, paprika, thyme, tarragon, pepper, and salt and continue cooking 3 more minutes — no more! Transfer to blender or food processor, and purée with cream cheese and soaked bread. Transfer to serving crock. Cover with plastic wrap. Refrigerate 4 or more hours. Sprinkle with parsley. Serve from the crock with cornichons and toasted triangles of bread. SERVES 6–8.

Rillettes

Rillettes are a slowly cooked pâté of either pork, goose, rabbit, or duck, or a combination thereof. Like our *soupe aux poireaux,* which I personally consider our national French soup, rillettes, too, is our national pâté. More humble in its ingredients — and less costly — than its cousins foie gras or country pâté, it appears on virtually every menu throughout the country.

I started making rillettes many years ago, when I could not find any in America. Today they are available in some fancy food shops here, but still not many. So in offering them to your guests, you'll probably be the first on your block, or in your town, to do so.

I make my rillettes frequently, but come Christmastime, a large production often takes place in my kitchen, from which I make presents, in pretty crocks, for my friends. (Rillettes have the added virtue of keeping well under their protective layer of fat in the refrigerator.)

> 2 pounds pork shoulder, cut into ½-inch pieces
> 2 onions, finely chopped
> 1 pound lard
> ½ teaspoon grated nutmeg
> pinch of ground cloves
> ½ teaspoon sweet paprika
> pinch of ground cinnamon
> pepper and salt

In a deep kettle, combine ingredients, cover, and cook patiently 3 hours over very low flame, stirring occasionally to make sure rillettes don't stick or burn. If you find they are getting crisp, or too dry, stir in a few spoonfuls of water. Rillettes should be soft — not crisp. Cool.

With a big fork, mash mixture, making "threads" of the meat. Transfer to a crock. Cover and refrigerate. SERVES 10–12.

Tip: If you make duck, rabbit, or goose rillettes, add duck or chicken fat instead of lard. Proceed in the same manner as with pork.

Gâteau of Marinated Chicken in Aspic

If the name of this attractive dish sounds as though it is for professional chefs only, be reassured: It is an easy recipe. The term *aspic* should not put you off; it simply means "in a jelly." It will perhaps take a little more time than you are accustomed to, but it is very much worth it. Perfect for a picnic with a crisp green salad, it cuts like pâté, and a slice offers an elegant first course.

> 1 (5-pound) chicken
> 1 onion
> 4 whole cloves
> 4 peppercorns
> salt
> 2 shallots, finely chopped
> 1 garlic clove, minced
> 2 ½ cups white wine
> ½ cup flat parsley leaves, finely chopped
> 1 teaspoon finely chopped fresh rosemary leaves
> 1 teaspoon finely chopped fresh thyme leaves
> pepper
> 4 tablespoons unflavored gelatin
> ½ pound fatback, boiled 15 minutes, drained, and thinly sliced
> cornichons
> warm French bread

Have your butcher bone and skin the chicken. (If you bone it yourself, an easy process with a sharp knife, remove skin first and cut all meat away from bone). Wash chicken under running water. Chicken should remain in large pieces as they come off the bones — not diced.

Make a stock with the bones by covering them with 4 inches water, the onion studded with cloves, the peppercorns, and salt. Cook 3 hours over medium-low heat. (You may add a little water if needed.) You will obtain a strong stock. Cool. Strain and discard bones. You should have 2 cups. (If you don't, add a little store-bought stock.)

FOR THE MARINADE

In a bowl, mix chicken pieces with shallots, garlic, 2 cups wine, 2 tablespoons chopped parsley, rosemary, thyme, pepper, and salt. Cover and refrigerate overnight to marinate.

Remove from refrigerator, and remove chicken pieces from marinade. Reserve marinade.

FOR THE ASPIC

In a small saucepan, dilute gelatin with cold stock and remaining half cup wine. Heat to boiling, add a little salt, and simmer three minutes. Turn heat off. You should have 2 good cups gelatin liquid.

Preheat oven to 275°. Line a loaf pan with slices of fatback. Lay chicken pieces over fatback. Pour marinade and 1 cup gelatin over chicken.

Put loaf pan in a large baking dish. Add enough hot water to dish to come 2 inches up the sides of the loaf pan. Cover with a sheet of tin foil into which you poke small holes with a knife. Bake 2 hours.

Remove pan from oven. Cool.

Pour remaining cup cooled gelatin over chicken in loaf pan. Refrigerate overnight. Remove from refrigerator. Run a knife along sides. Place platter on top and flip to unmold. Slice. SERVES 4–6.

Pâté de Campagne

I hesitated to include this entire section and this pâté recipe in particular. Is it really "Mediterranean"? Do Mediterranean diners eat pâté? What about its high fat and cholesterol content? The answer to the first two questions is a resounding "of course!" When it comes to pâté, people who live around the Mediterranean are no different than their fellow gourmands elsewhere in the world. Pâté is indeed an integral part of their culinary repertory. As for its contribution to your health, I must confess that pâté has absolutely nothing to recommend it. But, doesn't the soul have to be fed as well from time to time?

Throughout France, in virtually every village and town north or south, *charcuteries* — shops that have a long history in France of specializing in pork meat cooked in infinitely different preparations — shops so popular in fact sometimes there are two charcuteries per block — are a main feature. In tiny villages or large cities, one can't help but stop in awe in front of charcuterie display windows, where the owners always proudly display an impressive variety of succulent pâtés and pork preparations. All restaurants, big or small, offer their *assiette de charcuterie,* which comprises several different homemade terrines or pâtés.

Pâté, it is safe to say, since time immemorial, is engrained in daily French gastronomy. All the French seem to have a gastronomic — if not moral — obligation to visit their *charcuterie* at least once a week for their *tranche de pâté.*

I make my pâté by popular demand — if I may be forgiven for this undue modesty — at least twice a year, or for a special occasion: a party or special dinner for people who love food. Because I don't always use the same proportions (there are times I happen to have one or more ingredient handy) the result differs slightly. But only I know the difference.

1½ pounds lean boneless pork (from the loin preferably),
   coarsely cut
2 cups diced ham
2 small containers chicken livers, about 1 pound total
6 tablespoons butter, duck fat, or lard, plus extra for greasing
   pans
2 cups minced onions
4 garlic cloves, minced
3 eggs
5 slices French bread, soaked in water and squeezed dry
1 cup parsley leaves, finely chopped
½ cup pistachios, shelled and coarsely chopped
3 tablespoons flour
1 teaspoon chopped fresh thyme leaves
1 teaspoon rosemary leaves, finely chopped
½ teaspoon grated nutmeg
½ teaspoon sweet paprika
pepper and salt
1 cup heavy cream
1 pound fatback, boiled 15 minutes, drained, and cut into fine
   strips
3 ounces brandy or Armagnac
warm sliced French bread
cornichons

In a food processor, grind half the pork and half the ham. With a small, sharp knife, remove sinews and gristle from liver. Chop coarsely. In a large bowl, mix ground pork, coarsely cut pork, ground ham, coarsely cut ham, and liver. In a skillet, heat butter, duck fat or lard, and sauté onions until translucent. Add garlic and sauté 2 minutes.

In a medium bowl, beat eggs and add bread, 1 cup parsley, the pistachios, flour, thyme, rosemary, nutmeg, paprika, pepper, salt, cream, and brandy. Combine with meats. Mix well with two big spoons several minutes, or with your rinsed hands. Cover and refrigerate overnight. (I put all this in plastic bags; it is easier to find room in the refrigerator with a bag rather than a big bowl.)

The next day, preheat oven to 325°.

Have 2 or 3 loaf pans ready. Grease loaf pans with duck fat or butter. Line with strips of fatback. Fill three-fourths full with mixture. Put another strip of fatback on top to cover pâté. Sprinkle with pepper and salt. Close each pan tightly with tin foil. With a sharp knife, poke holes every half inch to let steam escape. Put loaf pans in baking pan and add enough hot water to baking pan to come 1 inch up the sides of the loaf pans. Bake 1½ hours.

Remove from oven. Cool. Put several tin cans (soup cans, bean cans, any cans) on top of each loaf pan — to pack down the pâté. Refrigerate for at least 24 hours — 48 hours are preferable. It will season well and have the right consistency.

Remove from refrigerator, run a knife along edges of terrine, place a serving platter over terrine and flip. Sprinkle with remaining parsley. Slice and serve with cornichons and warm French bread. SERVES 10–12.

Antipasto

Once in a while I cannot resist the temptation to serve a platter of Italian antipasto as a first course. We tend to forget how attractive and inviting such a platter is as it comes on to the table. While some may think it not especially original, for me it still remains a most convivial and colorful opener, especially with warm bread. Most of the ingredients on this antipasto platter can be store-bought, which makes it easy for any dinner party. The only (slight) effort is in arranging the platter.

olive oil
1 bunch fresh basil, shredded
pepper and salt
1 ball fresh mozzarella cheese, sliced
4 thin slices Italian salami
4 paper-thin slices prosciutto
Genoa salami, cut into sticks
2 slices mortadella
black olives
green olives
roasted red peppers with olive oil, basil, and capers (see red-pepper coulis recipe, page 40)
1 small jar anchovies in olive oil
marinated artichokes
1 red beet, cooked and sliced

Add olive oil, shredded basil, pepper, and salt to sliced mozzarella and mix well. Assemble mozzarella mixture and remaining ingredients on a large serving platter. SERVES 4–6.

MAIN COURSES

SEAFOOD MAIN COURSES

Shrimp, Spanish Style, on a Griddle

In Spain, shrimp are often cooked on a *plancha* — the equivalent of our griddle. Quick and easy to prepare, this dish, cooked this way, is especially succulent.

2 pounds tiger shrimp, heads removed, with their shells
5 garlic cloves, minced
1 red chili, seeded and finely chopped
½ cup olive oil
1 teaspoon finely chopped fresh thyme
pepper and salt
1 lemon, cut into wedges

With a sharp knife, carefully cut an opening on the shells the length of the shrimp. Remove the black line (the shrimp's intestine) from each. Wash shrimp under running cold water and dry with a paper towel. Transfer to a bowl, add garlic, chili pepper, olive oil, thyme, pepper, and salt. Cover and leave to marinate 2 hours in the refrigerator.

Heat your griddle (if you do not have a griddle, simply heat a frying pan). Remove shrimp from marinade; reserve marinade. Cook 3 minutes, until they turn pink. Use a set of tongs to turn them over. Add marinade, toss a few seconds. SERVES 4–6.

Shrimp in a Piperade Sauce, Basque Style

Basque is the language spoken by people who live between northern Spain and the border of southwest France. *Piperade* is the Basque term for a preparation of peppers and tomatoes sautéed with some onion, and it is one of the region's signature dishes. At Biarritz, Saint-Jean de Luz, and on the whole southwestern coast of France to Bilbao and other points along the northern coast of Spain, you'll find piperade often served with an omelet or as a side vegetable.

2 tablespoons of olive oil
1 onion, finely chopped
2 tomatoes, peeled and cubed
1 yellow pepper, white membrane removed, seeded, and finely cubed
1 green pepper, washed, white membrane removed, seeded, and finely cubed
1 cucumber, peeled and finely cubed
juice of ½ lemon
20 shrimp, peeled and deveined
3 garlic cloves, minced
2 tablespoons tarragon leaves, finely chopped
2 tablespoons red wine vinegar
1 tablespoon tomato paste
½ teaspoon saffron
½ teaspoon cayenne pepper
pepper and salt

Start the piperade first. In a skillet, heat olive oil and sauté onion until translucent. Add tomatoes, yellow and green peppers, and cucumber and cook 10 minutes.

In same skillet, sauté shrimp 2 minutes. Sprinkle with lemon juice. Stir in garlic, tarragon, vinegar, tomato paste, saffron, cayenne, pepper, and salt and cook 1 more minute. Turn off heat. SERVES 4.

Spaghetti with Clams

In Italy, Spain, and France — and America — there are countless versions of this popular recipe — all good. I've tried a dozen variations, and this is my favorite.

½ cup olive oil
1 large onion, finely chopped
1 large green pepper, seeded, membrane removed, and diced
6 garlic cloves, minced
4 slices pancetta or other unsmoked bacon, cut into small pieces
1 bunch flat parsley, chopped
⅓ teaspoon cayenne pepper
pepper and salt
40 clams
½ cup white wine
1 pound thin spaghetti

In a kettle, heat olive oil. Over medium heat, sauté onion until translucent, and add green pepper, garlic, and pancetta. Cook 10 minutes. Sprinkle with parsley, cayenne, pepper, and salt. Turn heat off. Set aside.

In a separate kettle, cook clams, covered, 10 minutes, until they open. With a slotted spoon, remove half the clams from their shells, reserving the liquid from all the clams. Discard shells. Add both shelled and unshelled clams, wine, and clam liquid to first kettle with onion mixture.

In a pot of boiling, salted water, cook spaghetti 8 minutes. Drain. Combine with clams and onion/pepper mixture. Toss. SERVES 4.

Nathalie's Salmon on a Bed of Smoked-Eggplant Caviar with a Julienne of Cucumber

It seems as though virtually every Mediterranean country has its version of eggplant purée. My daughter Nathalie introduced this wonderful recipe to me.

The subtle blend of smokiness, lemon juice, onion, and cilantro elevates the eggplant into one of the most fragrant and exquisite dishes served throughout the

Mediterranean. Again, each country touts its own version as being "the real one." I prefer to maintain the delicacy of the smokiness by not adding garlic — just onion — for flavor.

Some people think that baking the eggplant in the oven is sufficient. I disagree. While baking the eggplant is indeed far easier and cleaner than my method of charring, nothing can substitute for the delicious flavor that results from actually *smoking* the eggplant directly over the flame.

The preparation of Nathalie's exquisite dish is a bit messy, yes, but please don't let that deter you. Thoroughly smoking the eggplant and peeling the charred skin off will, indeed, create a momentary chaos on your stove — and in your sink — but the result far outweighs that early minor inconvenience.

Under running water, peel off the eggplant skin, which will come off easily. As for the charred skin invading your sink, a sponge will return it to its pristine state in a matter of minutes. My recommendation is to prepare this recipe a day or more ahead. The smoke in the air will have long dissipated, and you'll thus keep your worried guests from dialing 911.

Note: Better yet, if weather permits, by grilling eggplant on an outdoor grill, you will altogether eliminate any such problems. The combination of flavors as well as texture in this recipe is delectable.

The smoked eggplant caviar needs to be prepared ahead of the salmon.

FOR THE EGGPLANT CAVIAR
1 large eggplant
1 medium onion, chopped
juice of 1 lemon
1 bunch cilantro, coarsely chopped
1 teaspoon ground cumin
pepper and salt

Directly on the grill, or on the flame of your stove top, char eggplant on all sides. The eggplant should look burned, shriveled — and indeed pathetic. That's to be expected.

Under running water, peel off all charred skin and put eggplant in food processor. Purée with remaining ingredients. Correct seasoning to taste, transfer to a bowl, and set aside. This caviar does not require refrigeration if you are going to serve this dish the same day. Simply keep it covered on your kitchen counter for later use. For longer conservation, of course, refrigeration is in order.

FOR THE SALMON

Salmon has been highly recommended both for lowering cholesterol and preventing cancer in recent years by nutritionists and doctors. As a result, a huge industry of farm-raised salmon has developed in America, making salmon accessible and affordable. Recently, however, a study has shown that farmed salmon contains considerably more "bad" fat than wild salmon, and it is also injected with red coloring. I recommend you buy only wild salmon.

> 1½ pounds wild-salmon fillets
> juice of ½ lemon
> pepper and salt
> dill sprigs

Preheat oven to 350°.

Brush fish with lemon juice, season with pepper and salt, surround with a few sprigs of dill, and encase salmon securely in aluminum foil. Bake 15 minutes. Remove fish from foil, let cool, and cut into 4 pieces.

FOR THE JULIENNE OF CUCUMBER

> 1 seedless cucumber, peeled and shredded
> salt
> 1 cup plain yogurt (Greek-style preferably)
> 1 tablespoon finely chopped fresh mint

Mix shredded cucumber and salt and let stand 10 minutes in a colander, over a bowl. Rinse and dry shredded cucumber.

In a bowl, mix cucumber, yogurt, and mint. Set aside.

FOR FINAL PRESENTATION

Spread a layer of eggplant caviar on each plate, add a salmon piece, and top with cucumber julienne. SERVES 4.

Tip: This dish is best served at room temperature. (If you've prepared the eggplant caviar ahead, remove from refrigerator at least 2 hours before serving.)

Halibut in a Crown of Stuffed and Baked Vegetables

Halibut is a delicate fish with a firm flesh and a rather flavorless taste. The crown of small stuffed vegetables adds zest and more than a touch of festivity to the dish. Don't let the long list of ingredients for this recipe deter you; it really is easy to prepare. Your only investment of time — and that's relatively little — is in stuffing the vegetables.

½ cup olive oil
1 white onion, minced
4 small white mushrooms, wiped clean, and stems removed
   and chopped
1 cup parsley leaves, finely chopped
pepper and salt
1 cup breadcrumbs
1 cup basil leaves, finely chopped
4 small tomatoes, tops cut off and insides scooped out and set
   aside
1 small eggplant, washed and halved lengthwise
½ cup green olives, pitted and finely chopped
½ cup herbes de Provence
1 small zucchini, washed and halved lengthwise
4 small or 2 medium red onions
3 garlic cloves, minced

In a skillet, heat 2 tablespoons olive oil. Sauté 1 tablespoon minced white onion until light brown. Stir in chopped mushroom stems, add 2 tablespoons parsley, and continue cooking another 5 minutes. Season with pepper and salt. Fill mushroom caps with stem mixture. Top with some of the breadcrumbs and a few drops of olive oil. Set aside.

In same skillet, heat 1 tablespoon olive oil and sauté 1 tablespoon white onion until light brown. Add scooped-out tomato pulp and cook 5–8 minutes, until liquid subsides, adding 2 tablespoons basil. Season with pepper and salt. Fill tomato cavities with contents of skillet. Top with breadcrumbs and a few drops olive oil. Set aside.

With a knife, cut inside eggplant and scoop out pulp. Dice eggplant meat. In a skillet, heat 2 tablespoons olive oil and sauté eggplant meat until soft and light brown. Add green olives. Sprinkle with 1 tablespoon herbes de Provence, pepper, and salt. Fill eggplant shells with cooked eggplant mixture and top with ½ cup breadcrumbs and a few drops olive oil.

With a knife, cut inside zucchini and scoop out. Dice zucchini meat. In same skillet, heat 1 tablespoon olive oil and sauté remaining white onion, until light brown. Stir in zucchini pulp and cook 10 minutes. Add basil, pepper, and salt. Fill zucchini shells. Top with breadcrumbs and a few drops olive oil.

Preheat oven to 350°.

In a kettle, bring 2 cups water to a boil. Cook red onions 10 minutes. Drain, peel, and cut tops off. Sprinkle with 1 teaspoon olive oil, salt, pepper, and 1 teaspoon breadcrumbs.

In a large, lightly oiled casserole dish, place your stuffed vegetables and the onions side by side. Bake 20 minutes.

FOR THE FISH
1½ pounds halibut
a few sprigs tarragon
juice of ½ lemon
pepper and salt

Place halibut on a sheet of aluminum foil, top with a squeeze of lemon juice, tarragon, pepper, and salt, and seal tightly. Bake 15 minutes. (Put the halibut in the oven 5 minutes after your casserole of vegetables. They will both be ready at the same time.) On a serving platter, arrange stuffed vegetables around fish. SERVES 4–6.

Gratin of Fresh Cod with Spinach and Anchovies

This great dish came to my attention one day in Cannes, when, desperate and starved, and having explored, to no avail, all manner of restaurants in town — it was during the film festival — we drove a few miles westward, and arrived in a postcard-perfect village perched on a hill above the sea. Convinced we had pioneered a fine new spot away from the madding crowd, we walked into a restaurant there, only to discover that several of the festival crowd had beaten us to it and were already well into their dinners.

Relieved, nevertheless, to find a table on the terrace, we sat, perusing the menu, when the owner/chef made a beeline to our table and, in his charming southern accent, recommended his *specialité*. His detailed description won us over immediately. When it arrived, it exceeded our already high expectations.

        olive oil
        1½ pounds fresh cod
        squeeze of lemon juice
        pepper and salt
        6 anchovy fillets
        1 cup cream sauce, also known as béchamel sauce, recipe follows
        2 pounds fresh spinach, well washed, thick stems removed
        ½ cup breadcrumbs

Preheat oven to 350°. Grease a casserole dish with olive oil.

Place cod on a piece of aluminum foil, sprinkle with a squeeze of lemon juice, some pepper, and salt, and bake 10 minutes. Remove foil. Cut cod into 2-inch pieces. Run cold water over anchovies to take out some of the salt. With a fork, mash into a purée. Set aside.

FOR THE CREAM SAUCE
        2 tablespoons olive oil
        ½ cup all-purpose flour
        1½ cups half-and-half or milk
        pepper and salt

In a saucepan, heat olive oil, add flour, and slowly stir in half-and-half. Cook, stirring over low heat about 5 minutes, until it thickens. Season with pepper and salt. Turn off heat and reserve.

In a steamer, cook spinach 5 minutes. Drain. Squeeze out all liquid. Coarsely chop cooked spinach and, in a bowl, combine with anchovies and 1 cup cream sauce.

In the oiled casserole dish, spread first a layer of spinach mixture, then pieces of fish, and so on. Finish with a layer of spinach. Trickle a little olive oil over the top. Dust with breadcrumbs. Bake 10 minutes. SERVES 4.

Broiled Trout

One of the many typical Mediterranean ways of serving trout, most often in Greece and in Greek restaurants in America, but also in France, Italy, and Turkey, is grilling or broiling, which keeps the fish firm and maintains its flavor. Quick and easy to prepare, this recipe makes a light, attractive main course.

> 4 (1-pound) trout, cleaned and whole
> olive oil
> a few sprigs tarragon
> pepper and salt
> juice of 1 lemon

Heat broiler or outdoor grill. With a sharp knife, slit trout lengthwise. Lightly oil fish on both sides. Open trout, and insert tarragon. Close trout. When broiler — or grill — is red hot, cook trout 3 minutes on each side, carefully turning over with the help of 2 spatulas (the flesh should be opaque). Depending on your broiler or grill heat, and your own preference, you may want to cook fish a minute or so longer.

With a fork and knife, gently peel off skin. Again with care, and with the help of a spatula, lift fillet off bone and place filleted trout on serving platter or individual plate. Trickle a few drops of olive oil, pepper, salt, and lemon juice over trout. Repeat with remaining trout. SERVES 4.

Stuffed Squid

This typical Mediterranean dish exists in slightly different guises in Spanish, Italian, Turkish, and French cuisines. Stuffed squid requires a little more cooking preparation than most of the recipes in this book, but I urge you to give it try. I hope you'll share with me that exploring new territories — culinary or other — always ends up a rewarding experience. What's more, you'll appreciate the immediate impression this dish makes on the gourmands around your table.

The stuffing can be made ahead and stored, covered, in the refrigerator.

4 squid, rinsed and dried

FOR THE STUFFING
4 anchovy fillets, cut into small pieces
2 small tomatoes, peeled and chopped
2 garlic cloves, minced
1 egg, lightly beaten
1 cup breadcrumbs
1 cup parsley leaves, finely chopped
2 tablespoons capers, finely chopped
pepper and salt
1 tablespoon olive oil
1 medium onion, finely chopped

In a bowl, mix anchovy fillets, tomatoes, garlic, egg, breadcrumbs, parsley, capers, pepper, and salt.

In a skillet, heat olive oil over medium heat and sauté onion until translucent, about 10 minutes. If (as he should) the fishmonger gave you the squid's tentacles, rinse and chop them finely. Add tentacles to onion. Continue cooking 10 more minutes, until squid liquid has evaporated. Combine skillet liquid and contents to tomato-anchovy mixture. Mix well. Set aside.

With a spoon, stuff squid, making sure, however, not too pack them too tightly. (Squid tend to reduce in cooking, so you need to leave a bit of space, otherwise the stuffing might burst out.) Close squid with a tooth pick or some twine.

COOKING SQUID
      2 tablespoons olive oil
      1 medium onion, finely chopped
      2 tablespoons vodka
      ½ cup white wine
      1 teaspoon herbes de Provence
      pepper and salt

In a skillet, heat oil and over medium heat, sauté onion until translucent, about 10 minutes.

Raise heat to medium-high, add squid, and sauté 5 minutes, shaking the skillet to ensure they cook on all sides. When flesh has turned opaque, pour in vodka and with a long match, ignite. When flame has subsided, add wine. Sprinkle with herbes de Provence, pepper, and salt. Cover. Simmer on very low heat 50–60 minutes. SERVES 4.

Trout with Sorrel

Sorrel looks a little like spinach. Unlike spinach, however, it has a slight lemony flavor, and because of its pleasantly tangy taste it is often used in fish preparations. This is a light and different way to serve trout.

½ cup olive oil
1 medium onion, finely chopped
3 pounds fresh sorrel, washed
pepper and salt
4 (1-pound) trout, whole, cleaned and cut down the middle,
    lengthwise
½ cup white wine
4 ounces yogurt (or, for sinners, crème fraîche)

Preheat oven to 350°. Use a little of the oil to grease a sheet of parchment.

In a skillet, heat remaining olive oil and sauté onion until light brown. Add sorrel, and cook 5 or so minutes. (It will shrink and should make about 1 cup). Add pepper and salt. With a slotted spoon, remove sorrel from skillet, discarding liquid. Press remaining liquid out with a fork. Stuff onion-sorrel mixture inside each trout and press closed. Place trout in ovenproof dish. Pour wine over fish, add pepper and salt. Cover with oiled parchment paper. Bake 15 minutes. Remove from oven, and serve with a dollop of yogurt (or crème fraîche) over trout. SERVES 4–6.

Salmon and Olive Tart

This original, scrumptious, and easy-to-make tart, with its crunchy potato crust and soft salmon filling, offers a nice contrast in textures.

> 2 baking potatoes, shredded in a food processor or on a grater
> 1 onion, minced
> ½ cup finely chopped dill
> ⅓ cup olive oil
> 2 tablespoons flour
> 1 cup milk
> 2 cups cooked wild salmon, separated into flakes with a fork
> 15 black Kalamata olives, pitted and halved
> ½ cup Gruyère or white cheddar cheese, shredded
> 1 lemon, not peeled, cut into thin slices

Preheat oven to 400°.

In a small bowl, combine potatoes, onion, and dill. Brush an 8-inch pie plate with a bit of the olive oil. With a fork, line mold with potato/onion mixture, pressing down as you go. Spray potato crust with a few more drops of olive oil. Bake 40 minutes. Remove from oven. The potato "piecrust" should be crisp and golden brown. If for some reason your crust is not crisp enough, continue baking a few more minutes. Remove from oven.

In a saucepan, heat 2 tablespoons of the olive oil and stir in flour and milk. Keep stirring over low heat until you obtain a cream sauce. Remove from heat. Intersperse salmon and olives on top of potato piecrust. Cover with cream sauce. Sprinkle evenly with cheese. Top with lemon slices and a sprinkle of remaining olive oil. Bake 15 minutes. Serves 4–6.

Fillets of Salmon, à la Bourguignonne

The red wine sauce — more often associated with boeuf bourguignon — gives this salmon recipe a nice kick, elevating it to a delicate haute cuisine level. Don't be tempted to use ordinary wine. It is necessary — as it is for beef bourguignon — to utilize a good Burgundy wine of your choice, one you would enjoy drinking. (Sorry about that, but sometimes sacrifices have to be made for good causes.)

>	juice of 1 lemon
>	1½ pounds fillet of wild salmon, cut into 4 pieces
>	pepper and salt
>	2 tablespoons olive oil
>	8 small potatoes, cooked and sliced
>	1 cup Italian parsley leaves, finely chopped
>	1 zucchini, washed and sliced
>	1 teaspoon finely chopped fresh sage
>	1 shallot, minced
>	2 cups red Burgundy wine
>	½ cup beef stock
>	2 tablespoons tomato paste
>	1 teaspoon finely chopped fresh thyme

Preheat oven to 350°.

Rub most of the lemon juice on fish and sprinkle with a little pepper and salt. Wrap tightly in aluminum foil. Bake 15 minutes.

While salmon bakes, in a skillet, heat 1 tablespoon olive oil and sauté potatoes until golden. Toss half the parsley and all the zucchini with sage, add to the potatoes, and continue sautéing 5 more minutes. Set aside.

In a shallow pan, heat remaining oil and sauté shallot until light brown. Stir in wine, beef stock, tomato paste, thyme, a few drops of lemon juice, pepper, and salt. Cook over low heat 10 minutes, until sauce thickens and is reduced by one-third. Unwrap salmon.

Place baked salmon on a serving platter, pour reduced red-wine sauce over it, and sprinkle with remaining parsley. Garnish with zucchini and potatoes. Serves 4–6.

Gratin of Cod with Leek, Olives, and Truffle (optional)

½ cup olive oil
1½ pounds fresh cod
6 leeks, washed, trimmed, white part only, sliced
1 cup black olives, pitted and chopped
½ cup chicken stock
1 cup breadcrumbs
1 truffle, optional

Preheat oven to 350°. Grease 4 gratin dishes with some of the olive oil.

Wrap cod in aluminum foil and bake 10 minutes. Remove from foil, cool, and cut into 1-inch pieces.

In a kettle, heat olive oil and over medium heat and cook leeks, covered, 10 minutes. Toss in olives and stock, and continue cooking over low heat for an additional 15 minutes. Add breadcrumbs and stir well — the contents of the kettle will quickly swell. Incorporate cod pieces into leek mixture and drizzle a few drops olive oil. Transfer to prepared gratin dishes. Bake 15 minutes, until tops are light brown and crusty. Remove from oven and bring to the table.

If you are using a truffle, bring it on a separate little plate with its grater. Shave the truffle over each dish, and serve. (These near-priceless truffles deserve this kind of "show.") SERVES 4–6.

Gigot of Monkfish

When we say "gigot" we immediately think lamb. In this case, however, the term gigot is merely used as a culinary method of cooking. This said, one could argue that this exquisite Mediterranean fish recipe could fairly qualify as gigot. I recommend carving and serving it at the table, which will make a stronger statement than plating it in the kitchen.

3–4 pounds filleted and skinned monkfish
6–7 garlic cloves, peeled and cut into slivers, plus 2 garlic cloves, minced
½ cup rosemary leaves, finely chopped
3 tablespoons olive oil
1 tablespoon flour
pepper and salt
1 onion, finely chopped
4 carrots, peeled and sliced
½ pound mushrooms, sliced
1 tablespoon herbes de Provence
½ cup white wine

In the same way you would when preparing to roast a leg of lamb, make small incisions all over the fish with the tip of a sharp knife — every ½ inch or so. Insert a sliver of garlic and a pinch of rosemary in each incision. Rub fish with some olive oil and dust with some flour. Fold fish onto itself to form a "roast." Sprinkle with more flour, rosemary, pepper, and salt.

In a skillet, heat remaining olive oil and sauté onion until translucent. Add carrots, mushrooms, and minced garlic. Cook 5 minutes. Sprinkle with herbes de Provence. Set aside.

Preheat oven to 350°.

In an ovenproof dish, spread carrot mixture and place monkfish on top. Pour wine over fish and roast 25 minutes. Remove from oven and let sit 5 minutes. Serves 4–6.

Salmon with Onion Confit, Spanish Style

Do not be put off by the term *confit*. Remember, the verb *confire* merely means to cook something very slowly at a low temperature. Here it simply translates into cooking the onions over low flame for a while until they become like marmalade, thus creating an intense essence of onions.

> 1 tablespoon ground cumin
> 1 tablespoon paprika
> 1 teaspoon finely chopped fresh thyme leaves
> ¼ teaspoon cayenne pepper
> pepper and salt
> 2 pounds wild salmon fillet
> juice of ½ lime
> 4 tablespoons olive oil
> 4 large onions, peeled and sliced
> 3 garlic cloves, minced
> ½ red bell pepper, cut into thin strips
> ⅔ cup white wine
> 1 tablespoon capers
> 1 cup fresh cilantro leaves, chopped

In a small bag (paper or plastic), make your dry marinade by mixing together cumin, paprika, thyme, cayenne, pepper, and salt. Shake vigorously.

Brush salmon with lime juice and rub both sides well with dry cumin-paprika marinade. Refrigerate, covered, 30 minutes.

Preheat oven to 375°.

In a skillet, heat 2 tablespoons olive oil and sauté onions, garlic, and red pepper 5 minutes. Sprinkle with ⅓ cup wine and pepper and salt. Reduce heat, cover pan, and cook 30 minutes, stirring once in a while, until mixture thickens and looks a little like marmalade. You've just made your onion confit.

In an ovenproof dish, spread onion confit evenly.

Heat skillet to very hot. Add remaining olive oil, and sear salmon 1 minute on each side. Turn off heat. Cut salmon into 4 steaks and place them in a row on top of onion confit. Scatter capers and remaining wine over salmon. Bake 8–10 minutes. Salmon steaks should be served on top of bed of onion confit. Sprinkle with cilantro. SERVES 4–6.

Fillets of Skate in an Oyster Emulsion, on a Bed of Spinach

The more traditional recipe for skate calls for poached skate with brown butter. This recipe is slightly more ambitious but not more difficult. Don't be put off by the title. It is not a recipe best left to professionals, let me assure you! The preparation is infinitely easier than the title suggests, and besides, you'll have fun with the blender (or a small manual foamer — easy to find, and inexpensive — used for steaming milk in cappuccino), while creating an airy, bubbly, and light sauce. You'll be pleasantly surprised at how easy it really is to make this fancy, haute cuisine "foam."

In fact, chances are as you arrive at the table bearing this dish you will immediately be elevated to a four-star chef by your dinner guests.

> 2 pounds fresh baby spinach, washed and cut into fine strips
> 2 shallots, minced
> 3 tablespoons olive oil
> 1 tablespoon balsamic vinegar
> pepper and salt
> 4 cups vegetable stock
> 4 (½ pound) pieces of skate
> 6 oysters, shucked (with their liquid)
> juice of 1 lemon
> 4 ice cubes
> pinch of sugar
> ½ cup capers

In a bowl, toss spinach with shallots, olive oil, vinegar, pepper, and salt. Spread spinach salad in center of a platter. Set aside.

In a kettle, bring stock to a boil. Poach skate 5 minutes. With a slotted spoon, remove skate to a plate. With a spatula and a fork, gently slip skate pieces out of their bones.

Arrange skate around spinach, in a fan-like manner. (Skate lends itself naturally to this shape.)

In a blender, quickly emulsify oysters, lemon juice, ice cubes, sugar, and a pinch of salt for a few seconds. (If you are using one of the little manual foamers, immerse oysters, lemon juice, sugar, and salt in a bowl and turn manual foamer on.) Pour foamy mixture over skate. Sprinkle with capers and serve.

This dish is best served tepid. SERVES 4.

Grilled Snapper with Chili and Garlic

Light and easy to prepare, this snapper recipe is quite flavorful. If you find it too hot, simply decrease the number of chili peppers.

FOR THE FISH
    1 (2-pound) snapper
    1 teaspoon coarse salt
    3 tablespoons olive oil
    2 garlic cloves, minced
    1 bunch watercress, washed and stems removed

FOR THE CHILI SAUCE
    3 tablespoons olive oil
    1 garlic clove, minced
    4 red chili peppers, minced
    juice of ½ lemon
    pepper and salt

Have your fishmonger scale and split open the snapper for you. Open the fish out flat. Salt it lightly and leave 30 minutes. Rinse and pat dry.

Preheat grill or broiler.

Brush some of the olive oil on both sides of snapper. Lay fish skin-side down on the grill, or skin-side up under the broiler. Cook 8 minutes. Do not turn fish. Simply test to make sure it's done by poking with a knife. If the flesh is opaque, your fish is cooked.

While fish cooks, make the chili sauce: In a skillet or saucepan, heat olive oil and sauté garlic and red chili pepper a few seconds. Stir in the lemon juice, pepper, and salt. Set aside.

Spread some watercress with seasoning on each plate. With a spatula and a fork, carefully lift fish off its spine, divide into 4 serving portions, and place one on each plate. Sprinkle with chili sauce. SERVES 4.

Salmon in Cabbage Purses on a Bed of Roasted Vegetables

Both salmon and cabbage are known to be medicinally beneficial for a variety of ailments, including reducing the risks of heart disease and cancer. Each time I make this dish, I not only enjoy the delicacy of a salmon patty encased in a cabbage leaf, I also feel virtuous.

½ white cabbage, leaves separated
juice of ½ lemon
1 pound fillet of salmon (wild or Atlantic)
2 shallots, minced
1 egg, lightly beaten
1½ cups breadcrumbs
1 cup finely chopped dill
1 cup celery, peeled, washed, and diced
⅓ cup mayonnaise
1 tablespoon Worcestershire sauce
1 teaspoon Tabasco sauce
pepper and salt
oil for frying
1 bunch chives

Preheat oven to 350°.

In a kettle, bring 1 quart water to a boil. Cook cabbage 3 minutes. Drain. The leaves should be soft and malleable. Dry leaves with paper towels. Set aside.

Sprinkle lemon juice on salmon, wrap in foil, and bake 15 minutes. Remove from oven and cool.

FOR THE SALMON PATTIES

In a bowl, mix salmon, shallot, egg, 1 cup breadcrumbs, the dill, celery, mayonnaise, Worcestershire sauce, Tabasco, pepper, and salt. Spread remaining breadcrumbs on a sheet of foil. With your hands, form cakes roughly 2 inches in diameter and coat them in the breadcrumbs.

In a skillet, heat a little olive oil and cook salmon patties over low flame 2 minutes on each side. Drain on paper towels. You should have about 8 or 10 patties.

Arrange 10 cooked cabbage leaves on counter. Place a salmon patty in each leaf (if the leaves seem too small, overlap two leaves to form a "purse"). Enclose by tying each purse with strands of chives.

In a kettle, heat 2 tablespoons olive oil and brown "purses" 3 minutes. Serve 2 "purses" per person, with a couple extra for good measure. SERVES 4.

Tiger Shrimp with Feta and Tomato

Quick to prepare, this Greek dish is as good as it is simple. (Tiger shrimp are simply jumbo shrimp with a more colorful name.)

> ¼ cup olive oil
> 5 tomatoes, peeled and chopped
> 2 garlic cloves, minced
> 1 green pepper, seeded, white membrane removed, cut into chunks
> 1 cup flat parsley leaves, finely chopped
> ½ teaspoon cayenne pepper
> 16–20 tiger shrimp, peeled and deveined
> pepper and salt
> 1 cup feta cheese, crumbled

Preheat oven to 400°.

In a skillet, heat olive oil and sauté tomatoes, garlic, pepper, parsley, and cayenne. Cook 10 minutes. Add tiger shrimp, stir, and cook 1 more minute. Sprinkle with pepper and salt. Transfer to casserole dish, add feta, and bake 8 minutes. SERVES 4.

Spanish Tiger Shrimp with Cream, Lemon, Chili, and Pappardelle

Wonderfully spiced, this shrimp and pasta dish, prepared in minutes, is as easy to make as it is delightful to eat.

1 teaspoon salt, plus extra for seasoning
1 pound pappardelle or wide fettuccine pasta
1½ cups heavy cream
2 tablespoons butter
pepper
3 tablespoons olive oil
16–20 tiger shrimp, shelled, shells retained
3 garlic cloves, minced
3 hot peppers, minced
juice of 2 lemons

In a kettle, heat 4 quarts water and 1 teaspoon salt to boiling. Cook pasta 8 minutes. Drain. Toss 1 cup cream, butter, pepper, and salt. Transfer to serving platter.

In a skillet, heat olive oil. Sauté shrimp shells 2 minutes. Add garlic, peppers, and lemon juice. Stir in shrimp and cook 2 more minutes until they turn pink. Turn heat off.

With a slotted spoon, remove and discard shells. Put shrimp on top of pasta on serving platter. Heat skillet and stir in remaining ½ cup cream; boil 1 minute. Pour over shrimp. SERVES 4.

Angel Hair with Trout Caviar

Let me be blunt: I *love* this dish, and so do my guests. Surprisingly easy and quick as well as elegant, it never fails to become everyone's instant favorite. There is something magical about taking the first bite and tasting those little pearls of caviar with chives and butter on angel-hair spaghetti — a combination of textures and flavors unlike anything you've ever tasted!

Finding trout caviar is the only problem. Trout caviar looks like salmon roe, but is more delicate and has less of a fish flavor. For some reason, trout caviar is readily available in several Mediterranean countries, but despite the fact that trout can be found at all fishmongers in America, its roe seems virtually unavailable. However, very similar results can be obtained with salmon roe.

> salt
> 1 pound angel-hair pasta
> 2 tablespoons vodka
> 4 tablespoons butter
> 1 bunch fresh chives, finely chopped
> pepper
> 4 ounces trout caviar or salmon roe

In a kettle, bring 2 quarts water and 1 tablespoon salt to a boil. Cook angel-hair pasta 5 minutes. Drain. Return to kettle, pour in vodka (the addition of vodka makes the pasta silky), and add butter, chives, pepper, and salt. Turn heat back on, cook 2 minutes, and toss well, making sure angel hair is good and hot. Turn heat off at once. Add trout caviar or salmon roe and toss quickly to mix. Serve immediately. SERVES 4.

Tip: Do not keep heat on after trout caviar or salmon roe has been incorporated into the pasta. If you do, the tiny eggs will cook and turn opaque and the whole dish will be ruined!

Note: This recipe, in half-portions, is also a welcome first course.

Le Grand Aioli

Aioli is a garlic mayonnaise, and the *grand aioli,* as the southern French call it, is a festive, colorful, and convivial one-dish summer meal consisting of fish and a multitude of vegetables served with the garlic mayonnaise. It is always fun to present the big platter with its many colors. Considering that most food you really enjoy is not always recommended by your nutritionist, the grand aioli also happens to be very healthy — offering mainly poached fish and a generous array of vegetables. The only sin here is the aioli itself. But so little sinning for so much enjoyment!

Grand aioli is also ideal for a large summer buffet party, in which case, simply multiply the ingredients appropriately.

6 young carrots, peeled, steamed 5 minutes
6 small potatoes, washed, unpeeled, and cooked
3 tomatoes, peeled and quartered
1 fennel bulb, stalks and leaves cut off, cut into quarters
1 small cauliflower, separated into florets and blanched 5 minutes
1 beet, cooked, peeled, and halved or quartered
½ pound green beans, trimmed and steamed 2 minutes
½ pound asparagus, trimmed and steamed 3 minutes
1 cup black olives, pitted
1½ pounds fillets of fresh cod, cooked 15 minutes, drained, cooled, and divided into 2-inch pieces
3 eggs, hard boiled, peeled, and cut into quarters

FOR THE AIOLI

2 eggs
2 cups olive oil
6 garlic cloves, minced
salt and pepper

I used to make my aioli by first pounding the garlic in a mortar, beating in the egg yolks, and slowly trickling the oil until it formed a mayonnaise, a process that often took 20–30 minutes. I am sure that gastronomic purists will throw up their arms in horror at the way I make my aioli today. Thanks to the electric blender, I achieve the same result — in minutes. I break the whole egg — I use 2 eggs here — into the blender, add garlic, pepper, and salt, and while the machine is on, I trickle in the olive oil until the aioli thickens. I then transfer my aioli into a serving bowl. *Voilà*!

On a large serving platter, arrange the vegetables, cod, and eggs according to your personal aesthetic taste. Place the bowl of aioli in the center. SERVES 6.

Grilled Sea Bass with Fennel and Herbs

All Mediterranean cuisines feature some version of grilled fish. Here, the fennel, used in Greece, France, and Italy, enhances the fish with its anise perfume, giving it an irresistible summer flavor.

FOR THE SEA BASS
2 small sea bass, cut in half lengthwise
juice of 1 lemon, plus 2 lemons, quartered
4 or more sprigs fennel cut off from fennel bulbs
4 sprigs thyme
a few sprigs parsley
pepper and salt
¼ cup olive oil
3 tablespoons flour

FOR THE LEMON BASIL SAUCE
juice of 1 lemon
½ cup fresh basil leaves, finely chopped
⅓ cup olive oil

In a small bowl, combine juice of 1 lemon, basil, and ⅓ cup olive oil. (You may emulsify the above ingredients in the blender for smoother sauce.) Set aside.

Wash fish and pat dry. Pour lemon juice over fish and rub in well. Stuff fennel sprigs, thyme, parsley, and lemon quarters into cavities and sprinkle with pepper and salt. Brush olive oil on all sides of fish. Sprinkle with flour.

Heat grill or broiler and cook 4 minutes on each side. Lift fish with two spatulas onto serving platter, remove thyme and fennel, and carefully lift fillets off the center bones — leaving the backbones on platter. Place sea-bass fillets onto individual plates with a little of the fennel. Trickle with lemon-olive and basil sauce. SERVES 4.

Bouillabaisse

Bouillabaisse — *La grande! La merveilleuse!*

Famous, fragrant, and delectable, this southern French specialty, a one-dish meal consisting of different fish, shellfish, and soup, and accompanied by aioli, and a hotter mayonnaise version, the rouille, originated in Marseilles — the important, bustling fishing harbor. Now other towns and cities along the Mediterranean coast claim it as well. In fact, it would appear that bouillabaisse predates the Greeks, who had invaded Marseilles and mention a soup recipe dating from the pre-Christian era — a recipe as tantalizing as today's bouillabaisse. Be that as it may, bouillabaisse conjures up an image of Marseilles, and it is referred to by many as Marseilles's property. French gourmands, and Marseillais especially, approach eating bouillabaisse with the reverence and anticipation of a sacred ritual. If in doubt, I suggest you walk along the Marseilles harbor at lunch or dinner time. Watching people at all the restaurant terraces bordering the harbor will confirm the high esteem in which this dish is held. And with good reason.

The name bouillabaisse comes from Old French and literally means: to boil — *bouillir* — in a pot. The strict rules as to which fish to include, and in what proportion, has over the years intimidated many a home chef. The one constant seems to be *rascasse* fish. Since it is not available on this side of the Atlantic, one simply omits it — or substitutes — when preparing one's own bouillabaisse. Many food experts and cooks say it's impossible to make a real bouillabaisse in America — the native fish being so different. I disagree.

Years ago, I decided to overcome my initial intimidation and began experimenting with my own version of bouillabaisse — fully aware I might be breaking some sacred rules. In any case, this recipe, of the twelve or fifteen I have tried and tested, is my favorite, and comes close to the original.

The more varieties of fish you are able to include, of course, the tastier your bouillabaisse will be.

FOR THE FISH STOCK

If you have time, making your own fish stock is so much better than the ready-made variety. Strained in small containers, it can be frozen and kept for later fish soups.

I usually ask the fishmonger to give me a bag of bones and fish heads.

In a large kettle, cover fish bones and heads with 2 cups white wine, 5 inches water, ½ teaspoon peppercorns, 1 teaspoon salt, 1 large onion, celery stalks, 3 carrots, 1 teaspoon thyme, and 1 bunch parsley. Bring to a boil, reduce heat, and simmer 2 hours. Cool. Strain and discard solids and fish bones.

FOR THE BOUILLABAISSE
: ½ cup olive oil
: 3 onions, finely chopped
: 5 tomatoes, peeled and cubed
: 7 garlic cloves, minced
: 1 bunch basil leaves, washed and chopped finely
: 2 tablespoons fresh thyme leaves
: 3 pints or more good fish stock
: 1 cup white wine
: ½ cup Pernod
: 1 tablespoon Tabasco sauce
: zest of ½ orange, cut into strips
: ½ teaspoon saffron
: 8 small potatoes, cooked 15 minutes in water and drained
: 10 little clams, scrubbed
: 2 pounds fresh fillets of monkfish
: 1 pound fresh cod
: 1½ pounds shrimp, peeled, deveined, and tails removed
: 10 mussels, scrubbed
: 1 cup sea scallops
: 1 cup parsley, finely chopped
: cheese toasts, recipe follows
: aioli, see recipe on page 102
: rouille, recipe follows

FOR THE BOUILLABAISSE SOUP

In a large kettle, heat olive oil and sauté onions until wilted. Add tomatoes, garlic, basil, and thyme and cook 5 minutes, stirring. Add fish stock, white wine, Pernod, Tabasco sauce, orange zest, and saffron and simmer, covered, 15 minutes, over low heat. Taste and adjust seasoning to taste.

In a blender, put fish stock, 2 ladles at a time, with tomato mixture, and half the potatoes, and, holding blender top down, tight — anytime you blend hot food, you must hold on tight to the top, otherwise the liquid tends to spurt out — purée remaining liquid. You will obtain a pinkish, creamy soup.

Transfer puréed soup back to kettle and stir.

Clams go in soup first because they take longer to open. Cover and cook 10 good minutes. Add remaining potatoes, monkfish, cod, shrimp, mussels, and scallops. Cover again, and continue cooking over low heat for another 5–8 minutes. If all the mussels haven't yet opened, cover and cook a few more minutes. Stir in the parsley.

Bring the bouillabaisse kettle to the table and ladle soup liquid first, and apportion a little of each fish and seafood to each soup plate. Top with one toast covered with cheese. Add a dollop of rouille and one of aioli to the soup plate, and serve.

Pass both bowls of rouille and aioli around for those who wish to add more to their bouillabaisse.

The bouillabaisse is traditionally served with aioli, and a rouille sauce, and accompanied by garlicky toasts topped with grated Swiss cheese.

Note: If you prefer, you may omit the grated Swiss cheese and merely spread rouille and aioli on the toasts.

FOR THE AIOLI: SEE PAGE IO2

FOR THE CHEESE TOASTS
⅓ cup olive oil
8–10 thin slices of French bread
1 garlic clove, peeled but left whole (for rubbing toasts)
1 cup grated Swiss cheese

In a skillet, heat some olive oil and fry bread slices on both sides. Rub garlic clove on each fried toast. Top each toast with cheese. Transfer to serving platter.

FOR THE ROUILLE
3 garlic cloves, minced
3 slices French bread, soaked in water and squeezed dry
1 egg
1 small hot red pepper, minced
1 tablespoon tomato paste
saffron
1 cup olive oil
3 tablespoons liquid from bouillabaisse soup
pepper and salt
cayenne pepper, optional

In a blender, put the garlic, bread, egg, red pepper, tomato paste, and saffron. Turn machine on. Trickle in olive oil until you have a red-looking mayonnaise. Season with bouillabaisse liquid, pepper, and salt. Check and adjust seasoning. You may wish to make it stronger and add a few more grains of cayenne. Transfer to serving bowl. SERVES 10–12.

Cod Purée with Garlic and Truffles

The pride of Provence, it is called *brandade de morue* — cod purée with olive oil and garlic. The *brandade* stands out as one of Provence's specialties, one of its crown jewels. Each Provençal cook, of course, whether home chef or professional, claims to hold the "real" *brandade* recipe.

How much thyme or garlic one uses, whether one adds a potato or two, or whether one adds cream elevates the *brandade* or banishes it as blasphemy; it depends on how purist a gastronomic position one takes. My *brandade*'s success rests mainly on using a few potatoes and cream, which neutralizes the fish while preserving its integrity.

Tip: When making *brandade de morue,* it's a good idea to plan ahead at least three days. You'll need that much time to allow the cod, submerged in water, to rid itself of its salt (at least 24–48 hours, because the cod is packed in salt), and be reconstituted prior to baking. Only then can the actual preparation of the final recipe be completed.

1½ pounds dried, salt cod
2 cups milk
2 medium potatoes, cooked
½ cup or more olive oil
½ cup heavy cream
garlic
pepper and salt
2 tablespoons fresh thyme leaves, finely chopped
1 or 2 black truffles, cleaned with a small brush (optional)
1 baguette, sliced

Preheat oven to 350°.

In a shallow dish, immerse dried, salted fish in cold water. Place fish in its water, covered, in the refrigerator. Change water every few hours. Do this over the course of 2 days. The cod should come out looking fluffy. Remove from refrigerator. Drain. Discard water.

Place fish in an ovenproof dish and cover with milk. Bake 20 minutes. Drain and discard milk.

In a food processor, purée cod, adding potatoes, ½ cup olive oil, cream, garlic, thyme, pepper, and salt. Adjust for taste. (It may perhaps need a touch more olive oil, more cream, or more garlic, even a touch more salt, etc.) Transfer to serving platter. Shave truffles over cod purée and serve. For better dramatic effect, given the luxury aspect of serving truffles, I recommend shaving truffles, if you go that route, over the *brandade* right at the table.

Toast 20 slices of French baguette. Rub a garlic clove over each toast and sprinkle on a few drops olive oil. Put toasts in a basket. Serve alongside the *brandade*. SERVES 6–8.

Tip: This sumptuous dish is obviously commonly served *without* truffle. The truffle, however, does add that *je-ne-sais-quoi* to the already acclaimed dish, that "superfluous touch of luxury" that elevates it to the level of true gastronomic elegance. But even without truffles, this is a dish your family and friends will love.

MEATLESS MAIN COURSES

Leek Tart

When crates of fresh leeks arrive on the market late in the season, it confirms that summer is nearly over and it's a time for a change in your cooking habits.

A delicious main course, this leek tart can be prepared ahead. You may use any piecrust recipe you prefer. I use my mother's, finding it always easy and foolproof.

FOR THE CRUST
> 3 ounces cream cheese
> 8 tablespoons butter
> 1½ cups all-purpose flour
> 1 egg beaten with 1 tablespoon water (egg wash)

FOR THE FILLING
> 3 pounds leeks, well washed, white part only, sliced
> 3 tablespoons olive oil
> 1 tablespoon flour
> 1 tablespon herbes de Provence
> pepper and salt

Preheat oven to 400°.

In a food processor, combine cream cheese, butter, and flour. Pulse until it forms a dough. Wrap and refrigerate 30 minutes.

In a skillet, heat olive oil and 2 tablespoons water. Add leeks, herbes de Provence, pepper, and salt. Cook over medium heat about 10 minutes, until leeks are tender and liquid has evaporated. Set aside. Remove pastry dough from refrigerator.

On a floured surface, roll out pastry dough into a thin round roughly 10–12 inches in diameter. Transfer dough round to a baking sheet. Sprinkle flour over dough. Spread leeks in the center, leaving a good inch space to the edge of dough. Fold edge of dough over filling forming a loose shell. Brush dough edges with egg wash. Bake 35 minutes. SERVES 4–6.

Galette of Potatoes and Wild Mushrooms

This potato pie is succulent but rich, and although the regions of Provence, like their neighbors in Dordogne, tend to make this recipe with duck fat, it may perhaps not be recommended for those for whom cholesterol is a concern. Olive oil can nicely be substituted for the duck fat.

> 4 tablespoons duck fat (or olive oil)
> 2 garlic cloves, minced
> 8 ounces or a little more wild mushrooms, cleaned and chopped
>   coarsely
> 1 cup flat parsley leaves, finely chopped
> pepper and salt
> 4 baking potatoes, peeled and finely sliced

Preheat oven to 375°.

In a pan, heat 1 tablespoon duck fat over low heat and cook garlic and mushrooms 15 minutes, until liquid subsides (you may have to add a little more duck fat). Toss in half the parsley, pepper, and salt. Set aside.

In a frying pan, heat remaining duck fat. Remove from stove and line frying pan (sides included) with a layer of sliced potatoes, overlapping a little. Spread mushroom mixture over potato and cover with remaining potato slices. Drizzle a touch more duck fat, and sprinkle with pepper and salt.

Over medium heat, cook potato galette until bottom becomes light brown and crisp. Remove from stove top and place in oven. Bake 20 minutes. Check to make sure potatoes are tender, light brown, and crisp on top, and cooked through when you poke with a fork. Remove from oven and sprinkle remaining parsley. Carve like a pie and serve. SERVES 4–6.

Tip: Frivolous but delectable tip: If you happen to have a small jar of truffle cream, add a tablespoon to mushrooms when they are cooked, as you fill your potato pie.

Roast Portobello Mushrooms with Gremolata

The large and meaty portobello mushroom can be a good substitute for a satisfying meatless main course, especially prepared in this Italian recipe with lemon and garlic. (Braised radicchio will provide a delicious accompaniment for roast portobello.)

zest of 1 lemon
2 garlic cloves, minced
½ cup flat parsley leaves, finely chopped
4 portobello mushrooms, stems removed, caps wiped clean, and
   cut into thick slices
6 tablespoons olive oil
pepper and salt

FOR THE GREMOLATA:

In a mini food processor, grind zest, add garlic and parsley, and process until finely ground. Transfer to bowl. Set aside.

Preheat oven to 350°.

In a roasting pan or (preferably) individual ovenproof dishes, arrange mushroom slices, drizzle with some olive oil. Sprinkle with pepper and salt. Roast 15–20 minutes, until soft and golden. Remove from oven, drizzle a few drops olive oil, and sprinkle a generous amount of gremolata. SERVES 4.

Soupe au Pistou

This soup is featured in the main course section because in the South of France, *soupe au pistou,* consisting of three different beans and other vegetables, is considered a full meal (followed by a salad). Marvelously rich and satisfying, this hearty soup originated in seventeenth-century Italy, and some hundred years ago it made its way over to Provence, where it has been firmly ensconced ever since.

Because of the many ingredients, as with several other recipes in this book, it is unrealistic to prepare this dish for only four people; plan on serving it when you expect several guests. If you are only four, you can safely keep the leftover in the refrigerator for a few days.

1 tablespoon herbes de Provence
pepper and salt
½ pound dried white (Great Northern) beans, soaked overnight
   and drained
½ pound dried cranberry beans, soaked overnight and drained
3 tomatoes, peeled and coarsely chopped
2 leeks, washed, white only, and sliced
2 onions, sliced
1 yellow squash, washed and cut into ½ cubes
1 large baking potato, peeled and diced
½ pound carrots, peeled and cut lengthwise into sticks
1 zucchini, washed, coarsely chopped
1 cup short macaroni
1½ cups green beans, trimmed and cut in half
pistou, recipe follows
warm, crisp French bread

In a kettle, put 8 cups water, herbes de Provence, pepper and salt. Bring to a boil. Add both Great Northern and cranberry beans. Reduce heat, cover, and cook 40 minutes. Add tomatoes, leeks, onions, squash, potato, and carrots and continue cooking 20 minutes. Add zucchini and pasta. Cook another 10 minutes over low heat. Add green beans. Cook another 5 minutes. Turn heat off. The soup should be thick and hearty.

Stir and serve with a generous spoonful of *pistou* on each plate, together with some warm, crisp French bread.

FOR THE PISTOU
4 garlic cloves, minced
2 cups basil leaves
1 tomato, peeled and cut into quarters
¾ cup olive oil
½ cup freshly grated Parmigiano-Reggiano cheese
pepper

In a food processor, combine garlic, basil, tomato, olive oil, cheese, and pepper. Unlike pesto — more familiar in America — this pistou has a tomato and doesn't call for pine nuts. You may, however, add some if you prefer. SERVES 8–10.

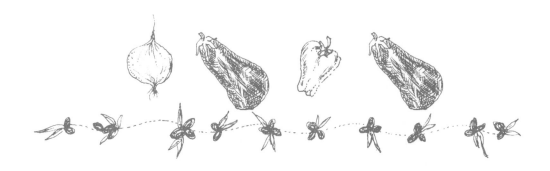

Eggplant Roulades

Eggplant is a substantial vegetable, and these roulades, as you will see, provide a fine main course. I suggest you start by making the sauce.

FOR THE SAUCE

2 tablespoons olive oil
1 onion, finely chopped
1 pound tomatoes, peeled and chopped coarsely
4 red peppers, seeded, white membrane removed, and diced
2 garlic cloves, minced
½ cup red wine
½ cup fresh basil, chopped
pepper and salt
2¼ cups freshly grated Parmigiano-Reggiano cheese

In a skillet, heat olive oil and sauté onion until translucent. Add tomatoes, red pepper, garlic, red wine, basil, pepper, and salt. Simmer 20 minutes. Toss in cheese. Transfer to sauceboat. Set aside.

FOR THE ROULADES

olive oil
2 long and wide eggplants, peeled and cut lengthwise into slices
1 shallot, minced

1 small eggplant, peeled and cubed
1 garlic clove, minced
½ cup fresh basil leaves, chopped
1½ cups feta cheese, crumbled
½ cup freshly grated Parmigiano-Reggiano cheese, grated
pepper and salt

Preheat oven to 350°. Grease a casserole dish with some oil.

Rub some olive oil on eggplant slices. Grill under a broiler or cook on top of the stove, in a skillet or a griddle about 3 minutes on each side. Set aside.

In the same skillet, heat 1 tablespoon olive oil, sauté shallot 3 minutes, stir in cubed eggplant, and cook 10 minutes. Add garlic, some basil, feta cheese, Parmigiano-Reggiano, pepper, and salt. Cool slightly.

Spoon out some eggplant-cheese mixture into center of eggplant slices. Roll lengthwise if you can, otherwise widthwise is fine; the roulades will be smaller but just as good. In prepared casserole dish, place eggplant rolls, seam down, side by side. Trickle with few drops olive oil. Cover with foil and bake 10 minutes. Heat sauce 2 minutes. Spoon out sauce and cover each eggplant roulade. Sprinkle with remaining basil. SERVES 4–6.

Eggplant Cutlets Milanese with a Yogurt Sauce

I have a weakness for crisp breaded veal cutlets — Viennese or Milanese — served with a wedge of lemon. Some years ago I discovered, to my great pleasure, this wonderful eggplant variation on the same theme. If you cut thick eggplant slices, they can pose as a first cousin of the meat cutlet. It's a perfect main course for vegetarians, and I have found carnivores love it as well. I have sometimes served it without announcing it wasn't veal or chicken, and my guests were fooled . . . at least for a minute or two.

> 2 medium eggplants, peeled and cut lengthwise into thick slices
> salt
> ½ cup all-purpose flour
> 2 egg whites, lightly beaten with a little milk
> ½ cup or more breadcrumbs
> 1 cup olive oil
> pepper
> 1 lemon, cut into wedges
> yogurt sauce, recipe follows

Place eggplant slices in a colander over a bowl and sprinkle salt over them. Let stand 30 minutes. Rinse and dry.

Have 3 soup plates ready on your counter, one for the flour, the second for the egg-white and milk mixture, and the third for the breadcrumbs.

Coat each eggplant slice first with the flour. Then dip in egg mixture, and, lastly, coat with breadcrumbs on both sides.

In a skillet, heat the olive oil, and fry each "cutlet" on both sides, turning them with the help of a spatula. The "cutlets" should be crisp and golden brown. They should look — and actually taste more than a little — like a breaded veal cutlet. Remove onto a platter lined with paper towels. Salt and pepper. Remove paper.

Serve each cutlet with a wedge of lemon and a generous helping of the yogurt sauce.

Tip: If you are pressed for time, just plain yogurt will do fine.

FOR THE YOGURT SAUCE

Greek, Turkish, and Indian cuisines all share variations of this yogurt sauce. I find that it is always a welcomed accompaniment to most grilled meats, fish, and vegetables.

> 2 cups plain yogurt (I favor the Greek variety)
> 1 cup mint, finely chopped
> ½ cup cooked spinach
> ½ cup raisins
> 2 garlic cloves, minced
> pepper and salt

In a bowl, combine the ingredients. Keep refrigerated until serving time. SERVES 4–6.

Morel and Truffle Tart

If this sumptuous dish seems a bit extravagant, save it for that special occasion. I assure you that, whenever you do serve it, you won't regret it.

Both fresh morels and truffles — among gastronomy's gems — are luxurious and costly gourmet items. Still, the unique aroma wafting from your kitchen is certain to permeate the whole house and envelop your soul. Enough said.

> 1 pound fresh morels, stems removed, and sliced (or 6 ounces dried ones)
> 1 tablespoon wine vinegar
> ⅓ cup olive oil
> 2 tablespoons butter
> 2 shallots, minced
> 2 slices cooked ham, diced
> 2 fresh (or canned) truffles, gently scraped clean and sliced
> 1 cup heavy cream
> ½ cup flat parsley leaves, finely chopped
> 2 sheets frozen puff pastry, thawed according to package directions
> 1 egg yolk mixed with 2 tablespoons water (egg wash)

Preheat oven to 425°.

Soak fresh morels in water and vinegar 5 minutes. Rinse several times to get rid of the grit. Drain and dry in a cloth or paper towels, squeezing out as much liquid as possible. (If using dried morels, soak 1 hour. Drain. Dry on towels and slice.)

In a skillet, heat a little olive oil and butter, sauté shallots until translucent, stir in morels, and continue cooking 5 minutes. Add ham, truffles, and cream. Cook 5 more minutes. Stir in parsley. Turn off heat.

On a lightly floured board, roll out pastry sheets. Lightly oil a cake pan and line it with one pastry sheet, letting it overhang a bit. Freeze 30 minutes. Roll out second sheet, spread on a plate, and freeze along with the one in the cake pan. Remove cake pan and fill with morel mixture. Remove second puff pastry sheet from freezer and place over filling. With wet fingers, seal top and bottom layers of pastry by pinching with thumb and forefinger all around. Brush "hat" of pie with more egg wash. Run a fork on the "hat" to create designs. (If you happen to have a little excess pastry, and are so inclined, roll it out, cut out shapes like flower petals, brush with egg wash, and add to top of "hat.") With a sharp knife, poke small incisions in the top crust (to allow steam to escape and prevent top crust from bursting).

Bake 50 minutes. Cool. With two pot holders, carefully unmold by lifting bottom of cake pan out of its rim and sliding it onto a serving platter. Slice. SERVES 4–6.

Lemon and Artichoke Risotto

Given my predilection for lemon and artichoke, I always enjoy making this fragrant risotto.

>4 cups chicken stock
>2 tablespoons olive oil
>2 tablespoons butter
>1 onion, finely chopped
>1½ cups Italian rice (Arborio)
>3 celery stalks, peeled and diced
>1 garlic clove, minced
>⅔ cup white wine
>juice and grated zest of 4 lemons
>2 artichoke hearts, cooked and diced
>½ cup fresh basil leaves, chopped
>pepper and salt
>½ cup freshly grated Parmigiano-Reggiano cheese
>½ cup crème fraîche or sour cream

Tip: It is best to zest lemons when whole.

In a pan, heat stock. In a kettle, heat olive oil and butter and sauté onion until translucent. Add rice, celery, garlic, and cook 5 minutes. Pour in wine, and continue stirring until wine is evaporated. Gradually pour in hot stock one ladle at a time, until all is absorbed. Stir in lemon zest, lemon juice, artichoke, basil, cheese, crème fraîche, pepper, and salt. SERVES 4–6.

Tip: In the absence of fresh artichokes, a jar of marinated artichokes will do fine. Drain and use as above.

MEAT MAIN COURSES

Moroccan Lamb Meat Balls with Prunes and Almonds

Tagine is the term used in Morocco not only for a round, spectacular-looking earthenware (or ceramic) dish covered with a conic top, but also for the actual dish cooked therein. Tagine comes in many ways: with chicken, lamb, meat balls made from lamb or beef, and fish. Always spicy and aromatic, the meat is braised and served with a grain such as couscous or rice, into which a variety of dried fruit, olives, or preserved lemons has been incorporated. The following is one of the many traditional tagines made with lamb meat balls, called *kefta* in Moroccan.

Tip: I find it handy to prepare kefta tagine a day or even two after serving a roast of lamb, when leftover lamb from the roast — 2–3 cups — is just about what is required to make this dish.

> 2 cups instant couscous
> 1 cup prunes, pitted
> ½ cup sugar
> olive oil
> 1 teaspoon ground cinnamon, plus extra for sprinkling
> 2 pounds onions, finely chopped
> 2 bunches cilantro, washed and chopped

1 bunch flat parsley, chopped
3 garlic cloves, minced
1 teaspoon ground cumin, plus extra for sprinkling
1 teaspoon paprika
1 cup almonds
pepper and salt

FOR THE MEAT BALLS
olive oil
1 medium onion, finely chopped
2–3 cups cooked lamb, ground
½ teaspoon ground cumin
½ teaspoon ground cinnamon

Prepare couscous according to package directions, fluff it with a fork and set aside, covered.

In a saucepan, heat 2 cups water, the prunes, sugar, 1 tablespoon olive oil, and 1 teaspoon cinnamon. Reduce heat and simmer 25 minutes. Drain prunes, discard liquid, and set aside.

In another saucepan, bring 1 cup water to a boil. Plunge almonds in boiling water 1 minute. Remove from water, and peel skin off. Set aside.

In a skillet, heat 3 tablespoons olive oil. Sauté onions until translucent. Add half the cilantro, the parsley, garlic, 1 teaspoon cumin, and paprika. Stir in 2 cups water and simmer 15 minutes. It will become thick like a marmalade. Set aside.

In a skillet, heat 1 tablespoon olive oil. Sauté onion until translucent.

In a bowl, combine meat, cumin, cinnamon, and cooked onion. Form little meat balls. In same skillet, heat 1 tablespoon olive oil, brown meat balls on all sides.

Preheat oven to 350°.

In a tagine dish, or an ovenproof dish, combine prunes, meat balls, almonds, onion mixture, and couscous. Sprinkle with more cumin, cilantro, cinnamon, pepper, salt, and a few drops olive oil. Cover and cook 20 minutes. Sprinkle remaining cilantro and serve.

If you happen to have cooked the kefta in a tagine dish, bring it to table with its conic lid on. Ceremoniously, remove lid. SERVES 4–6.

Tip: The meat of choice is lamb, which imparts a special Middle-Eastern flavor, but beef tagine is also good, following exactly the same steps as above.

Chicken Tagine with Preserved Lemons and Olives

The lemon aroma from preserved lemons in this easy-to-prepare tagine gives this variation a special exotic tang. The green olives add a crunchy, tasty element.

1½ cups green olives, pitted
¼ cup olive oil
1 onion, finely chopped
1 chicken, cut into 2-inch pieces
2 preserved lemons, flesh and pith scrapped off, peel cut into
   wedges
2 garlic cloves, minced
1 teaspoon paprika
1 teaspoon ground cumin
pepper and salt
1 cup chicken stock
1 cup fresh cilantro leaves, chopped

In a saucepan, bring 1 cup water to a boil and cook olives 5 minutes. Drain and set aside.

In a kettle, heat olive oil. Sauté onion until translucent. Add chicken and cook 10 minutes. Add olives and lemon. Sprinkle with garlic, paprika, cumin, pepper, and salt. Stir in chicken stock. Transfer to casserole (or tagine dish). Cover and cook 30 minutes. Sprinkle with cilantro. Serves 6–8.

Note: Preserved lemons may be obtained in specialty food stores. To make preserved lemons, cut lemons into wedges, salt them well. Cover with lemon juice and let stand covered in a jar for a week or more.

Greek Pork Loin in a Dried Figs Sauce

The sweetness of the figs works well with the roast here. Remember, pork loin is, as the ads tell us, the "other white meat." A loin of pork provides many an exquisite meal, takes relatively little cooking time, is flavorful, and can often be a fine substitute for veal.

1 tablespoon chopped fresh thyme leaves
1 tablespoon fresh rosemary leaves, finely chopped
1 teaspoon ground cumin
pepper and salt
1 pork loin
½ cup olive oil
3 carrots, peeled and sliced
2 onions, finely chopped
2 tomatoes, peeled and chopped
1 garlic clove, minced
juice of 1 lemon
1 cup white wine
1 cup dried figs, cut into very small pieces

Preheat oven to 300°.

In a bowl, mix thyme, rosemary, cumin, pepper, and salt. Rub dry marinade all over the loin.

In a skillet, heat olive oil and brown meat on all sides. Add carrots, onions, tomatoes, garlic, lemon juice, and 1 cup wine, reduce heat, and continue cooking 20 minutes. Transfer to ovenproof dish. Drizzle a little water over meat. Cover. Bake 40 minutes.

With a slotted spoon, remove meat from sauce, and set aside on carving board. Purée contents of ovenproof dish in a blender. Pour puréed mixture in a colander over a bowl, pressing with a fork to extract all liquid. Discard solids. Pour strained sauce into saucepan, bring to simmer, add figs, and cook 5–8 minutes.

Slice pork.

Arrange slices on serving platter, cover with sauce and figs. SERVES 6.

Tip: Orzo — a small pasta in the shape of rice — with parsley and butter is a fine accompaniment for this roast.

Chicken Bouillabaisse

Like its namesake, the great fish bouillabaisse, this one offers chicken, vegetables, and plenty of garlic and basil. It also originated in Marseille and its coastal environs. Chicken bouillabaisse is easy to prepare, and particularly welcome when vegetables and herbs are in season. A one-dish meal, it is very handy for a crowd. This recipe is for four, but if you wish to make it for more, simply multiply the ingredients accordingly.

½ cup olive oil
3 chicken breasts, cut in half
3–4 thighs, preferably boned
1 large onion, finely chopped
4–5 tomatoes, skinned and quartered
4 small russet potatoes
2 garlic cloves, minced
1 cup fresh basil, chopped
½ cup fresh thyme sprigs
½ cup fresh oregano sprigs

pinch of saffron
pepper and salt
2 cups chicken stock
1 cup white wine
1 zucchini, sliced
pesto, recipe follows

In a deep kettle, heat the oil and brown chicken on all sides. Stir in onion, and cook 10 more minutes. Add tomatoes, potatoes, garlic, basil, thyme, oregano, saffron, pepper, and salt. Pour in stock and wine, reduce heat, cover, and simmer 20 minutes. Add zucchini, cover, and continue simmering 10 more minutes. Serve by ladling liquid with chicken and vegetables into each soup plate, and top with a dollop of pesto.

Tip: While your chicken bouillabaisse simmers, prepare your pesto.

FOR THE PESTO

Not so many years ago, this pungent — and for me essential — sauce was unavailable, except in Italian restaurants. I used to make it using a pestle and mortar — somewhat time consuming. I have long since abandoned this method for the food processor.

Today, ready-made pesto can be purchased in most food stores and supermarkets throughout the land. Many are actually quite good. But for me fresh has no rival. Besides, to make your own is so easy and quick — it can literally be done in minutes — so there is no excuse *not* to make pesto.

4 garlic cloves
1 bunch basil, washed
½ cup pine nuts
½ cup freshly grated Parmigiano-Reggiano cheese
½ cup olive oil
pepper and salt

In a food processor, purée all ingredients to form a thick, green pesto sauce. SERVES 4–6.

Cassoulet

This exceptional dish emanates from Languedoc, but virtually every southern French village or town — from Carcassone and Castelnaudary to Toulouse and Provence — claims to hold the "real and authentic" cassoulet recipe. Endless debates continue still today to determine whose is the best. Cassoulets do vary, not only from place to place, but from cook to cook. There are some with goose and duck only, others with a combination of goose and pork and tomatoes, or goose and lamb meat. They all share however, a smoky and garlicky pork sausage called *saucisse de Toulouse* — the equivalent here is a combination of the Polish kielbasa and pure pork sausage.

I once traveled with some "foodie" friends through the southern regions of France *à la rechèrche du cassoulet,* sampling different versions for practically every meal — yes, for breakfast, lunch, and dinner — in a half dozen towns including Carcassonne and Castelnaudary. All were delicious. As I felt my waistline expanding, I was hard pressed as to which I preferred.

Aromatic, mouthwatering — and very rich — this one-dish-meal is always presented with great pride, no matter who the chef and which part of the country he or she hails from. Many home chefs find making cassoulet daunting, but I urge you to try. I guarantee you'll find it rewarding.

Of the many "real" cassoulet recipes I have tried and made over the years, this is my favorite.

Note: No cassoulet recipe, by definition, can be conceived for less than 8–10 people, or many more. What is left over keeps well for a few days, covered, in the refrigerator, or may even be successfully frozen.

Tip: Keep in mind that by making your cassoulet ahead, little by little, in several "acts," you will find it much easier. Cassoulet is like a play in four acts:

Act One: Soaking overnight and cooking beans
Act Two: Cooking various meats — separately
Act Three: Making the stock
Act Four: Assembling and baking the cassoulet

2 ducks, boned
3 carrots, plus 1 cup cut-up carrots
1 onion, peeled, plus 2 onions, finely chopped
1 bunch flat parsley, finely chopped
3 bay leaves
½ teaspoon peppercorns
¼ teaspoon ground cloves
salt
2 pounds dried French white beans (flageolets) or Great
    Northern beans
duck fat
1 tablespoon dried thyme leaves
3 teaspoons fresh rosemary leaves, finely chopped
pepper
4 kielbasa sausages
2 pork sausages
6 slices lamb steak from the leg
4 garlic cloves, minced
4 tomatoes, peeled and cut up
1 pound salted fatback, boiled 20 minutes, drained and cut into
    small cubes
4–5 cups duck broth made from the bones, or chicken stock
½ bottle white dry wine
½ cup brandy
1½ cups breadcrumbs

Preheat oven to 250°.

Tip: At little extra cost, the butcher will bone your ducks, and give you the bones from which to make a fine, strong stock.

ACT ONE

As I embark on my cassoulet preparation, I put the duck bones, 3 carrots, 1 peeled onion, some parsley, 1 bay leaf, peppercorns, ground cloves, and salt in a large kettle. I cover the bones with 4 inches water. Bring to boil, reduce heat, and simmer 3 hours. Cool. Strain. Discard solids. Reserve stock.

ACT TWO

In a kettle, combine beans with enough water to cover by 2 inches and soak overnight. Next day, drain and rinse beans in a colander. In a kettle, heat 2 tablespoons duck fat. Sauté chopped onions until translucent. Add beans, cut-up carrots, 1 teaspoon thyme, 1 teaspoon rosemary, 2 bay leaves, pepper, and salt. Add enough water to cover by 3 inches, reduce heat, and cook, covered, until tender — about 50 or more minutes. You may need to add a little water from time to time. Drain, discard bay leaves — but keep liquid. Set aside.

ACT THREE

Preheat oven to 275°.

Put ducks in ovenproof pan, make some gashes to allow fat to escape, sprinkle with pepper and salt, and slowly cook for 3 hours. Remove from oven. Cut duck into 2-inch pieces. Reserve fat.

In a kettle, bring 2 quarts water to a boil and cook kielbasa sausages 15 minutes. Drain. Peel and slice sausages into 1-inch pieces. Set aside.

Prick pork sausages with a fork and sauté in 1 tablespoon duck fat until cooked — about 15 minutes. Slice and set aside.

In a kettle, heat 2 tablespoons duck fat and brown lamb, reduce heat, and cook 40 minutes over medium heat with 1 minced garlic clove, 1 teaspoon rosemary, ½ teaspoon thyme, salt, and pepper. Stir in ½ cup water. Set aside.

ACT FOUR

Now comes the final step of assembling and baking, which I recommend doing the day before serving. Cassoulet gains in fragrance and taste when reheated the next day.

Preheat oven to 350°.

In a large casserole dish, arrange your duck pieces, sausages, lamb pieces with the pan drippings, tomatoes, pork fat cubes, beans, 2 cups duck stock, wine, brandy, remaining thyme, rosemary, and garlic, 3 tablespoons duck fat, wine, and brandy. Cover with a thick layer of breadcrumbs. Bake 1 hour. With a spoon, press down on the crumb crust to let liquid come to the surface. Cool. Remove from oven. Refrigerate covered overnight.

The next day, add bean liquid and stock to cassoulet — the cassoulet *must* remain well lubricated and moist — and stir well (more liquid may be required to moisten the dish, in which case feel free to add more stock, even a little more duck fat).

Preheat oven to 275°.

Sprinkle more breadcrumbs in an even layer, especially after you've added more liquid, it will prevent your casserole from overflowing in your oven. (I usually line the bottom of the oven with a sheet of foil). Bake cassoulet slowly 2 hours. The cassoulet should be bubbling, and breadcrumbs should form a golden crust. Sprinkle with remaining parsley. SERVES 8–10.

Note: For those put off by the time it might take to perform these "acts," remember, you are doing this over several days at your leisure. I, like many, work outside the home full time. I manage to fit the cassoulet acts in the interstices of my life, with no problem, and in fact enjoy seeing the edifice "cassoulet" being built, piece by piece. SERVES 8–10.

Tip: I often serve a hot, clear broth, sprinkled with chopped parsley *before* serving the rich cassoulet. It is a soothing, healthy prologue for what is to follow.

Marinated Grilled Rabbit in a Mustard Sauce

This delectable stew is both light — low in calories — and satisfying.

Being French, I often feasted on rabbit meat as I was growing up, as do most Europeans. I am still surprised to see so many Americans today — even sophisticated gourmands — who tend to be prudish when it comes to eating rabbit. It's unfortunate, for rabbit is very lean and tasty. Marinated, it becomes tender and wonderfully delicate. With a mustard sauce, it is particularly flavorful.

Tip: One cautionary note, beware of tiny bones in rabbit. Somehow, when the meat is cut up, the brittle bones tend to chip. Mind these little shard-like pieces.

1 rabbit, washed and cut up into pieces

FOR THE MARINADE
3 garlic cloves, minced
1 onion, finely chopped
4 cups rosé wine
1 tablespoon chopped fresh thyme leaves
1 tablespoon chopped fresh rosemary leaves
1 tablespoon chopped fresh sage
1 tablespoon peeled and grated fresh ginger
3 tablespoons olive oil
2 tablespoons soy sauce
pepper and salt

In a blender, purée ingredients.

In a ziptop plastic food storage bag, combine rabbit pieces and marinade. Seal bag, and refrigerate overnight. If possible, shake and turn bag from time to time to distribute marinade evenly.

Remove plastic bag containing marinated rabbit from refrigerator. Reserve marinade. Pat dry rabbit.

FOR THE SAUCE
1½ cups half-and-half
¾ cup Dijon mustard

In a small saucepan, heat ½ cup marinade and simmer 5 minutes. Add half-and-half and mustard. Set aside.

FOR THE COOKING
olive oil

Brush a little olive oil on rabbit, and grill or broil 10 minutes on each side, until nice and crisp. If on outdoor grill, reduce heat. If you are broiling, lower rabbit rack and baste with 2 tablespoons marinade. Continue cooking 10 more minutes on each side, making sure it doesn't burn. Heat sauce. Transfer to sauceboat.

Remove rabbit from grill (or broiler), and serve accompanied by the sauce. SERVES 6–8.

Broiled Duck Breasts with Grilled Peaches

Once a specialty rare to obtain, breasts of duck can readily be found these days at your local butcher. They tend to come with a thick layer of fat, much of which I slice off horizontally before broiling. (Make sure to insert a sheet of foil underneath the broiler rack, so that what leftover fat remains can drip onto it rather than onto the bottom of your oven.) Breasts of duck take minutes to cook. Have everything else you plan to serve ready before cooking the duck.

4 tablespoons soy sauce
2 tablespoons honey
2 duck breasts, roughly 1 pound each
¼ cup olive oil
4 peaches, halved and stones removed

In a bowl, combine soy sauce and honey. Let duck breasts marinate 4 hours (or overnight) covered, in the refrigerator.

Preheat broiler or grill.

Remove duck from bowl, pat dry with paper towel. Reserve marinade. Rub a little olive oil over peaches.

Broil or grill duck 5 minutes on each side. Place peaches, cut side down on the grill — or cut side up under the broiler — and cook alongside duck. Pour marinade over duck, continue broiling a few seconds (watch that the honey doesn't burn), slice, and serve duck breasts with a crown of peaches. SERVES 4.

Roast Leg of Lamb Provençal with Pastis-Pernod Flambé

For those who enjoy the taste of anise, pouring some anise-flavored alcohol and igniting it over the meat adds to the flavor and elevates an otherwise good but traditional lamb roast into a festive and dramatic event. Pastis is one of the Mediterraneans' favorite drinks. Many years ago, Pastis was the name brand for this aperitif. Pernod and Ricard are today the current brands, as they have since taken the lion share of the market in France.

In any case, Pastis over the *gigot* imparts a lovely hint of anise which blends well with the lamb.

This recipe unavoidably yields more than four. Lamb keeps well in the refrigerator. And so much can be created with leftover lamb.

8 garlic cloves
1 (6-pound) leg of lamb, bone in
¼ cup fresh rosemary leaves
2 tablespoons olive oil
1 tablespoon herbes de Provence
pepper and salt
10 medium potatoes, peeled and sliced
1½ cups chicken stock
1 cup finely chopped parsley
½ cup Pernod

Preheat oven to 350°.

Cut 4 garlic cloves into slivers.

With a sharp knife, make incisions every inch or so in the leg of lamb. Insert garlic slivers and rosemary into incisions. Rub roast with olive oil and sprinkle with some herbes de Provence, pepper, and salt. Line an ovenproof dish with sliced potatoes. Pour stock over potatoes, and sprinkle with some herbes de Provence and a bit of the remaining garlic, chopped. Place leg of lamb and remaining garlic cloves in roasting pan. Roast in the oven for 1 hour. Check with an instant-read thermometer; it should read 130° for medium rare.

Remove lamb from oven, and let stand 15 minutes. Sprinkle parsley over potatoes.

In a small saucepan, warm up Pernod with drippings from the pan.

Carve lamb and place slices on a serving platter surrounded with the potatoes. Pour warm Pernod and sauce drippings over meat and ignite. Wait until flames have subsided. Serve with potatoes. SERVES 6–8.

Roast Chicken with 40 Caramelized Garlic Cloves

This traditional and very flavorful Provençal preparation has inspired many a chef. James Beard fell in love with the recipe and adopted it, touting it in several of his books. If the number of garlic cloves seems excessive, remember that garlic, when baked and caramelized, loses much of its pungency and becomes almost sweet. Keep in mind, too, that garlic in any form is, by all accounts, good for your health.

> 1 (5-pound) roasting chicken, or a small capon
> ⅓ cup olive oil
> 1 whole lemon
> 40 garlic cloves, peeled and left whole
> 1 tablespoon herbes de Provence
> pepper and salt

Preheat oven to 350°.

Wash and dry chicken. Rub a little olive oil over chicken and place lemon and a few garlic cloves inside chicken. Sprinkle with herbes de Provence, pepper, and salt. Roast 50 minutes.

Place remaining garlic in dish around chicken, and continue roasting 40 minutes, until chicken is golden and crisp, and garlic is caramelized. Transfer to serving platter, surrounding the chicken with the garlic. Degrease ovenproof pan with ½ cup water — scraping up browned bits from pan. Bring to boil, reduce heat. Pour pan drippings into gravy boat. Carve chicken. SERVES 4–6.

Roast Chicken with 50 Garlic Cloves

If I may test your garlic endurance, I recommend this sensational variation on the same theme. It will transport you to garlic heaven.

An older version of the preceding recipe, from which this one obviously emanates, is served in many villages of *la Provence profonde,* deep Provence. It calls for no fewer than 50 cloves of garlic! But for true garlic aficionados, this older version of the same recipe is even more intense and infinitely more fragrant. First, the chicken is placed in a baking dish. Olive oil is rubbed inside the cavity as well as all over the chicken, and then the bird is seasoned with a good sprinkling of fresh thyme, pepper, and salt. Fifteen garlic cloves are smashed and inserted inside the chicken. The remaining 35 garlic cloves are distributed around the bird in a baking dish and drizzled with a little olive oil. The dish is sealed with foil, or a lid, and roasted 1½ hours. The foil or lid is removed at the table, releasing its aroma to the delight of everyone! Serves 4–6.

Roast Chicken in "Mourning Clothes" — with Truffle

Truffle is an acquired taste, but if you feel a bit extravagant and happen to be among those who, like me, love truffles, I recommend indulging in this chicken recipe. The truffle slices are inserted underneath the chicken skin, turning it black — in "mourning," as French gastronomes call it — with the incredible perfume from the truffle enveloping both the chicken and you. The elegance of this dish has few rivals. This said, given the price of truffles, this dish is obviously for very special occasions.

1 plump 5-pound chicken
2 or 3 fresh truffles, brushed and thinly sliced
6 tablespoons butter
pepper and salt

Preheat oven to 350°.

The trick here is gently lifting the skin of the chicken by inserting a knife and sliding the truffle slices under the skin. Your chicken will indeed look "in mourning." Place the chicken in a baking dish, cover with foil, and refrigerate 24 hours, which will allow the aroma of the truffles to penetrate the whole chicken. Remove from refrigerator. Cover chicken with dabs of butter, sprinkle with pepper and salt, and roast 1 hour. SERVES 4–6.

Roast Squab with Olives

The original Mediterranean recipe calls for pigeon and is appreciated in all Mediterranean countries. Pigeon meat is dark, juicy, and more flavorful and tender than that of chicken. Most Americans, however, are generally squeamish about cooking pigeon for a variety of reasons, so I have substituted squab.

One squab is usually ample for one person. For this recipe, ask your butcher to cut each bird into four pieces.

> 36 green olives, pitted
> 2 tablespoons olive oil
> 4 squabs, washed, dried, and quartered
> 6 ounces salt pork, boiled 10 minutes, drained, and cubed
> 1 medium onion, finely chopped
> 1 tomato, peeled and cut into small pieces
> 1 cup white wine
> 1 tablespoon flour
> ½ cup chicken stock

In a small pan, bring 2 cups water to a boil. Reduce heat and cook olives 5 minutes. Drain. Set aside.

In a kettle, heat olive oil, and, in batches, brown squab pieces 10 minutes on each side. Add salt pork and onion and continue cooking over low flame 15 minutes. Add tomato, wine, pepper, and salt. Cook 10 more minutes. In a small bowl, blend flour with stock. Pour and stir into kettle. Continue cooking over low heat another 10 minutes.

Add olives, stir, cook 5 minutes. SERVES 4–6.

Moussaka

This national and always-satisfying Greek one-dish-meal has penetrated the American food landscape and become very popular here. For the cook, moussaka comes in especially handy the day after roasting a leg of lamb. Its leftovers are often enough for the moussaka preparation.

⅓ cup olive oil
1 onion, finely chopped
1 large eggplant, peeled and cubed
3 tomatoes, peeled and cubed
1 teaspoon fresh thyme leaves, finely chopped
pepper and salt
3–4 cups cooked lamb, ground
½ cup fresh mint leaves, chopped
1 cup cream sauce, recipe follows
2 cloves garlic, minced

Tip: I recommend making the cream sauce first.

FOR THE CREAM SAUCE
1 tablespoon olive oil
1 tablespoon butter
2 tablespoons flour
2 cups milk
1 cup feta cheese, crumbled

Preheat oven to 350°.

In a saucepan, over low flame, heat olive oil and butter. Stir in flour and cook a few seconds. Gradually pour in milk, stirring all the while, and cook until sauce thickens. Stir in feta cheese, and cook 3 more minutes until cheese is melted. Set aside.

In a skillet, heat some of the olive oil and sauté some of the onion until translucent. Add eggplant and tomatoes. Cook 15 minutes, until mixture becomes soft. Sprinkle with thyme, pepper, and salt. Transfer and spread in ovenproof dish.

In the same skillet, heat a few drops of olive oil and sauté some more onion until translucent; add lamb, stir, and cook 5 more minutes. Sprinkle with mint, pepper, and salt. Spread lamb evenly over eggplant mixture. Cover with cream sauce. Bake 20 minutes. Serves 4–6.

Tip: Rice goes well with moussaka as does a side dish of yogurt.

Moussaka of Artichoke and Veal

This is a delicate and elegant variation on the original theme. I have, on occasion, substituted white turkey meat for veal.

FOR THE ARTICHOKE MIXTURE
6 artichoke hearts, fresh or frozen
juice of ½ lemon
¼ cup olive oil
4 tablespoons butter
1 large onion, finely chopped
2 pounds veal (or white turkey meat), ground
2 tomatoes, peeled and quartered
1 garlic clove, minced
½ teaspoon fresh thyme leaves, finely chopped
¼ teaspoon grated nutmeg
pepper and salt
½ cup white wine
1 cup breadcrumbs
1 cup flat parsley leaves, finely chopped
3 eggs, lightly beaten

FOR THE CREAM SAUCE
3 cups milk
4 tablespoons butter
2 tablespoons flour
½ teaspoon grated nutmeg
pepper and salt

Bring milk to near boiling in a saucepan. Turn heat off. In another saucepan, heat butter. Add flour. Stir for a few seconds, and gradually pour in scalded milk. Stir until mixture thickens to form a smooth cream sauce. Turn heat off. Add nutmeg, pepper, and salt. Set aside.

If using fresh artichokes, remove artichoke leaves and choke, and cook in water with lemon juice 35 minutes. Drain. If you are using frozen hearts, follow package instructions. Drain. Slice artichoke hearts. Set aside.

Preheat oven to 300°. Grease an ovenproof dish with some of the olive oil.

In a skillet, heat remaining olive oil and the butter. Cook onion until translucent. Over medium heat, add meat and cook 15 minutes. Add tomatoes, garlic, thyme, nutmeg, pepper, and salt, and continue cooking 10 more minutes. Stir in wine and cook another 5 minutes. Stir in 3 tablespoons cream sauce. Turn heat off.

In the prepared ovenproof dish, spread half the breadcrumbs. Arrange half the artichokes evenly on top. Spread with meat mixture. Sprinkle with half the parsley. Continue with a layer of artichoke and meat. Whisk eggs into cream sauce. Top with cream sauce. Bake 30 minutes. Sprinkle with remaining parsley. SERVES 4–6.

Greek Roasted Lamb Stuffed with Baby Spinach, Dill, and Feta Cheese

This Greek lamb recipe is slightly different than the French *gigot,* but equally delicious. I like to make it from time to time as a variation of the more familiar roast lamb.

With the boned leg of lamb, make sure to cut out all sinews and extra fat before stuffing, and tie it securely with twine or kitchen pins to ensure that the stuffing doesn't escape during cooking.

4 tablespoons olive oil
1 (4-pound) leg of lamb, flattened with a mallet, boned, and
    trimmed of all its fat and sinews
1 pound baby spinach, washed and dried
4 garlic cloves, minced
2 eggs, lightly beaten
2 cups fresh dill sprigs, washed and chopped
2 cups fresh mint leaves, chopped coarsely
1 cup small cubes of feta cheese

1 cup grated Gruyère cheese
1 teaspoon chopped fresh thyme leaves
pepper and salt
1 onion, finely chopped
6 tomatoes, peeled and diced
1 cup red wine

Preheat oven to 400°.

Rub some of the olive oil on all sides of meat.

In a large mixing bowl, with your hands — wear thin plastic gloves available in most drugstores — mix spinach, garlic, eggs, dill, mint, feta and Gruyère cheeses, 2 tablespoons olive oil, pepper, and salt. (It's actually fun to do this step. It will remind you of summer camp or even farther back, kindergarten days.) Tightly pack this filling, making a kind of sausage of it, along one side of the meat. Roll meat (with filling) onto itself, forming again a kind of sausage-like roll with the filling securely encased. Tie well with twine or kitchen pins. Sprinkle with thyme, pepper, and salt.

In a roasting pan, cook roast 30 minutes or until meat thermometer registers 135° — for medium rare.

In a saucepan, heat remaining olive oil and sauté onion until light brown. Add tomatoes and cook 10 minutes, until mixture forms a thick sauce. Set aside.

Remove roast from oven and let stand 15 minutes. Cut twine off, or remove pins.

Warm a serving platter in low-temperature oven.

On a cutting board, slice meat and transfer slices to warm serving platter. Add pan drippings to saucepan with tomato/onion, bring to a boil. Turn heat off, and transfer to gravy boat. SERVES 6–8.

Beggar's Purses of Stuffed Chicken

Chicken breasts are lean and versatile, but I find that they often have a tendency to be a bit dry and bland. Brining and marinating them gives them flavor and renders them tender. This dish may be prepared ahead and stored in the refrigerator, or even frozen. The chicken breasts are folded over to look like purses.

4 skinless, boneless chicken breast halves
salt
olive oil
2 shallots, minced
1 boneless chicken-breast half or 2 boneless thighs, ground in a
     food processor
½ cup parsley leaves, finely chopped
2 tablespoons finely chopped fresh tarragon leaves
2 tablespoons finely chopped fresh rosemary leaves
6 tablespoons dried porcini mushrooms, reconstituted in boiling
     water, squeezed dry and finely chopped
pepper
2 egg whites
1 cup half-and-half
4 slices prosciutto di Parma
1 large onion, sliced
½ cup sliced shiitake mushrooms
1½ cups parsley leaves, finely chopped
zest of 1 lemon

Start by immersing chicken breasts in a bowl of water with 2 tablespoons salt. Cover and refrigerate at least 4 hours — preferably more. When you are ready to cook the chicken breasts, remove them from bowl, rinse well, and pat dry. Set aside.

In a kettle, heat 1 tablespoon olive oil and sauté shallots until translucent. Add ground chicken meat, stir in herbs and porcini, pepper and salt. Cook 10 minutes. Let cool. Mix in egg whites and 2 tablespoons half-and-half. Set aside.

Place chicken-breast halves between sheets of plastic wrap. With a mallet or rolling pin, pound breasts, making sure they are evenly flattened. Remove plastic wrap. Cover each breast with a slice of prosciutto. Spoon a tablespoon or so of stuffing in center of breast. Roll and enclose stuffing in chicken breast as tightly as you can with the help of some twine or pins to avoid stuffing from escaping. Wrap in plastic wrap and refrigerate purses 1 hour.

Remove from refrigerator and, in a heavy kettle, heat olive oil and brown purses over medium heat. Add onion slices and shiitake mushrooms. Stir, cover, and simmer 25 minutes.

Transfer to serving platter. Stir remaining half-and-half, the parsley, and lemon zest into kettle, stir a few seconds, pour over purses. Serves 4.

Grand Pot-au-Feu with Warm Marrow Brioches

One of France's national dishes, *pot-au-feu,* with its fragrant and rich broth served with various cuts of long-simmered beef, an array of vegetables, some coarse salt, and some mustard, is a permanent fixture in virtually every home and restaurant throughout the land — south or north. For me, it automatically conveys the warmth of family suppers, or of many friends around the dinner table. One simply can't make a small pot-au-feu; no matter how modestly one starts out, it inevitably ends up in a quantity that calls for a crowd to appreciate it.

In France it's called pot-au-feu, but Italy has its own called *bollito misto,* with different cuts of meat — not only beef, but sausage, veal, and even chicken and side condiments like *mustarda,* a fruit and mustard concoction. I can still smell the exceptionally fragrant pot-au-feu my mother made at least every other week, especially during winter. I have since elaborated on the theme, and have often added a smoked sausage or two, and even at times, a ham shank — boiled separately so as not to "smoke" the rest. What has made my pot-au-feu much in demand through my years of entertaining, are my little warm brioches stuffed with marrow and parsley and served along with the clear broth; and, as an additional side dish, my shallot-dill vinaigrette, which dresses both meat and vegetables.

Traditionally, onions into which a few whole cloves have been pushed go into making the basis for the soup. My mother's secret to her amazing broth was the addition of a good third of a teaspoon of ground cloves and a bunch of dill. The combination of these two elements gives the broth of her pot-au-feu its *je-ne-sais-quoi*, an unforgettable elixir.

4 pounds beef short ribs
2 pounds beef chuck
4 marrow bones
4 leeks, trimmed, and well washed
6 whole cloves
2 large onions
1 bunch carrots, peeled and whole
1 bunch celery, peeled
1 bunch dill
1 bunch flat parsley, plus ½ cup chopped and extra for sprinkling
2 turnips, peeled and halved
2 bay leaves
1 tablespoon salt
½ teaspoon peppercorns
½ teaspoon ground cloves
8 small potatoes, washed and whole
5 parsnips, peeled and halved
1 or 2 Polish kielbasa sausages
10 small brioches or 10 baguette slices, toasted
coarse salt for serving
mustard for serving

FOR THE VINAIGRETTE
2 shallots, minced
½ bunch fresh dill, finely chopped
6 tablespoons olive oil
2 tablespoons balsamic vinegar
pepper and salt

Wash ribs, chuck, and marrow bones under running water. Cut off green part of leeks and wash well. Push cloves into onions. In a large and deep kettle, put meat, bones, the green part of leeks, onions studded with cloves, 2 carrots, the leafy part of celery, dill, parsley, 1 turnip, bay leaves, salt, peppercorns, and ground cloves. Cover with 4 inches water. Bring to a boil, reduce heat to low, and cook 1½ hours, skimming and discarding gray foam from time to time. Turn heat off and cool. Remove marrow bones to a plate. Cool, cover, and refrigerate overnight. Strain stock through a colander placed over a bowl. Refrigerate, covered, overnight. Store meat and vegetables in a bowl, cover, and refrigerate.

The next day, remove stock from refrigerator. With a slotted spoon, lift layer of fat and discard. In the clean kettle, combine meats, degreased stock, the white part of leeks, hearts of celery, remaining carrots and turnip, potatoes, and parsnips. Bring to a boil, reduce heat to low, and cook 20 minutes. In a separate pot, cook sausage 10 minutes. Drain.

Preheat oven to 350°. With a knife and a small spoon, scoop marrow out of bones into a small bowl. Mix in ½ cup chopped parsley and some pepper and salt. Cut brioches crosswise, make a small indentation inside each, and stuff with marrow. Bake brioches on a baking sheet 15 minutes. If you are using baguette slices, spread marrow mixture on toasts and serve. (I do all this before dinner, and keep them warm, covered with foil in the oven, until serving time.)

Whisk the vinaigrette ingredients together in a bowl.

On a serving platter, arrange meats and sausage surrounded with vegetables. (Discard boiled bay leaves, parsley, and dill.) Sprinkle some fresh parsley over platter. Keep warm, covered.

First, ladle broth and serve with warm marrow brioches — or toasts spread with marrow. Second, for your main course, serve the platter of pot-au-feu along with shallot-vinaigrette and a few small bowls of coarse salt and mustard. Serves 8–10.

Rack of Lamb

Lambs are raised in abundance throughout most Mediterranean countries — France, Italy, Spain, Morocco, Tunisia, and Israel. As such, lamb constitutes the main meat in virtually all of the cuisines bordering the coast. No matter where and on what occasion it is served, rack of lamb is inevitably considered — and rightly so — to be elegant and festive.

> 2 garlic cloves, minced
> ½ cup Dijon mustard
> 2 tablespoons fresh rosemary leaves, finely chopped
> 2 tablespoons fresh thyme leaves, finely chopped
> 2 tablespoons soy sauce
> pepper
> 2 racks of lamb, each of 8 ribs

Preheat oven to 400°.

In a bowl, make a paste by mixing mustard, rosemary, thyme, garlic, soy, and pepper. Spread paste all over lamb — fat side as well as meat. Refrigerate lamb 1 hour. Remove racks from refrigerator and place on baking sheet. Roast 18 minutes. Remove from oven, check for doneness with an instant-read thermometer: it should read 140° for medium-rare. Cover with aluminum foil, and let stand 15 minutes.

Remove foil from lamb, carve racks, and arrange ribs on warm serving platter. In as much as most people carve the racks in the kitchen — 2 or 3 ribs for each plate, depending on the diner's appetite — I much prefer carving at the table, where the arrival of the aromatic racks heightens the appetite and generally elicits an enthusiastic response. SERVES 4–6.

Couscous of Lamb and Chicken

One of Tunisia's, Algeria's, and Morocco's national dishes is couscous, both the name of the dish as well as the semolina cereal served with it. It is definitely a perfect one-dish meal that requires no first course. Rich in ingredients and flavor, couscous remains, nonetheless, surprisingly light and healthy.

Most often in Tunisia, Algeria, or Morocco, the couscous comes with its meats boiled along with the vegetables. *I* prefer my meats grilled and served along side the couscous. Grilled meats, very simply, have more flavor and enhance the dish.

The list of ingredients may seem terribly long — again, please don't let this deter you. A goodly number of them are spices, all of which are necessary to flavor the couscous.

Because of its many ingredients, there is no way to prepare couscous for fewer than 8–10 people (or more), no matter how hard you try. By the time all the vegetables and meats have been assembled, you will inevitably have enough for at least two, maybe even three, meals if you are serving only four. So again, keep this dish high on your list when your guest list is 8–10.

This said, couscous keeps refrigerated for a few days. (To prevent the vegetables from becoming soggy, I remove them from the broth, and refrigerate them, the broth, couscous, and meats in separate containers and reassemble everything at the time of another meal.)

2 pounds boneless lamb meat from the leg, cut into 2-inch pieces
2 pounds boneless chicken from both breast and leg, cut into
    2-inch pieces
1 teaspoon chopped fresh thyme leaves
1 teaspoon chopped fresh marjoram
pepper and salt
¼ cup olive oil
1 onion, peeled and quartered
2 leeks, well washed and cut into 1-inch pieces
2 white turnips
1 bulb celeriac, peeled and cut into chunks
¼ teaspoon ground ginger
¼ teaspoon ground cinnamon
¼ teaspoon ground cardamom

¼ teaspoon ground cloves
¼ teaspoon ground coriander
¼ teaspoon freshly grated nutmeg
pinch of cayenne pepper
5–6 cups stock — vegetable or chicken
2 small zucchini, washed and cut into 1-inch pieces
2 cups cooked chickpeas
1 cup raisins
5 cups instant couscous
1 cup fresh cilantro, finely chopped
1 cup fresh mint leaves, torn into small pieces
½ cup finely chopped scallions
harissa, recipe follows

Preheat the broiler or grill. Sprinkle lamb and chicken with thyme, marjoram, salt, and pepper. Put chicken on skewers and grill 10 minutes on each side. The lamb only needs 5 minutes on each side. Set aside.

In a large kettle, heat oil and sauté onion until translucent, add leeks, turnips, celeriac, all the spices, and the stock. Reduce heat, cover, and cook 30 minutes. Add zucchini and continue cooking for 10 minutes. Add chickpeas and raisins.

Cook couscous according to package instructions, making sure to toss well until it becomes fluffy.

On a serving platter, make a mound of couscous in the middle, and crown it with vegetables and grilled meats. Ladle broth over the whole platter. Sprinkle with fresh coriander, mint, and scallions. Serve and pass the harissa (see below).

Pour remaining broth into a soup terrine and pass it around so that each person can ladle additional broth to his or her preference. SERVES 8–10.

Note: There are some who serve couscous in soup plates.

Harissa

This fiery North African condiment flavors practically every food throughout not only Tunisia and Morocco, but all the neighboring North African countries, and is a traditional accompaniment to couscous. Harissa is an integral part to the North

African culinary culture, and there are many who even enjoy it spread on a slice of bread or pita. Here again, as a matter of personal pride, each home chef claims to hold the secrets to the *real* recipe.

Growing up in Paris, I remember a close Tunisian family friend who, each time he came to dinner — and no matter what my mother's menu offered — would pull out of his elegant vest pocket a little ceramic miniature jewelry box that contained harissa. As we watched with utter curiosity, he would then take, almost ceremoniously, a teaspoonful of the mysterious red paste out of the box, and delicately place it at the edge of his plate. My mother would smile, later wondering aloud why she had gone to the trouble of preparing gourmet food for him if he immediately anaesthetized it with his hot condiment.

Like ketchup in American coffee shops, harissa also is a permanent fixture on every table of most North African eateries. Essential to enjoying couscous, it does impart a special, indescribable zip to the vegetables and grilled meats.

1 teaspoon caraway seeds
1 teaspoon cumin seeds
1 teaspoon coriander seeds
¼ teaspoon cardamom pods
3 garlic cloves, smashed
6 tablespoons sweet paprika
1 teaspoon cayenne pepper
¼ teaspoon turmeric
¼ teaspoon freshly grated nutmeg
½ teaspoon salt
1–2 tablespoons olive oil

In a dry skillet, roast caraway, cumin, coriander seeds, and the cardamom pods for 1 minute. Remove from heat and cool. In a spice (or cleaned coffee) grinder, grind to fine powder. Pour mixture into a bowl, add garlic and remaining dry ingredients, and stir with 1 tablespoon olive oil to form a paste. If the harissa seems too thick, add a little more olive oil. Cover and set aside. (Note: One should take harissa with caution — a spoonful on the side to start.)

Molded Egyptian Baked Rice Stuffed with Chicken and Mushrooms with a Turkish Walnut Sauce

I have adapted this traditional Egyptian cake-like chicken-and-rice dish — one that, apart from being delicious, also makes a dramatic entrance to the table — by adding a layer of mushrooms, and by serving it with a Turkish walnut sauce. I can only hope Egyptian purists will forgive me, and even appreciate my version.

Here again, it is impractical to prepare this dish for only four, so it's best prepared when you anticipate 6–8 guests.

Tip: I prepare the walnut sauce ahead.

FOR THE WALNUT SAUCE
2 slices French bread
1½ cups walnuts
1½ cups chicken stock
½ cup fresh parsley leaves, finely chopped
½ cup finely chopped onion
½ teaspoon paprika
pepper and salt

In a blender, purée all ingredients. Transfer to a serving bowl and set aside.

FOR THE RICE AND CHICKEN
2 half chicken breasts, boned and skinless, cut into 2-inch pieces
2 thighs, boned and cut into 1-inch pieces
2 tablespoons olive oil, plus extra for brushing chicken and
    casserole dish
1 tablespoon herbes de Provence
2 cups sliced white mushrooms
1 tablespoon ground cumin
pepper and salt
2 tablespoons butter
2 cups uncooked long-grain rice
1½ cups milk
1 cup heavy cream
3 cups chicken stock

Place chicken in a broiler pan. Brush chicken pieces with a little olive oil and sprinkle with herbes de Provence. Broil 15 minutes, until crisp and golden on both sides. Set aside.

In a skillet, heat 2 tablespoons olive oil, and sauté mushrooms 5 minutes. Season with cumin, pepper, and salt. Set aside.

Preheat oven to 400°.

Brush bottom and sides of a deep 3-quart casserole dish with olive oil and a little of the butter. Spread 1½ cups rice evenly. Arrange chicken pieces on top and sprinkle with pepper and salt.

In a saucepan, heat milk, cream, and stock. Pour 2 cups of the liquid over chicken. Bake 15 minutes. Remove from oven, and spread remaining ½ cup uncooked rice over chicken. Spread with a layer of cooked mushrooms. Dot with remaining butter. Bake, uncovered, another 15 minutes. Pour 1 more cup of simmering stock, and continue baking another 5 minutes. Pour last of the liquid and continue baking 20 more minutes. Remove from oven, cover, and let stand 20 minutes. (These 20 minutes are *important;* they will allow the dish to set properly so that it can successfully be unmolded.)

To unmold, run sharp knife along the sides of the dish. Place a serving platter upside down over the top of the casserole dish. Grasping both the casserole and the platter, invert them. Remove mold. It will look like a cake. Serve accompanied by the walnut sauce. Serves 6–8.

"In a Kettle (comma)..."

Roasted Cornish Game Hens with Fresh Figs

Cornish game hens always present well and for that reason probably seem to appear at many formal dinners. I find them generally lacking in taste, however, and always welcome anything that will give them a little zest. Fresh figs, readily available in most Mediterranean countries, make a perfect complement.

> 2 tablespoons olive oil, plus extra for brushing figs
> 2 Cornish game hens, washed and dried, cut in half
> 1 onion, finely chopped
> pepper and salt
> 1 tablespoon herbes de Provence
> 1 cup white wine
> 2 pounds fresh figs, halved

Preheat oven to 350°.

In a kettle, heat 2 tablespoons olive oil. Brown Cornish hens 10 minutes. Add onion, continue cooking 10 minutes. Season with pepper, salt, and herbes de Provence. Transfer to ovenproof dish. Add wine, ½ cup water, and half the figs. Cover with foil, and cook 20 minutes. Remove from oven. Turn broiler on. Place remaining figs on a baking sheet and brush with olive oil. When broiler is red hot, place figs under broiler a few minutes, until roasted. Arrange figs around Cornish game hens. SERVES 4.

Lamb Stew, Avignon Style
(Ragout d'Agneau à la mode d'Avignon)

Is a lamb stew always a lamb stew? Not always. This one has the distinction of being dressed with typical Provençal spices. And a chef, whose name, alas, is no longer remembered, coined it *Ragout d'Agneau à la mode d'Avignon* — Avignon stew.

> 2 pounds lamb shoulder, cut into 1-inch pieces
> 2 onions, minced
> 1 carrot, peeled and sliced
> 2 garlic cloves, minced
> 1 bay leaf
> 1 cup parsley leaves, finely chopped
> 2 cups white wine
> 1 tablespoon fresh rosemary leaves, finely chopped
> ¼ teaspoon freshly grated nutmeg
> ¼ teaspoon ground cloves
> pepper and salt
> ½ cup olive oil
> 1 package frozen (or canned) artichoke hearts

Combine lamb, 1 onion, carrot, garlic, bay leaf, parsley, wine, rosemary, cloves, nutmeg, and pepper and salt. Put in a sealed plastic bag, and refrigerate overnight.

Remove meat from marinade, pat dry. Set aside marinade.

In a kettle, heat olive oil, brown meat. Stir in second onion. Cook 5 minutes. Pour in marinade, stir, and cover. Simmer over low heat 2 hours. (Yes, 2 hours!) Add artichoke hearts and continue simmering 30 minutes. Check to see sauce doesn't stick. It may require a few more drops of water or wine. SERVES 6–8.

Tip: Serve with steamed potatoes and parsley.

Turkish Lamb Dumplings with a Yogurt Sauce

Traveling through the Middle East and Turkey and seeing field upon field of white lambs with their lonely shepherds makes one understand the prevalence of lamb in Middle Eastern and Turkish cuisine.

When I first sampled these dumplings, called *manti* in Istanbul, I liked them so much I ended up ordering them more than once during my stay. At home, the day after I have roasted a leg of lamb and have just a few pieces left over, I find that this delectable dish becomes a good second act. Don't be put off by what might appear at first glance the many steps in the recipe. They are all short and extremely easy.

FOR THE DUMPLING DOUGH
  1 cup all-purpose flour
  1 egg
  ¼ teaspoon salt
  2 tablespoons olive oil

Make a well with the flour. Pour in egg, salt, oil, and 3 tablespoons water. Working with your hands, knead until dough becomes soft and shiny. Cover this dough with plastic wrap, and refrigerate 1 hour.

FOR THE FILLING
  2 tablespoons olive oil
  1 onion, finely chopped
  2–3 cups cooked lamb — fresh, or from a previously served
      roast — finely chopped
  pepper and salt

Remove dumpling dough and roll out to ⅛ of an inch. Cut out squares and place a spoonful of filling in the center. Seal with wet fingers. Set aside.

In a skillet, heat olive oil and sauté onion until light brown. Add lamb, stir 5 minutes, and season to taste. Set aside.

FOR THE SAUCE
      3 garlic cloves, minced
      16 ounces plain yogurt

In a bowl, mix garlic and yogurt.

FOR THE TOPPING
      4 tablespoons olive oil
      4 tomatoes, skinned, finely chopped
      1 garlic clove, minced
      1 teaspoon paprika
      ½ cup fresh mint leaves, finely chopped

In a skillet, heat olive oil and sauté tomatoes, garlic, and paprika for 3 minutes. Set aside.

COOKING THE DUMPLINGS
In a kettle, bring 2 quarts salted water to a boil.

Remove dumpling dough from refrigerator. On a floured board, divide dough into four equal pieces — it's easier to handle in small amounts — and roll each piece out into a thin strip. Cut out 1-inch squares. Place 1 tablespoon meat filling in center of each square and, with wet fingers, seal into little dumplings that look a little like ravioli.

Drop dumplings into boiling water, reduce heat, and cook 10 minutes until they all rise to the surface. Drain. Keep warm, covered with a towel or bowl. Place serving platter on a heating tray, or in low oven for 15 minutes.

Arrange dumplings on warm serving platter. Cover with garlic sauce. Drizzle tomatoes/garlic on top. Sprinkle with mint. SERVES 6–8.

Stuffed Crown Roast of Pork

Presenting this roast is a glorious way of entertaining. It's also a wonderful way of appreciating pork. True, it calls for a little more preparation time than most recipes, but again the result is definitely rewarding. I suggest you save this dish for festive or special occasions. Appetites will be whetted the minute people enter your house, from the irresistible aromas emanating from your kitchen.

For those who are concerned about pork being too fatty, the meat of the crown roast is very lean.

1 (6-to-8-pound) crown roast of pork
zest and juice of 1 orange
6 garlic cloves, minced
3 tablespoons, plus ⅓ cup olive oil and a little bit for oiling the
    casserole dish and cooking the sausage
2 tablespoons fresh rosemary leaves
2 tablespoons fresh sage leaves, plus 1 tablespoon chopped
pepper and salt
4 cups wild rice, cooked
1 cup white rice, cooked
1 medium onion, minced
2 celery stalks, yellow part only, strings removed by peeling,
    diced in ½-inch pieces
½ cup flat parsley leaves, finely chopped
1 pound sweet Italian sausage, casings removed
4 Granny Smith apples, washed, cored, and cubed
15 dried apricots, chopped
½ cup dried cranberries
½ cup slivered almonds, roasted
½ cup apple brandy (Calvados)

Ask your butcher to prepare the crown roast by removing the chine (backbone), and any excess fat from the roast. Cover ends of ribs with aluminum foil to prevent burning.

Preheat oven to 450°. Use a little olive oil to oil a large casserole dish.

Remember to zest the orange *before* extracting its juice — it's easier that way. In the blender, make a paste with the zest, orange juice, half the garlic, 2 tablespoons rosemary, sage, 3 tablespoons olive oil, pepper, and salt. Rub crown roast inside and out with the paste. Refrigerate 1 hour. Remove from refrigerator and roast 15 minutes. Reduce heat to 375° and continue roasting 1½ hours.

Cook both wild and white rice in separate pans according to package instructions. Set aside.

In a skillet, heat ⅓ cup olive oil and sauté onion until translucent. Add remaining garlic, sage, rosemary, and the celery, and continue cooking 8 minutes. Toss in parsley and transfer to a large bowl. In the same pan, heat a few more drops olive oil and cook sausage meat 15 minutes. Combine wild and white rice, sausage, apples, apricots, cranberries, almonds, and apple brandy in bowl with celery mixture. Mix well and transfer to an oiled casserole dish. Cover with foil and bake 45 minutes.

Remove crown roast from oven and place on a serving platter. Cover with aluminum foil and let sit 20 minutes. Spoon some rice stuffing in the center of roast. Bring casserole with remaining stuffing to the table.

Carve roast and serve about 3 ribs per guest along with some stuffing. Serves 10–12.

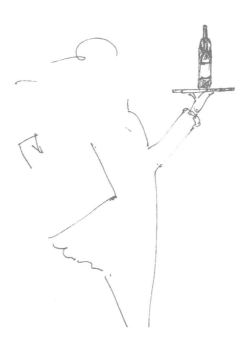

Broiled Chicken with Rosemary and Lemon

Broiled chicken is a fragrant presence in all outdoor markets in Mediterranean countries, where one's appetite is mercilessly teased as one walks among portable rotisseries. Rosemary has a pungent perfume as it roasts. This once exotic dish is increasingly available in grocery stores and delis. Still, in my view nothing rivals the home-cooked version.

> 2 garlic cloves, minced
> juice of 1 lemon
> zest of 1 orange
> ½ cup fresh rosemary leaves, finely chopped
> ¼ cup olive oil
> pepper and salt
> 1 chicken, split in half

Purée garlic, lemon juice, orange zest, rosemary, olive oil, pepper, and salt in a blender. Put chicken and marinade into a plastic bag. Seal and refrigerate 2 hours.

Preheat the grill or broiler. Remove chicken from bag, draining it of its marinade. Reserve marinade for basting. Grill or broil chicken 10 minutes on each side, basting as you go. When chicken is crisp on the outside, but tender on the inside, remove from heat. SERVES 4–6.

Polenta Squares with Sautéed Swiss Chard, Broccoli Rabe, and Pancetta

This delicious Italian comfort food recipe is also a satisfying meatless meal. Broccoli rabe tends to be more bitter than other vegetables, and many shy away from it for that reason. I, like most Italians, actually like that bitterness, but, for those who don't, I have devised a compromise by mixing broccoli rabe with Swiss chard, which acts as a neutralizing agent, allowing broccoli rabe to shine.

4 tablespoons olive oil, plus extra for oiling casserole dish and
    drizzling over polenta
2 cups chicken stock
salt
1 cup polenta or cornmeal
2 cups diced pancetta or unsmoked bacon
2 large onions, sliced
3 garlic cloves, sliced
pinch of cayenne pepper
2 pounds Swiss chard, leaves only, chopped coarsely, blanched,
    and drained
1 pound broccoli rabe, chopped coarsely
juice of ½ lemon
⅔ cup Pecorino Romano cheese, grated
pepper

Preheat oven to 350°. Oil a casserole dish.

In a saucepan, bring chicken stock, 2 cups water, and 1 teaspoon salt to a boil. Reduce heat. Pour cornmeal in gradually, stirring with a wooden spoon, and cook 40 minutes. Pour contents of saucepan into oiled casserole dish, smooth top evenly, drizzle with some olive oil, and bake 1 hour. The top should be golden and crisp. Remove from oven.

In a skillet, heat 3 tablespoons olive oil. Add diced pancetta (or unsmoked bacon), reduce heat, and cook 5 minutes. Add onions, and cook a few minutes, until translucent, then add garlic and cayenne.

In a separate pan, heat remaining 1 tablespoon olive oil and cook Swiss chard, covered, 15 minutes. Add to onion/pancetta. Stir in broccoli rabe, add lemon juice, and continue cooking 5 more minutes. Stir in half the cheese, some pepper, and salt.

Cut polenta into squares. Using a spatula, place a square on each plate. Top each square with pancetta/broccoli rabe mixture. Sprinkle with remaining cheese. Serves 4–6.

Daube of Venison

The term *daube* comes from a large Provençal earthenware pot called *daubière,* in which slowly simmered meat stews are traditionally cooked. *La Daube Provençale* — a slow cooked beef stew with herbs and vegetables — is an intrinsic part of that region's everyday cuisine. Venison daube is a departure from the traditional daube made with beef. A leaner meat, it has the advantage of having fewer calories and less cholesterol than beef. It's difficult to make a daube for only four.

6 garlic cloves, minced
4 carrots, peeled and sliced
2 medium onions, finely chopped
1 bunch flat parsley, finely chopped
4 sprigs fresh thyme, leaves only
1 teaspoon fresh rosemary leaves
10 juniper berries
1 bottle red Burgundy wine
½ cup orange juice
2 tablespoons brandy
pepper and salt
4 pounds venison meat, cut into 3-inch pieces
1 slab lean salt pork, cut into thin 1-inch pieces
3 tablespoons olive oil
½ pound cremini mushrooms, cleaned and sliced
4 cups veal or beef stock
1 pig's foot, split in half and blanched
5 ounces pork rind
zest of 1 orange
4 tomatoes, peeled and chopped
1 cup black olives, pitted

FOR THE MARINADE

In a blender, purée garlic, carrots, onions, parsley, thyme, rosemary, juniper berries, half the wine, orange juice, brandy, ½ teaspoon freshly ground pepper, and some salt.

Make a small incision in venison pieces and insert a piece of salt pork in each. In a large plastic bag, combine marinade and meat. Seal bag and refrigerate overnight.

Preheat oven to 350°.

Remove meat from marinade. Pat dry. Reserve marinade.

In a skillet, heat 3 tablespoons olive oil and brown meat on all sides until golden brown. Add mushrooms and cook 5 more minutes. Transfer to ovenproof casserole dish. In a sauce pan, heat marinade with stock and remaining wine and pour over meat. Add pig's foot, pork rind, orange zest, tomatoes, olives, pepper, and salt. Cover and bake 2 hours. Remove and discard pork foot. SERVES 8–10.

Note: This dish is delicious served with potato gnocchi or a purée of potatoes and celeriac.

Note: You may, if you wish, substitute the traditional counterpart for venison, beef chuck, which is also extremely good, though a tad heavier.

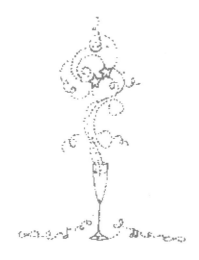

An Italian Slow-Roasted Pork Shoulder

This flavorful pork roast recipe calls for basting regularly every 20 minutes or so — in this case, the basting is with olive oil and lemon juice.

The slow and long roasting of the pork at low temperature is a little like the method used to "confire" duck. And, as for the duck confit, this fragrant lemony pork roast becomes both crunchy on the outside — with its very crisp skin — and meltingly soft and tender inside.

Because pork shoulders don't usually come under at least six or eight pounds, this recipe serves eight or more people.

FOR THE DRY MARINADE
>12 garlic cloves, peeled
>zest of 3 lemons
>½ cup fennel seeds
>½ teaspoon crumbled dried hot chilies
>pepper and salt
>1 tablespoon olive oil

In a mini processor, purée lemon zest, fennel, chilies, garlic, pepper, and salt with one tablespoon olive oil.

FOR THE PORK ROAST
>1 (7-pound) pork shoulder with its skin on
>juice of 6 lemons
>5 tablespoons olive oil

With a sharp knife, score the entire surface of the shoulder every ½ inch with deep and long gashes. Push some of the marinade inside each cut. Rub excess marinade over skin. Allow dry marinade to flavor the roast for an hour (or overnight) in the refrigerator.

Preheat oven to 450°.

Remove pork from refrigerator and roast 30 minutes, until skin begins to turn light brown and crackle a little. Reduce oven heat to 200°. Pour juice from 5 lemons and 4 tablespoons olive oil over roast, and bake for at least 6 hours. Baste every 20 minutes, adding more lemon juice and olive oil as needed.

Remove from oven, place roast on carving board, cover with foil, and let stand 20 minutes. Scrape bits of meat and pan drippings in roasting pan, and add 1 tablespoon olive oil and juice of another lemon. Bring to a boil, reduce heat, and stir well one more minute. Pour sauce into gravy boat. Bring sauce and roast to the table. Carve. SERVES 10–12.

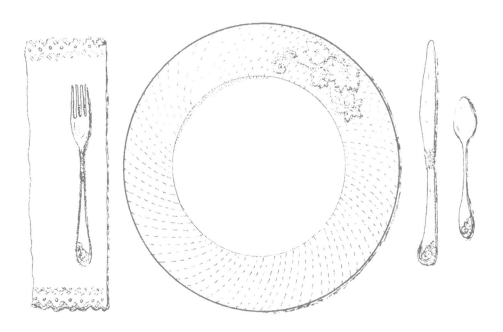

Individual Beef Wellingtons

The Duke of Wellington became a national British hero when he defeated Napoleon in 1815. History — or legend — has it that the duke liked his beef topped with goose pâté and mushrooms and wrapped in puff pastry. He apparently also insisted on serving that dish whenever he was asked to host an official dinner. Subsequently, his name became associated with the dish. The French, who never quite accepted their emperor's defeat, serve the same dish (which originated in France), but to this day call it *boeuf en croute* or *boeuf en brioche*. If you ask for Beef Wellington in France, you usually get a blank stare in response.

Whenever I was served beef Wellington in the United States or in Europe, it was mainly at very chic affairs. Always impressed by it, I was long convinced that only a grand *chef de cuisine* could attempt it. Years later, as I traveled on my gastronomic journey, I plucked up my courage one day and decided to try and prepare this utterly elegant specialty, which to my surprise proved quite simple. If only I had known that years ago!

I prefer to make individual beef Wellingtons rather than serving a whole fillet encased in pastry and carved into single portions. They not only look so much better, but they are easier to handle. You will note that I have virtually no beef recipes in this book, but when I was recently served beef Wellington, or, rather, boeuf en croute, in Provence, I was reminded that Mediterraneans do enjoy beef as much as anyone. They simply eat it less frequently.

In order to fully appreciate this delicacy, and because the recipe is, by design, rather rich, I have also learned that one shouldn't exceed more than 3 ounces of beef fillet per serving. By the time the goose pâté and the duxelles of mushroom are added to the meat inside the pastry, the whole dish is more than satisfying.

Note: Duxelles is simply finely diced mushrooms sautéed in butter and olive oil with a shallot, a few drops Worcestershire sauce, and Madera or sherry wine and cooked until all liquid has evaporated and mushrooms are golden and soft.

> 2 sheets frozen puff pastry
> 2 tablespoons olive oil
> 1 tablespoon butter
> 1 shallot, finely chopped

1 pound white mushrooms, diced very small
3 tablespoons sherry wine
1 teaspoon Worcestershire sauce
½ cup flat parsley leaves, finely chopped
½ teaspoon finely chopped fresh thyme leaves
pepper and salt
8 ounces goose pâté
flour for rolling out pasty
4 (3-ounce) beef fillet steaks
1 egg, lightly beaten with 2 tablespoons water (egg wash)

Defrost frozen puff pastry sheets as package label directs.

In a skillet, heat olive oil and butter. Sauté shallot until translucent. Add and cook mushrooms, stirring, 15 minutes. Add sherry, Worcestershire sauce, parsley, thyme, pepper, and salt. Continue cooking a few more minutes, until all liquid has evaporated. Transfer contents of skillet to a bowl. Set aside.

Add goose pâté to bowl of mushrooms and combine well into a kind of paste.

Roll out puff pastry onto a floured surface and divide into 4 squares.

Place 1 little fillet steak in center of 1 pastry square. Spread a good layer of mushroom/pâté mixture over meat. Close pastry by pinching dough with wet fingers and sealing meat and mushroom paste into a little "package." Turn package seam side down and place onto a baking sheet. (If possible, try saving a little puff pastry dough to roll out and cut into petals as decoration for the top of the package). Brush with egg wash. Proceed with remaining meat, mushroom topping, and pastry in same manner.

Refrigerate 4 hours or longer, or freeze 40 minutes.

Preheat oven to 425°.

Remove individual Wellingtons from refrigerator and bake 15 minutes. Check with an instant-read thermometer; it should read 125° for medium-rare. (If temperature has not reached 125°, cook a bit longer until it does.) Remove Wellingtons from oven and let sit 5 minutes. SERVES 4.

Note: I do not precook — even briefly — the small fillet steaks, as is customary when preparing the whole fillet in the original beef Wellington. I find that that step risks overcooking the meat.

Duck Confit

I have always been intimidated when anyone even mentioned *canard confit*. I grew up with everyone around me respectfully saying *confire* was a great specialty best left to the experts. Thus, for years, I ordered it only in restaurants. Only recently, annoyed by my own passivity regarding confire, did I decide to pluck up my courage and give it a shot. Since then I have more than made up for all those years of timidity.

I ask the butcher to bone my duck (and set the bones on the side for a fine stock). I stuff the duck with leeks and, in a low oven, roast it for 3 hours. Unlike normal duck roasting, where I remove fat regularly in the course of cooking for the confit, I *never* remove any of the fat that has melted and accumulated. In so doing, I discovered the secret of confire: Leaving the duck to roast in its bath of fat and cooking it slowly is precisely what gives the meat its legendary confire moisture. And, sure enough, 3 hours later, the confit miracle happened! My duck came out golden crisp on the outside, and moist inside. In the south of France (especially in Dordogne where geese and ducks abound) duck confit is traditionally — and sinfully — served with cubed potatoes roasted in duck fat. (So much for cholesterol awareness! But oh so delicious!)

1 duck, boned
4 leeks, white part only, well washed
pepper and salt
3 baking potatoes, washed and cubed
2 garlic cloves, minced
½ cup fresh parsley leaves, finely chopped

Preheat oven to 350°.

Wash and pat dry duck inside and out. Place leeks inside cavity. With a sharp knife, prick duck all over, to allow the fat to escape. Sprinkle with pepper and salt. Place duck in roasting pan. Roast duck for 1 hour, reduce temperature to 200°, and continue cooking 2½ hours. Meanwhile, take a couple spoonfuls of the rendered duck fat and sauté potatoes in a skillet until golden brown and crisp. Sprinkle with garlic and parsley. If your duck doesn't seem crisp enough, place it for 2 minutes under the broiler. With a slotted spoon and a spatula, remove duck from its fat. Place on carving board, and carve. Serve with potatoes. SERVES 4–6.

Pork Tonnato

The original recipe calls for a veal roast. I have substituted pork for veal. Pork tenderloin is lean and tasty. I found it as tender as, if not more tender than, veal.

> 6 garlic cloves, peeled and minced
> ½ cup fresh rosemary leaves, finely chopped
> zest of 1 lemon
> 1 (5-to-6-pound) pork loin
> pepper and salt
> olive oil
> 2 jars anchovy fillets in oil
> 1 (6-ounce) can tuna fish, drained
> 1 egg
> juice of 1 lemon
> ½ cup capers
> 1 cup yogurt
> a few leaves fresh basil

Preheat oven to 350°.

In the food processor, purée garlic, rosemary and lemon zest. Rinse pork and pat dry. With a sharp knife, make incisions every ½ inch all around the roast. Insert some rosemary-lemon-garlic paste into each incision. Pepper and salt the roast. (If you have any leftover paste, rub the roast with it.) Brush with olive oil. Roast 1½ hours, until tender. Remove from oven and cool.

In a blender, put 1 jar anchovies with their oil, tuna, the egg, lemon juice, and half the capers, and turn machine on while drizzling in 1 cup olive oil. You will obtain a very tasty tuna and anchovy mayonnaise. Season with pepper first (the anchovies are salty; you should taste mayonnaise first before adding more salt). Transfer mayonnaise to a bowl, and with a whisk, beat in the yogurt. Set sauce aside.

When pork is cold, slice and arrange slices on serving platter. Cover slices with sauce. Sprinkle with remaining capers and the basil leaves and decorate with remaining anchovies. SERVES 10–12.

Note: I have successfully on occasion even used turkey loin as meat.

Coq au Vin

Why bother with *another* coq au vin recipe, you might ask?

Despite the relatively recent popularity in America of this traditional French way of cooking chicken with red wine — once exclusively the specialty of French restaurants — coq au vin has settled today comfortably into the American culinary repertory. There are, however, ordinary coq au vins, and good ones. I hope mine is among the latter.

One of the secrets of a good coq au vin is making sure to use an excellent, top-of-the-line red wine — one you would serve and enjoy drinking. A fine bottle of wine will immediately upgrade your recipe and is worth the extra expense.

Rather than using a whole chicken, quartered, I prefer 2 or 3 boned chicken breasts and 4 boned chicken thighs. Less waste, and easier to eat.

⅓ cup olive oil
2–3 chicken breasts, boned and cut into 1-inch pieces
4 chicken thighs, boned and cut into 1-inch pieces
8 bacon slices, cut into small strips
2 onions, finely chopped
2 garlic cloves, minced
4 sprigs fresh thyme, leaves only, finely chopped
2 sprigs rosemary, leaves only, finely chopped
pepper and salt
1 bottle red Burgundy wine
½ pound white mushrooms, stems removed, wiped, and sliced
1 bunch flat parsley, finely chopped

In a kettle, heat olive oil and brown chicken pieces on all sides. Add bacon, onions, garlic, thyme, rosemary, pepper, and salt. Cook 8 more minutes, until bacon and onions become translucent. Reduce heat, pour in wine. Stir. Cover and cook 30 minutes. Add mushrooms and parsley and continue cooking 10 minutes. SERVES 4–6.

Tip: If, like me, you don't enjoy the sauce so thin you can't properly eat the coq au vin without spilling some, thicken it at the last minute with a touch of cornstarch. Use 1–2 tablespoons cornstarch blended in a cup with 2 tablespoons from the wine sauce. Pour back into coq au vin kettle, stir 2 minutes, and serve. The thickened sauce nicely binds the whole recipe.

VEGETABLE MAIN COURSES

Braised Endives

One generally thinks of Belgian endives as a crispy salad unto itself or as part of a salad. Less known is its use as a side dish. In fact, braised Belgian endives, prized in Europe as a delicacy, are the unsung heroes of Mediterranean cuisine. Their delicate and sweet flavor enhances many a meat and fish course.

> 3 tablespoons butter
> 6 Belgian endives, cores removed, washed, halved
> juice of ½ a lemon
> ½ teaspoon freshly grated nutmeg
> salt

In a kettle, heat 2 tablespoons butter. Add endives. Sprinkle with lemon juice, nutmeg, and salt, and cook about 5–6 minutes, until golden brown on both sides. Reduce heat to low, cover, and simmer 30 minutes. SERVES 4.

Zucchini Alfredo Topped with Onion Rings

This crunchy and creamy vegetable dish, emanating from Italy, as its name implies, is an ideal accompaniment to any grilled meat. It can also be a delicious main course for lunch.

> 2 medium zucchini, washed but unpeeled, cut into thin strips
> salt
> 2 tablespoons olive oil
> 2 garlic cloves, minced
> 1 (8-ounce) package lowfat cream cheese
> 1 cup half-and-half (or plain soy milk)
> ⅔ cup freshly grated Parmigiano-Reggiano cheese
> ½ teaspoon freshly grated nutmeg
> 1 cup onion rings (or canned onion rings), recipe follows
> pepper

In a large colander, sprinkle zucchini with salt. After 30 minutes, rinse, squeeze, and pat dry.

Tip: Make your onion rings while the zucchini sits in the colander.

In a skillet, heat olive oil and cook zucchini and garlic 2 minutes. Transfer to a bowl.

In a food processor, purée cream cheese and half-and-half, pour into same skillet, and heat 2 minutes, stirring. Add ½ cup cheese. Stir zucchini back into skillet for 1 minute. Transfer to serving platter. Sprinkle with grated nutmeg, onion rings, pepper, salt and remaining cheese. SERVES 4.

FOR THE ONION RINGS

Making onion rings is easy and, in my opinion, they taste far better than the canned variety.

1 large onion, peeled and sliced
½ cup all-purpose flour
½ teaspoon salt
2 tablespoons water or buttermilk
peanut oil for frying

In a kettle, heat peanut oil.

In a bowl, mix flour, 2 tablespoons water, and the salt. Coat onion rings well with batter.

Fry onion rings in hot oil 2 minutes on each side, until they turn golden and are crisp. Drain on paper towels. SERVES 4.

Spinach, Mediterranean Style

Spinach, with all its oft-touted health-giving properties, can either be one of the dullest vegetables on earth or one of the most delectable. Overcooked, it is frankly awful. But as anyone who has been to Italy knows, spinach cooked al dente, with a lemon-juice and garlic zing, becomes a culinary delight.

3 pounds fresh spinach, cut into thin strips
2 garlic cloves, minced
juice of ½ lemon
⅓ cup olive oil
pepper and salt

Wilt spinach in a kettle, tossing over high heat for 2 minutes with no water or oil. You may press liquid out with a fork and discard. When all liquid is eliminated, toss in garlic, lemon juice, olive oil, pepper, and salt. Cook 1 more minute. SERVES 4.

Zucchini Cakes, Greek Style

Zucchini cakes with a garlic-yogurt sauce are a tasty accompaniment to lamb. They are also a good main dish for lunch.

> 2 small zucchini, unpeeled and washed
> salt
> 1 small onion, minced
> 2 eggs
> 1 cup crumbled fresh feta cheese
> 1 cup finely chopped fresh dill
> 2 tablespoons flour
> pepper
> olive oil for frying
> garlic and mint yogurt sauce, recipe follows

In a food processor, shred zucchini. Transfer shredded zucchini to a colander set over a bowl, sprinkle with 1 tablespoon salt, and let stand 30 minutes. Rinse off salt, squeeze zucchini, and pat dry. In a bowl, mix zucchini with onion, feta cheese, dill, egg, flour, pepper, and salt.

With your hands, form zucchini mixture into cakes or patties, like hamburgers.

In a frying pan, heat olive oil and cook zucchini cakes over medium heat until golden brown and crisp, about 5 minutes on each side.

Serve zucchini cakes with a dollop of yogurt sauce.

GARLIC AND MINT YOGURT SAUCE
> 1 pint Greek-style yogurt
> 2 garlic cloves, minced
> 1 cup fresh mint leaves, finely chopped
> 1 tablespoon olive oil
> pepper and salt

In a serving bowl, combine and mix ingredients. Set aside. SERVES 4–6.

Roasted Mediterranean Vegetables

Roasting is an ancient and traditional way of cooking vegetables in Mediterranean cuisines, and the same method of cooking vegetables has, in recent years, solidly taken its place in American cuisine as well. Fragrant and multicolored, roasted vegetables offer many attractive presentation possibilities. They sustain interest if served alone, but provide a most satisfying accompaniment to any meat or fish dish.

> 1 red onion, peeled and quartered
> 1 small eggplant, peeled and cut into 1-inch pieces
> 1 red beet, quartered
> 1 red or yellow pepper, seeded, white membrane removed, and
>   cut into 1-inch pieces
> olive oil to moisten all vegetables (about ⅓ cup)
> herbes de Provence
> pepper and salt
> 7 ripe tomatoes, quartered
> 1 small head of radicchio, leaves separated
> 1 small zucchini, washed and cut into 1-inch pieces
> 1 small bunch asparagus, trimmed and cut diagonally in 1-inch
>   pieces

Preheat oven to 350°.

In a baking dish, spread onion, eggplant, beet, and peppers, sprinkle with olive oil, herbes de Provence, pepper, and salt, and bake 20 minutes. Add tomatoes, radicchio, and zucchini. Continue cooking 20 more minutes, sprinkling with more oil, herbes de Provence, pepper, and salt, and, with a spatula, tossing every 5 minutes. Add asparagus; continue cooking 5 minutes. Toss and serve. SERVES 4–6.

herbes
de
provence

Broccoli with a Zing

Speaking of zing: Broccoli, another source of many virtues for the body and soul, offers as many detractions as overdone spinach. Here's a recipe I've cooked over the years that is guaranteed to turn broccoli haters into broccoli lovers.

> 2 tablespoons olive oil
> 1 medium onion, sliced
> 1 head broccoli, trimmed, stems peeled and sliced, florets separated
> 1 garlic clove, minced
> ½ cup chopped walnuts
> 1 teaspoon peeled and grated fresh ginger
> pepper and salt

In a skillet, heat olive oil. Cook onion 5 minutes until wilted but not brown. Add broccoli, garlic, walnuts, and ginger. Stir and cook 3 more minutes. Season with pepper and salt. SERVES 4.

Casserole of Zucchini and Tomatoes

This typical Provençal casserole of baked vegetables is often served in the local earthenware casserole dish called *tian*. It's usually served with a roast — any roast. Served with a salad, it also constitutes a fine lunch.

> ⅓ cup olive oil
> 3 tomatoes, sliced
> 2 zucchini, unpeeled and sliced
> 3 garlic cloves, minced
> herbes de Provence
> pepper and salt

Preheat oven to 350°.

Use some of the oil to lubricate an ovenproof dish. In the prepared dish, for color contrast, alternate tomato and zucchini slices. Sprinkle with garlic, herbes de Provence, pepper, salt, and remaining olive oil. Bake 30 minutes. SERVES 4–6.

Carrots Provençal

The Mediterranean abounds in olives, and Provençal cuisine in particular makes wide use of this bounty. My friend Marise, a farmer who lives in my village and sells her carrots — picked that morning — at our local *marché,* gave me her recipe. The sweetness of new carrots blended with the distinct flavor and saltiness of black olives provides an attractive contrast in taste and looks. It also gives some more substance to carrots.

>   2 tablespoons olive oil
>   3 cups new carrots, peeled and cut diagonally
>   2 garlic cloves, minced
>   30 or so black olives, pitted and halved
>   pepper and salt

Tip: To cut carrots diagonally, put your knife at an angle, and cut.

In a skillet, heat the oil and cook carrots 10 minutes, covered. Add garlic, stir, and continue cooking 10 minutes, covered. Stir in olives, pepper, and a little salt (not too much because olives bring their own salt). SERVES 4–6.

Swiss Chard Cakes

I don't know why Americans call this vegetable "Swiss" chard. Does it especially grow in, and come from, Switzerland? I am not sure. Be that as it may, there are fields and fields of Swiss chard throughout Italy and Southern France, where it's known as *blettes* and used in countless recipes in both cuisines.

½ cup olive oil
2 pounds Swiss chard, well washed, trimmed, and shredded
3 tablespoons flour, plus extra for dusting
1 teaspoon freshly grated nutmeg
pepper and salt
1 cup half-and-half
1 egg, lightly beaten

In a skillet, heat ¼ cup olive oil and sauté chard 5 minutes. Stir in flour, nutmeg, pepper, salt, and half-and-half. Continue cooking over low heat another 10 minutes. Remove from heat, transfer to a bowl, and cool. Wipe skillet.

When mixture is cool, add egg. Form patties with your hands, and dip patties in the flour.

In the same skillet, heat remaining olive oil and cook patties over low heat until crisp on both sides. SERVES 4.

Note: Serve with a roast — lamb is particularly recommended with this recipe.

The Fabulous *Purée Blanche* (Mashed Celeriac, Turnip, Garlic, Onion, and Potato)

An indulgence, yes. This remarkable purée with its subtle but multiple flavors ranks for me among the absolute best comfort foods. Whatever I happen to serve with it, be it a roast or fish, the attention inevitably goes to the *purée blanche,* making me wonder at times why I cooked anything else for the meal.

6 shallots, peeled and sliced
½ cup olive oil, plus 2 or more tablespoons
salt
1 pound celeriac, peeled and cut into 1-inch pieces
1 pound white turnips, peeled and cut into small pieces
1 pound potatoes, peeled and cut into small pieces
4 onions, finely chopped
1 head of garlic, cloves separated and peeled
2 Granny Smith apples, cored and cubed
pepper
1 tablespoon butter
fresh parsley, finely chopped

Preheat oven to 350°.

Put shallots in baking dish. Sprinkle with a little olive oil and bake 35 minutes, until they become light brown and crisp. Remove from oven. Set aside.

In a large kettle, bring 2 quarts salted water to a boil. Cook celeriac and turnips 15 minutes. Add potatoes, onions, and garlic, and continue cooking for an additional 15 minutes. Drain. (I have learned to keep and store the liquid. It always makes a good base for a future soup.)

Mash with a potato masher (the purée benefits from not being ultra smooth), adding olive oil, pepper, and salt. Incorporate cubed apples. Top with crisp shallots, fresh butter, and parsley. SERVES 6–8.

Roasted Radicchio

That red and tough cabbage-like vegetable emanating from Italy is now readily available in America as well, and is often mixed in salads, where it adds crunchiness and color. Italians, however, have wonderful ways of preparing this radicchio hot, which they serve with meat or fish.

> 3 heads radicchio, quartered lengthwise
> 2 tablespoons olive oil
> juice of ½ lemon
> 1 tablespoon balsamic vinegar
> pepper and salt
> ½ cup Parmigiano-Reggiano cheese shavings

Preheat oven to 350°.

In a kettle, bring 4 cups water to a boil. Blanch radicchio 1 minute. Drain.

In a skillet, heat 1 tablespoon olive oil. Braise radicchio 5 minutes on each side. Transfer to ovenproof dish. Pour pan drippings over radicchio, and sprinkle with remaining olive oil, the lemon juice, balsamic vinegar, pepper, and salt. Cover with cheese shavings. Bake 15 minutes. SERVES 4.

Purée of White Beans with Anchovies

This divine bean purée — *brandade de haricots* — is featured in Greek cooking as well as in southern French cuisine. A great first course by itself, it is also a good accompaniment to any fish or roast.

2½ cups dried Great Northern beans
a few sprigs parsley
1 carrot, peeled
1 celery stalk
salt
4 anchovy fillets
1 cup olive oil, plus extra for frying croutons
½ cup milk
2 garlic cloves, minced
juice of ½ lemon
pepper
4 slices bread, cut up in cubes

Soak beans overnight.

Discard water.

In a kettle filled with 6 cups water, the parsley, carrot, celery, and 1 teaspoon salt, cook beans, covered, over medium heat 1½ hours. Drain, but keep liquid for later use.

In a food processor, purée bean mixture with anchovies, trickling in oil and milk slowly while processing and stopping occasionally to check for consistency. (The purée should not be too thin, so you may not need to use all the oil.) Season with garlic, lemon juice, pepper, and a little salt.

In a skillet, heat a little olive oil and fry bread cubes for croutons. Transfer brandade to serving platter and top with croutons. Serves 4–6.

Tomato Tart

Melting in your mouth, this tomato tart is also a fine accompaniment to any roast, and can be served as a luncheon main course, followed (or preceded) by a green salad.

⅓ cup olive oil, plus extra for oiling baking dish
2 sheets frozen puff pastry
flour for rolling out pastry
1 egg beaten with ⅓ cup water (egg wash)
1 cup feta cheese, crumbled
½ cup Gruyère cheese, grated
5 ripe tomatoes, peeled and sliced
2 garlic cloves, minced
1 tablespoon herbes de Provence
pepper and salt
½ cup fresh basil leaves, finely chopped

Preheat oven to 350°. Oil a baking dish with some olive oil.

Defrost puff pastry according to package instructions. On a floured board, roll out pastry. Line the prepared baking dish with 1 pastry sheet. Cut second sheet into 4 strips. Place a strip on all 4 sides of the baking dish as if you were making a box. Make ridges along the sides with a fork. With a pastry brush, brush pastry with egg wash. Poke holes with a fork in center of pastry. Bake 20 minutes, until golden brown and puffy.

Remove tart shell from oven and spread feta and Gruyère cheese over bottom. Place tomato slices, overlapping, on top of cheeses. Sprinkle with garlic, herbes de Provence, pepper, and salt. Trickle olive oil over tomatoes. Bake 20 minutes. Sprinkle with basil. SERVES 6–8.

Gratin of Swiss Chard and Asparagus

This is a delicious Italian casserole that nicely accompanies poultry, fish, or any roast meat.

> 4 pounds Swiss chard, washed and chopped coarsely
> ⅓ cup olive oil
> 3 garlic cloves, minced
> 1 pound asparagus, trimmed and cut into small pieces
> pepper and salt
> 1 cup Gruyère cheese, grated

Preheat oven to 350°.

Blanch chard 3 minutes in boiling water. Drain. In a kettle, heat olive oil, and cook chard with garlic, stirring 5 minutes. In a steamer, cook asparagus 2 minutes. Transfer to ovenproof dish. Season with pepper and salt. Add Swiss chard. Top with cheese and cook 10 minutes, until Gruyère cheese is melted and forms a crisp topping. SERVES 4–6.

Note: Like spinach, Swiss chard reduces dramatically when cooked.

Braised Fennel

Like Belgian endive, fennel is more often eaten raw in salads than as a cooked side dish. Cooked fennel, however, well deserves recognition. Braised, with a licorice hint, it enriches any roast or fish.

> ¼ cup olive oil
> 2 or 3 fennel bulbs, trimmed and halved lengthwise, fennel leaves
>   washed and finely chopped
> 1 head of garlic, cloves separated but unpeeled
> ¼ cup white wine
> pepper and salt

In a large skillet, heat olive oil. Place fennel bulbs cut side down and put garlic cloves in between halves. Reduce heat to low and cook 15 minutes. Turn fennel over and continue cooking 15 minutes. Add half the wine, some pepper, and salt, cover, and braise 50 minutes or so. Add remaining wine from time to time and even a few drops water, as needed. Fennel should be tender and slightly caramelized. Sprinkle chopped fennel leaves on top. SERVES 4–6.

Casserole of Red Peppers Stuffed with Anchovies

This is a different, most flavorful way of preparing peppers.

> 6 anchovy fillets, rinsed
> 6 garlic cloves, minced
> 1 cup breadcrumbs
> ⅔ cup olive oil, plus extra for brushing casserole dish
> 8 red peppers, cut in half, seeded, and white membrane removed
> 1 teaspoon herbes de Provence
> pepper (no salt, because the anchovies, even after being rinsed,
>   retain a lot of salt)

Preheat oven to 350°. Brush a casserole dish with some olive oil.

In a mortar or mini-processor, make a paste with the anchovies, garlic, half the breadcrumbs, and ½ cup olive oil. Divide into 8 portions. Put 1 portion on 1 pepper half. Cover each with one of the remaining pepper halves — enclosing the paste. Line your stuffed peppers side by side in the casserole dish brushed with olive oil. Drizzle remaining olive oil over peppers and sprinkle with remaining breadcrumbs, the herbes de Provence, and pepper. Bake 20 minutes. SERVES 6–8.

Casserole of Eggplant, Tomato, and Chickpeas, Tunisian Style

Quite substantial, this casserole could well be a meal in itself, either for lunch or dinner, when served with a salad.

1½ cups dried chickpeas or 4 cups drained, canned chickpeas
salt
olive oil
2 medium eggplants, washed but not peeled, cut into 2-inch
    cubes
1 teaspoon paprika
1 teaspoon ground cumin
1 teaspoon ground cinnamon
¼ teaspoon cayenne pepper
pepper
3 medium onions, finely chopped
10 small tomatoes, peeled and finely chopped

If using dried chickpeas: in a bowl, soak dried chickpeas covered by 2 inches with water overnight. Drain.

In a kettle, cover chickpeas with fresh water, add some salt, and bring to a boil. Reduce heat and cook 2 hours, until peas are tender. You will need to add water from time to time. Obviously, the easier and faster way is using canned chickpeas, which need no cooking — merely draining and rinsing.

Preheat oven to 400°.

In a skillet, heat some olive oil and sauté eggplant 10–15 minutes, until light brown. With a slotted spoon, remove eggplant and transfer to casserole dish. Season with paprika, cumin, cinnamon, cayenne, salt, and pepper. In the same skillet, add a few drops olive oil and sauté onions until light brown. Spread onion with pan drippings over eggplant. Add pepper, salt, and layer of chickpeas. Cover with tomato. Dribble a little olive oil on top and season one more time. Bake 35 minutes. SERVES 6–8.

Eggplant Fritters

If you are looking for something new and different with eggplant — as a change from grilled or broiled — you will welcome these fritters. Mediterranean cuisine in general offers a wide variety of vegetable fritters, ranging from zucchini, mushroom, and olives to small artichoke fritters. All crunchy and delectable on their own, they are often served with fish or meat.

> 1 large eggplant, peeled, and cut into thick slices
> salt

Place eggplant slices in colander. Sprinkle evenly with salt and let rest 20 minutes. Rinse eggplant, pat dry, and set aside.

FOR THE BATTER
> 1 cup all-purpose flour
> 2 egg yolks
> ⅔ cup milk
> 1 tablespoon olive oil
> ½ teaspoon salt, plus extra for sprinkling
> 2 egg whites
> 4 cups peanut oil for frying

In a bowl, combine and whisk flour, egg yolks, milk, olive oil, and salt. Beat egg whites until stiff, and then fold them into yolk mixture.

In as wide a kettle as you can find, heat peanut oil.

Drop eggplant slices into batter, making sure each slice is well coated. When frying oil, wait until it is hot, but not smoky. (To test, drop a teaspoon of batter into oil. If it sizzles immediately, your oil is ready.) Fry eggplant slices 2 minutes or until underside of eggplant is golden brown. With the help of 2 forks, turn slices over and continue cooking until other side is golden as well. With a slotted spoon, drain slices and place on paper towels. Sprinkle fritters with salt and serve immediately. (If you wait, fritters will become soggy.) SERVES 4–6.

Mushroom Flan

This flan is a delicate side dish that accompanies roasted chicken or lamb with great elegance. I recommend not overcrowding the menu with too many other vegetables that would detract from this flan.

½ cup olive oil, plus extra for oiling baking dish or individual
  ovenproof dishes
1 onion, minced
½ pound white mushrooms, wiped and sliced
2 ounces dried porcini mushrooms, reconstituted with ½ cup
  boiling water, drained, squeezed, and chopped, soaking
  liquid strained and reserved
1 garlic clove, minced
½ teaspoon chopped fresh thyme leaves
½ teaspoon freshly grated nutmeg
pepper and salt
2 tablespoons flour
1 cup milk
4 eggs, lightly beaten

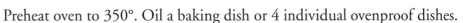

Preheat oven to 350°. Oil a baking dish or 4 individual ovenproof dishes.

In a skillet, heat olive oil. Sauté onion, until translucent. Add white mushrooms and chopped porcini to onion. Reduce heat and cook 20 minutes. Add garlic, thyme, nutmeg, pepper, and salt. Stir in flour and gradually pour milk and reserved porcini liquid. Stir 5 more minutes, until mixture thickens. Turn heat off. Cool a little.

In a food processor, purée contents of skillet. Add eggs.

Pour contents of processor into prepared baking dish or dishes. Place in a roasting pan and add enough hot water to come halfway up sides of baking dish or dishes. Bake 40 minutes. If using individual dishes, the cooking time is less by approximately 15 minutes. To check for doneness, insert a knife. If it comes out clean, the flan is cooked. If not, continue cooking a few more minutes. Serve. (I do not unmold the flan. It is either served from the baking dish in portions, or each person gets his or her own.) SERVES 4.

Spinach Dumplings

A pleasant variation, these light and flavorful spinach dumplings make an attractive side dish to any fish or meat. Served on their own as a lunch, 2 or 3 dumplings will suffice with a spoonful of either cheese sauce or tomato sauce, followed by a green salad.

2 pounds fresh spinach, cooked 3 minutes, squeezed dry, and chopped (the frozen, already chopped variety is fine, too; thaw and squeeze dry)
3 eggs
½ cup pine nuts, roasted
1 garlic clove, minced
1 cup ricotta cheese
1 cup freshly grated Parmigiano-Reggiano cheese
1 cup all-purpose flour, plus extra for dusting work surface
½ cup flat parsley leaves, chopped
½ teaspoon freshly grated nutmeg
pepper and salt
1 cup tomato sauce
4 tablespoons butter

Preheat oven to 400°.

In a mixing bowl, combine and mash spinach, eggs, garlic, ricotta, half the Parmigiano-Reggiano, 1 cup flour, parsley, the nutmeg, pinenuts, some pepper, and salt. The mixture should be firm. Generously flour a work surface. With your hands, form a long log-like shape. Cut each log into 2-inch pieces. Each cut piece is a dumpling. Roll again in flour.

In a large kettle, bring 2 quarts water and 1 teaspoon salt to a boil and reduce heat to a simmer. Drop well-floured dumplings into water. Simmer dumplings over medium heat 15 minutes, until they rise to the surface. When they do, remove dumplings with a slotted spoon and drain on paper towel.

In the bottom of an ovenproof casserole, spread tomato sauce and top with dumplings, side by side. Sprinkle with remaining Parmigiano-Reggiano and dots of butter. Bake 6 minutes. SERVES 4–6.

Note: You may opt to serve these dumplings simply with a butter and sage sauce instead of tomato sauce.

Cèpes, Mushroom, and Potato Ragout

Extremely fragrant, this ragout melts in your mouth, and is so delectable it should almost be served by itself to be properly appreciated. If you are unable to find fresh cèpes (porcini), substitute a combination of shiitake, portobello, and dried porcini mushrooms — it will still be a memorable dish.

⅓ cup olive oil
4–5 fresh cèpes, wiped dry and sliced, or 5 shiitake mushrooms,
    wiped dry and sliced
3 baking potatoes, peeled and cut into small cubes
1 portobello mushroom, cleaned and sliced
½ cup dry porcini mushrooms, covered with boiling water 30
    minutes and drained
pepper and salt
2 bay leaves
1 cup vegetable stock
1 bunch flat parsley, finely chopped

Preheat oven to 250°.

In a skillet, heat olive oil and sauté cubed potatoes until light golden brown. Add mushrooms, pepper, and salt. Cook 10 minutes. Transfer to casserole dish. Add bay leaves, porcini liquid, and stock. Bake 45 minutes. Remove bay leaves. Sprinkle with parsley. SERVES 4–6.

SALAD MAIN COURSES

In the Mediterranean region, and in European cuisines in general, fresh salads are sometimes served as a meal opener, but more frequently they are served after the main course, as a transition from the main course to the dessert. When I came to America, I was surprised to find that most often salads were served first on the menu. In the intervening years, France has followed that pattern, it seems, and today you'll see salads also being offered as first courses there as well. My preference remains "salad after the main course, before or with the cheese," but that may simply be because I was brought up that way. When I don't serve salad as a "transition" but as an opener, however, I like to dress up the salad with different additions such as walnuts, pear, goat cheese, bits of bacon, and other variants.

Tip: As a rule, toss in dressing *just* prior to serving salad: it wilts quickly when dressed and tossed ahead of time.

Baby Spinach Salad with Croutons

⅓ cup olive oil
1 garlic clove, peeled and left whole
4 slices French bread, cubed
5 handfuls baby spinach
½ red onion, finely sliced
juice of 1 lemon
1 teaspoon Dijon mustard
pepper and salt

In a skillet, heat a little olive oil and sauté garlic 1 minute. Discard garlic and fry croutons until they turn light brown. Remove from heat, and set aside.

In a salad bowl, make the dressing with remaining oil, the lemon juice, mustard, pepper and salt and toss with spinach and onion. Sprinkle with croutons. SERVES 4.

Chicory Salad

This crunchy salad is always a welcome transition between a rich gratin and dessert. It also provides a wonderful first course, with croutons, or with warm goat cheese on toasts. I recommend using only the "heart," the yellow center, and tossing it with a lemon vinaigrette.

Nathalie's Mint and Dill Salad with Mesclun

When my daughter introduced me to this particularly tasty salad, with its larger-than-usual quantity of mint and dill, I was immediately won over. Both mint and dill impart great flavor and freshness, and they become the salad even with some mesclun tossed in.

> 3 cups mesclun salad
> 2 cups fresh dill, washed and finely chopped
> 2 cups mint leaves, washed and finely chopped
> juice of ½ lemon
> 3 tablespoons olive oil
> 1 tablespoon Dijon mustard
> pepper and salt

Mix ingredients in salad bowl and toss with dressing made with lemon juice, olive oil, mustard, pepper, and salt just before serving. SERVES 4–6.

Arugula with Orange Slices and Red Onion, in a Lemon Vinaigrette

I first tried this tasty salad at my friend Carol Southern's house. The combination of red onion, arugula, and orange — the first two a little sharp, with the spark of the sliced orange — act as a perfect astringent, especially after a rich main course.

1 bunch arugula, washed and trimmed
1 eating orange, peeled and sliced (seeds and white membrane removed)
1 small red onion, sliced
juice of ½ lemon
3 tablespoons olive oil
pepper and salt

Into the salad bowl containing the arugula, add the other ingredients. It's best to hold off doing this until just before serving. Add the dressing, made with lemon juice, olive oil, pepper, and salt, and toss at the table. SERVES 4.

Boston Lettuce with Lemon Vinaigrette and Chives

In France, Boston lettuce is simply called named *laitue.*

juice of ½ lemon
4 tablespoons olive oil
pepper and salt
1 head of Boston lettuce, washed, dried, and leaves separated
½ cup chives, finely chopped

In a small bowl, mix lemon juice, olive oil, pepper, and salt. Pour over lettuce and chives in a salad bowl. Bring to the table and toss. SERVES 4.

Endive Salad

Endive with walnuts lends itself especially well as a first course.

> 2 tablespoons fresh lemon juice
> 2 tablespoons olive oil
> 1 tablespoon walnut oil
> 1 tablespoon Dijon mustard
> pepper and salt
> 4 Belgian endives, leaves separated, washed, and dried
> ½ cup toasted walnuts

In a salad bowl, prepare the dressing with lemon juice, olive oil, walnut oil, mustard, pepper, and salt and add endive leaves and walnuts. Toss. SERVES 4.

Endive, Watercress, and Beet Salad

This is a lovely mix of texture, colors, and flavors that works well both as a first course and later in the menu.

> 4 tablespoons olive oil
> 3 tablespoons fresh lemon juice
> 1 tablespoon Dijon mustard
> pepper and salt
> 3 endives, leaves separated, washed, and sliced
> 1 beet, peeled and sliced
> ½ bunch watercress, washed, stems removed

In the bowl, combine oil, lemon juice, mustard, pepper, and salt. Toss with endives, beet slices, and watercress. SERVES 4–6.

Watercress Salad

Watercress offers an astringent and refreshing transition to any main course, but particularly so when it follow a rich main course.

> 1½ bunches watercress, trimmed and washed
> juice of 1 lemon
> 2 tablespoons olive oil
> 1 tablespoon Dijon mustard
> pepper and salt

In the salad bowl, toss watercress with vinaigrette made from lemon juice, olive oil, mustard, pepper, and salt. Serves 4.

Chicory Salad with Roasted Shallots and Walnuts

> 2 shallots, peeled and sliced
> 2 tablespoons olive oil, plus extra for drizzling shallots
> 1 head chicory, washed and separated — yellow part only
> juice of 1 lemon
> 1 tablespoon toasted sesame oil
> 1 tablespoon Dijon mustard
> 1 teaspoon soy sauce
> 1 cup walnuts, toasted

Preheat oven to 400°.

In an ovenproof dish, spread out shallots, drizzle with a few drops olive oil, and roast 30 minutes, turning once in a while, until they turn crisp and light brown. Remove from oven.

In a salad bowl, mix chicory with dressing made with lemon juice, oil, mustard, and soy sauce. Top with shallots and walnuts. Serves 4.

DESSERTS

Throughout the history of gastronomy worldwide, no meal was ever considered complete without the conclusion of a proper dessert, which meant any preparation such as a cake — elaborate or not — a tart, or other baked sweet, served hot or cold. Fruit and chocolates were often passed around *after* the dessert.

There are, in fact, people who believe that a meal was merely an excuse for the grand finale, the culminating point, namely the dessert. Historically, *chefs pâtissiers* coveted their art and, indeed, were prized by both the court and the aristocrats. Today, they still covet their art of *pâtisserie*. And in Paris, more often than not, great chef patissiers like Ladurée, Dalloyau, Lenôtre, Fauchon, and many more, own their patisserie cum tea rooms bearing their names, where, each afternoon, people gather over a cup of coffee, hot chocolate, or tea and revel in the pâtissier's signature cakes or macaroons.

Desserts are still an integral and essential part of what is considered a good meal. In fact, despite restrictive measures — vis-à-vis sweets in general — that reflect today's health concerns, contemporary restaurants lead you directly to the dessert choices — often a separate menu — in order for you to end the repast with the right balance. Few are the chefs who can resist the temptation of creating the most sophisticated sweet constructions that they then proudly present — not without a degree of ceremony — to their eager guests.

Despite the rage of no-carb, no-sugar diets, which deprive their adherents of their once-prized desserts, I continue to enjoy and indulge in — in moderation — this part of the meal. The necessity to refresh one's palate and seek a change of taste from salty to sweet, especially after a rich meal, strikes me as both necessary and relevant.

In composing any menu, I like the challenge of creating an attractive dessert, one that would give the final touch with either panache or simply the right measure to a meal.

Desserts should and can be the dramatic conclusion of well-planned menus. And, like fireworks, the *bouquet* — the brilliant finale — is one of the key elements people both look forward to and remember.

You will note that most desserts in this book feature fruit as their base — a new departure for me that is the result of my increasing knowledge of Mediterranean dessert habits.

In summer, unable to leave farmers' markets anywhere without carrying away a crate of some fruit, I found myself rethinking desserts and conceived my menus accordingly. Thus, the irresistible Mediterranean bounty came into play and inspired many of the following desserts.

Roasted Peaches with Verbena

Verbena has a lovely lemony scent that imparts an exceptional and delicate fragrance to the roasted peaches. This dessert is as delicious served cold as hot.

1 cup verbena leaves
½ cup sugar
2 tablespoons, plus 1½ teaspoons butter
8-10 ripe peaches, peeled and left whole

Preheat oven to 200°.

In a food processor, pulse verbena until finely chopped and mix with sugar and butter (as if you were making pesto). Place peaches in an ovenproof dish. Top each peach with butter/verbena mixture. Bake 30 minutes. SERVES 4–6.

Optional: When I first tasted this dessert in France, the peaches were served on a small piece of French toast and topped with a spoonful of vanilla ice cream. My husband was ecstatic. I prefer the peaches plain.

Bananas Flambées

Bananas are so readily available throughout the year everywhere that they may, perhaps, appear too common to be considered for any dessert. But this dessert, so easy to prepare, is surprisingly delicious and provides a flamboyant conclusion to any meal.

> 8 tablespoons unsalted butter
> ½ cup brown sugar
> 6 bananas, peeled and sliced lengthwise
> ½ cup rum

In a skillet, melt butter, add sugar, and cook 3 minutes over medium heat until the mixture looks syrupy. Add bananas. Transfer contents of skillet to a serving platter. Bring to the table. In a small saucepan, heat rum. Pour rum over bananas, and ignite immediately. There will inevitably be some "oohs" and "aahs." When the flame has subsided, serve bananas with plenty of sauce. SERVES 4.

Broiled Pineapple Slices with Brown Sugar

Always fragrant, excellent, and extremely easy to prepare, I find that this is a welcome ending to a meal — provided the pineapple is ripe. (There is, by the way, a gadget that recently appeared on the market that peels and slices pineapples all in one motion!) The pineapple's aroma comes out particularly well when roasted or broiled.

> 1 pineapple, peeled, core removed, and sliced
> 1 cup brown sugar
> ½ cup fresh mint leaves, finely chopped

Place pineapple on a grill rack or broiler pan. Start grilling or broiling pineapple without the sugar for 3 minutes on each side. After both sides have cooked, pat sugar coating well on each slice and continue grilling 1 minute on each side. Place on serving platter. Sprinkle with mint. SERVES 4–6.

Chocolate and Strawberry Napoleon

Although I do not know the exact historical origin of the term "Napoleon," I have no doubt that the French emperor's pastry chef must have created this dessert for him. In any case, in culinary parlance, a Napoleon always refers to a multilayer dessert of either puff pastry or some kind of crisp dough and cream or fruit. Here I use chocolate wafers.

FOR THE WAFERS

butter for greasing parchment
2 large egg whites
8 ounces bittersweet chocolate, melted
½ cup sifted all-purpose flour
½ cup blanched whole almonds, ground
⅓ cup sugar
½ teaspoon salt
½ teaspoon vanilla extract
¼ teaspoon almond extract

Preheat oven to 350°. Butter a sheet of parchment.

In a bowl, whisk egg whites until frothy. Gradually fold in remaining ingredients. On a buttered parchment sheet, drop a tablespoon of the batter, leaving an inch space between each spoonful. Bake 8–9 minutes. Remove from oven. Cool a few seconds, and with a spatula, lift wafers onto a plate.

FOR THE FILLING
1 pound strawberries, washed, hulled, and sliced
1 tablespoon sugar
a few drops fresh lemon juice
½ cup heavy cream, whipped (optional)

In a bowl, toss strawberries with sugar and lemon juice.

On each dessert plate, place 1 chocolate wafer, spread with a thin layer of whipped cream, and top with a layer of strawberries, then another wafer, and another layer of cream and fruit. Top with a spoonful whipped cream. SERVES 4–6.

Apricot Crumble

What is the term "crumble" doing in a Mediterranean cookbook, you might ask? Somehow — most probably because so many British have settled in Spain, Italy, and southern France over the past several decades — "crumble" has now become part of Mediterranean culinary language. "Crumble" appears in many restaurant menus of the region, and I always smile when I hear farmers pronounce it with their rolling "r" Mediterranean accent.

The tartness of the apricot, with its astringent edge, provides a lovely dessert, anytime. In summer, fresh ripe apricots are plentiful throughout the whole Mediterranean basin.

1 cup almonds
1 cup brown sugar
½ cup white sugar
½ cup flour
8 tablespoons unsalted butter, plus extra melted butter for
    brushing casserole dish
1 tablespoon vanilla extract
8–10 apricots, washed, halved, and pitted

Preheat oven to 350°. Lightly brush casserole dish with melted butter.

In a food processor, grind almonds and combine with all crumble ingredients, except apricots, in a bowl. Place apricots in prepared casserole dish. Top with crumble. Bake 40 minutes. It is most often served cold. I prefer it warm. SERVES 6.

Cantaloupe with Beaume de Venise or Any Other Dessert Wine of Your Choice

I happen to favor this exquisite and fragrant Provençal dessert wine simply because I purchase it directly from the vineyard some 20 minutes from our house and feel a personal connection to it. There is, of course, a multitude of fine dessert wines from many other regions — all delicious, all perfectly suited for the melon.

> 2 cantaloupes
> 1 cup Beaume de Venise wine or another sweet dessert wine of
>   your choice

Cut melon in halves. Remove seeds and scoop out stringy insides. Pour Beaume de Venise or equivalent dessert wine into its cavity and refrigerate 1 hour. SERVES 4.

Raspberry Tart with Vanilla Custard

I always enjoy the nutty substance of this piecrust, and find it goes well with raspberries.

FOR THE PIECRUST
1 cup all-purpose flour, plus extra for rolling
1 cup ground almonds
12 tablespoons butter
¼ cup ice water

In a food processor, pulse all ingredients to form a coarse dough. Wrap with plastic wrap and refrigerate 2 hours or more.

Preheat oven to 350°.

Remove dough from refrigerator. On a floured board, roll out into a thin layer. Line a pie plate with the dough, prick little holes with a fork, and bake 20 minutes, until golden brown. Remove from oven. Cool.

FOR THE VANILLA CUSTARD
2 cups milk
4 eggs
¾ cup sugar
2 tablespoons flour
1 tablespoon vanilla extract
1 teaspoon unsalted butter
1 pint raspberries

raspberry tart

In a saucepan, heat the milk to scalding. Meanwhile, beat the eggs in a bowl with the sugar until creamy. Slowly add hot milk. Transfer back to saucepan, add the flour, and, beating with a whisk, cook over very low heat until it forms a custard, about 10 or more minutes. Stir in vanilla and butter. Cover. Cool. Refrigerate.

When pie crust has cooled, spread cold custard evenly with a rubber spatula. Top with raspberries. SERVES 4–6.

Rhubarb and Strawberry Soup with White Peaches

I have always found this cool, fragrant, and healthy dessert is greatly appreciated, whether it concludes a lunch or dinner.

1¼ cups sugar
3 rhubarb stalks, trimmed and cut into 1-inch pieces
1 pint fresh strawberries, washed, hulled, and sliced (or use
    frozen strawberries)
juice of 1 lemon
1 teaspoon vanilla extract
3 white peaches, peeled and sliced

In a small saucepan, heat 2 cups water and 1 cup sugar. Cook over low heat 15 good minutes, until mixture becomes syrupy. Cool. Set aside.

In a different saucepan, cook rhubarb with ¼ cup sugar and a few drops of water until soft. If a "few drops" seems too little, remember rhubarb renders its own juice. Purée rhubarb in a blender with syrup, half the strawberries, lemon juice, and vanilla. If mixture is too thick, add a little water for desired consistency. If you find it too sweet, squeeze in some more lemon juice to suit your taste. It should be soupy. Refrigerate in a serving bowl. At the time of serving, remove soup from refrigerator and add remaining sliced strawberries and peaches. SERVES 4–6.

Tarte Tropézienne

Traditional to the south of France, this light and irresistibly delicious cake can be found in every pastry shop or *boulangerie* throughout the Riviera. The cake originated in Saint-Tropez, the once beautiful fisherman's village on the Mediterranean coast that today has become a tony, overcrowded, international summer resort.

The Tropézienne is a kind of *brioche* cake with a layer of vanilla custard inside, that reminds one a little of Boston cream pie — without the chocolate icing.

1 tablespoon active dry yeast
¾ cup granulated sugar, plus a pinch for the yeast starter
1½ cups all-purpose flour, plus extra for rolling dough and 2
    tablespoons for custard
4 whole eggs, plus 2 eggs, separated
8 tablespoons unsalted butter, softened at room temperature,
    plus extra for buttering cake pan
pinch of salt
½ cup slivered almonds, plus extra for sprinkling on top
½ cup confectioners' sugar, plus extra for sprinkling on top
1 cup milk
1 tablespoon vanilla extract

In a bowl, dissolve yeast in ⅓ cup warm water with a pinch of granulated sugar. Let mixture stand until yeast is bubbly, about 5 minutes. Stir in half the flour; cover. Let dough double in volume, about 2 hours. Into another bowl, sift remaining flour. Incorporate 3 eggs, half the butter, ¼ cup granulated sugar with a pinch of salt, and the yeast mixture from the first bowl. Work the dough until it becomes shiny and soft. Cover and let stand 2 hours. (I usually do this before going off to work. It can stay risen until I return that afternoon.)

Preheat oven to 350°. Butter an 8-inch cake pan.

When the dough has risen to twice its size, punch to deflate. Roll out onto floured board. Lift the dough into the buttered 8-inch cake pan. In a small bowl, whisk 1 egg with a little water and brush dough with mixture. Sprinkle ½ cup slivered almonds on top of cake. Allow the dough to rise once more, 1 hour. With your hands, gently deflate dough. Bake cake 25 minutes.

Remove cake from oven and let cool.

While the cake bakes, in a bowl, beat 2 egg yolks, ½ cup granulated sugar, the remaining butter, and 2 tablespoons flour. In a saucepan, heat the milk to scalding. Gradually pour hot milk into the yolk/butter mixture. Transfer mixture back to saucepan, add vanilla, and over very low heat, stir until contents of saucepan becomes a custard. Cool completely. Beat egg whites until stiff. Fold into custard.

Cut the cake in half horizontally with a serrated knife. With a rubber spatula, spread vanilla custard evenly over the cut side of bottom portion, then cover with second half of cake. Sprinkle the top with slivered almonds and confectioners' sugar. SERVES 6–8.

Almond Tart with Strawberries

This is a somewhat richer-than-usual dessert. I recommend this splendid tart be served with a relatively light meal.

> 6 tablespoons sugar
> 3 eggs, plus 1 egg beaten with 2 tablespoons water (egg wash)
> 4 tablespoons flour, plus extra for rolling out pastry
> 1 cup milk
> 2 strips of orange peel
> 1 cup whole blanched almonds, ground
> 2 tablespoons orange-flower water*
> 1 pint ripe strawberries, washed and hulled
> 2 tablespoons orange juice
> 2 sheets frozen puff pastry, thawed according to package
>   directions a good hour before proceeding

Preheat oven to 375°.

In a mixing bowl, beat 6 tablespoons sugar and the eggs until they reach creamy consistency, add four tablespoons flour and milk, and continue beating. Transfer to saucepan, add orange peel, and cook 10 minutes over very low heat, stirring constantly until the mixture thickens. Turn off heat. Cool.

In a bowl, combine ground almonds and 4 tablespoons sugar with the orange-flower water. Incorporate into egg custard. Refrigerate, covered, 4 hours.

In a bowl, toss strawberries with a few drops of orange juice. Set aside.

As for puff pastry, I usually make my own, but not everyone has the time or inclination to do so, and I wouldn't want to burden today's busy home chef with the recipe when good puff pastry is readily available in most stores. However, if you do want to make your own, go to our website at www.arcadepub.com.

Onto a floured board, roll out first sheet of pastry. Remove custard/almond cream from refrigerator, remove and discard orange peel, and spread in center of pastry rectangle, leaving a ½ inch space to the border, all around. Roll out second sheet of pastry. Brush with egg wash. Place over first sheet, and pinch to seal all 4 edges with wet fingers. With a knife, prick top of pastry sheet, every inch or so. Bake 35 minutes. Transfer almond tart to serving platter, top with strawberries, and cool. SERVES 6–8.

*Orange-flower water is available in specialty stores and most gourmet shops, but if you are unable to find it, you may proceed without it.

Apricot Tart

When apricots bake, an irresistible fragrance fills the house. The fruit's pleasant tartness is always a welcome conclusion to a rich, or in fact any, meal.

FOR THE CRUST

2 cups all-purpose flour
⅓ cup sugar
⅓ cup ice water
⅓ cup vegetable shortening
12 tablespoons unsalted butter
1 egg yolk
pinch of salt

Preheat oven to 350°.

In a food processor, combine all ingredients and turn machine on a few seconds, pulsing until a coarse dough forms. Turn machine off, wrap dough in plastic wrap, and refrigerate 30 minutes. Remove from refrigerator, roll out, line a pie plate, and bake 20 minutes.

FOR THE FILLING

2 eggs
1 cup half-and-half
½ cup whole blanched almonds, ground
⅓ cup, plus 1 tablespoon brown sugar
2 tablespoons vanilla extract
1 tablespoon cornstarch
6–8 ripe apricots, halved and stones removed
butter for dotting

In a small saucepan, whisk eggs, half-and-half, almonds, ⅓ cup brown sugar, vanilla, and cornstarch. Cook mixture, stirring over very low heat 5 or so minutes, until it thickens a little. Pour into the baked pie crust.

Place apricot halves, cut side down, over the custard. Sprinkle 1 tablespoon brown sugar over apricots. Dot with butter. Bake 25 more minutes. Test to make sure the custard is firm. If not, continue baking a few more minutes. SERVES 6–8.

Amazing Lemon Macaroon Torte

For those with a penchant for lemon and marzipan, this is a rather rich cake — but again, fully worth the sinning. And if you serve very small portions, the "sin" reduces to almost nothing. The torte will keep well, covered, for up to a week in the refrigerator.

This, too, should be prepared a day ahead.

FOR THE BASE OF THE TORTE
1 (8-ounce) can almond paste
3 eggs

Preheat oven to 325°.

In a food processor, combine almond paste, 1 cup water, and the eggs. Trace 2 (8-inch) circles on parchment paper, and set paper on two baking sheets. Spread almond mixture into circles evenly with a spatula. Bake 20 minutes. Remove from oven. Cool, and peel off parchment paper. Set aside.

FOR THE FILLING
3 egg yolks
½ cup sugar
⅓ cup all-purpose flour
1 cup warm milk
1 tablespoon vanilla extract
3 teaspoons butter
¼ cup cornstarch
½ cup lemon juice
grated zest of two lemons
1 cup sugar

In a medium saucepan, over low flame, whisk 3 egg yolks, sugar, flour, and warm milk, 10 minutes, until mixture thickens and has the consistency of custard. Remove from heat; stir in vanilla and 1 teaspoon butter.

Blend cornstarch with 1 cup water in a saucepan over medium-high heat and stir until it comes to a boil. Reduce heat to low and cook 1 minute. Remove pan from stove and add lemon juice, zest, and 2 teaspoons butter. Combine custard with lemon/cornstarch mixture. Cool. This is your filling.

Spread filling evenly onto an almond circle. Top with second circle. Refrigerate torte 4 hours.

TOPPING FOR THE TORTE
⅓ cup sliced almonds, toasted
confectioners' sugar

Remove from refrigerator and garnish with almonds and confectioners' sugar. SERVES 8–10.

Blueberry Crumble

Blueberries are plentiful throughout the Mediterranean, as they are anywhere in the Western world today. In any event, this adopted crumble, using the healthy and flavorful fruit, appears increasingly on restaurant menus of the region.

8 tablespoons, plus extra for buttering a baking dish
1 pint blueberries, washed, stems removed
½ sugar
½ cup all-purpose flour
½ rolled oats
½ cup whole blanched almonds, ground

Preheat oven to 350°. Butter a baking dish.

In a buttered baking dish, spread blueberries evenly.

In a food processor, combine butter, sugar, flour, oats, and almonds to form a crumbly dough. Spread evenly over fruit. Bake 30 minutes. Serve hot or cold. SERVES 4–6.

Sinful, Flourless, Almond Chocolate Cake

My friend Becky Okrent once came to dinner bringing this wonderful chocolate cake, to the delight of everyone. She shared her Italian recipe with me.

Rich, yes, but oh so wonderful. It is perfectly marvelous, simply glazed with only the ganache of chocolate. But when sin calls, I add the mousse filling. With the addition of chocolate mousse, it is over the top.

> 1 cup unsalted butter (2 sticks), plus extra for buttering cake
>   pans
> 2 bittersweet chocolate bars, crumbled (8 ounces)
> 1½ cups whole unblanched almonds, ground
> 1 cup sugar
> 6 egg yolks
> 6 egg whites, beaten stiff
> pinch of salt

Preheat oven to 375°. Butter 2 cake pans. Line with parchment paper. Butter parchment paper.

Melt chocolate in the microwave a few seconds or over a double boiler and set aside to cool.

In a food processor, mix cooled chocolate, butter, almonds, and sugar. Add yolks, one at a time. Separately, beat egg whites with salt until stiff; fold into yolk/chocolate mixture.

Divide and pour chocolate batter into prepared pans. Bake 15 minutes. Reduce oven temperature to 300°, and continue baking 45 minutes. Cool. Unmold when cool.

FOR CHOCOLATE FROSTING
1½ cups bittersweet chocolate
⅓ cup heavy cream
2 teaspoons instant coffee, powder or granules

In a saucepan over medium heat, melt chocolate with the cream and instant coffee. (I use decaffeinated instant coffee). Stir well until all is integrated, about 5 good minutes. It should be shiny and thick. Let cool for 20 minutes.

FOR FILLING: CHOCOLATE MOUSSE (OPTIONAL)
5 ounces semisweet chocolate, melted
2 egg yolks
½ cup heavy cream, whipped
2 egg whites, beaten stiff

In a bowl, mix melted chocolate with yolks. Add whipped cream. Fold in beaten whites.

When the cake has cooled, cut horizontally in thirds. With a spatula, spread chocolate filling (mousse) in between the 3 layers of the cake. Pour chocolate frosting over cake. Refrigerate.

Remove cake from refrigerator to room temperature at the start of dinner, otherwise the chocolate will have become too hard and you'll end up serving a glorified bar of chocolate. SERVES 8.

Watermelon, Cantaloupe, and Honeydew with Ginger

The combination of fresh ginger, with a few shakes of black pepper, gives this chilled, simple melon salad an incredible "kick."

1 slice watermelon, cut into balls
½ cantaloupe, cut into balls
honeydew, cut into balls
1 cup fresh mint leaves, finely chopped
1 teaspoon peeled and grated fresh ginger
2 tablespoons crumbled, candied ginger
a few shakes of freshly ground black pepper

Combine the balls of the three melons with the mint and gingers. Refrigerate a couple of hours, and serve cold. SERVES 4–6.

Floating Islands

Isles Flotantes, as it is called, is one of French cuisine's classic desserts — widely served in the Mediterranean. I make my floating islands dressed with pralines (caramelized almonds), caramel angel hair, and fresh raspberries. All that is, of course, optional.

1¼ cups sugar
½ cup whole blanched almonds
5 eggs, separated
2 cups milk

1 tablespoon vanilla extract
½ pint raspberries

FOR THE PRALIN
In a small frying pan, over low heat, cook ¼ cup sugar and almonds. Cook a few minutes until sugar turns blond color. Turn heat off. Cool.

FOR THE VANILLA CREAM
In a bowl, whip egg yolks with ½ cup sugar until creamy.

In a saucepan, heat milk and vanilla to scalding point. Gradually pour into egg yolks. Transfer to saucepan, continue whisking and cook over low heat until it thickens. Turn heat off. Cool. Transfer to serving dessert bowl. Refrigerate several hours.

FOR THE "ISLANDS"
In a bowl, whip egg whites with ¼ cup sugar until it forms a peak.

In a large kettle, bring 6 cups water to a boil. Reduce heat, and with the help of a large spoon, take 1 spoonful of beaten whites at a time, and immerse each meringue in simmering water. Cook 2 minutes. Turn over and cook another 2 minutes. With a slotted spoon, carefully lift out meringues, drain, and place on paper towels.

ASSEMBLING
With a spatula, lift candied almonds and grind coarsely in the food processor. Place each meringue on top of vanilla cream. Add raspberries and pralin to bowl. Keep refrigerated until serving time.

FOR THE CARAMEL ANGEL HAIR
In a saucepan, put ¼ cup sugar and cook 5 minutes over low flame until it turns a blond color. Turn off heat. While syrup is still warm, take a wooden spoon, dip it in caramel, and immediately lift spoon as high as you can above the pan to create caramel strand or "hair." Continue this process to obtain several caramel strands. If the contents of pan hardens, turn heat back on a few seconds to melt it, and continue until you have enough strands. Transfer strands on top of meringues. SERVES 4–6.

Tip: You can create the caramel angel hair a few hours before serving, and keep refrigerated.

Cold Little Grapefruit Soufflés

Refreshing and out-of-the-ordinary, these elegant soufflés are served in the hollowed-out grapefruit shell, always a lovely presentation.

> 4 eggs, separated
> juice of ½ lemon
> ½ cup sugar
> 6 tablespoons unsalted butter, softened
> 3 grapefruits, halved
> ½ cup heavy cream

Beat egg yolks together with lemon juice and sugar until creamy. Add butter and continue beating for a couple of minutes. Squeeze juice of 1 grapefruit into mixture and transfer mixture to top of double boiler. Continue whisking until it becomes a custard — a good 10–15 minutes. Cool.

Scoop out meat from remaining 2 grapefruits, discarding white membrane, and mix part of the grapefruit into the custard. Check for sweetness. (Some grapefruits are sweeter than others; you may wish to add a bit more sugar.)

Whip cream and fold into custard. Beat egg whites until stiff. Fold into mixture. Fill grapefruit shells with mixture and refrigerate until serving time. Serves 4–6.

Tip: There will be some leftover, which will keep a few days, refrigerated, in case you want a repeat performance.

Cherry *Clafoutis*

A staple from what is known as French *cuisine bourgeoise,* this tasty cherry pudding belongs to a long tradition of Gallic desserts. The original *clafoutis* calls for cherries, but I often make this custard with plums, pears, apricots, grapes, or peaches, depending on the season and availability. In many villages, the cherries used for the clafoutis are stemmed, but to my constant surprise, left with their pit. I have never understood that. I much prefer taking the extra few minutes to pit the cherries beforehand — thus avoiding the unnecessary challenge — and danger — to one's teeth.

2 tablespoons unsalted butter, plus extra for buttering dish
1 pound cherries, stemmed and pitted
4 eggs
1 cup milk
⅔ cup sugar
½ cup all-purpose flour
¼ cup kirsch
1 tablespoon grated lemon zest
1 tablespoon vanilla extract
½ teaspoon almond extract
pinch of salt
2 tablespoons confectioners' sugar

Preheat oven to 400°.

Butter an ovenproof shallow dish, making sure sides are buttered as well. Spread cherries in bottom of dish. In the blender, purée eggs, milk, sugar, flour, kirsch, lemon zest, vanilla, almond extract, and salt. Pour over cherries. Dot with remaining butter. Sprinkle confectioners' sugar.

Bake 25 minutes, until top is golden. Remove from oven. Serves 4–6.

Note: Although the clafoutis can and is often served cold or at room temperature, I find it more delicious warm.

Apple Tart

American apple pie differs from French or Italian apple pie. The American version is mainly flavored with cinnamon and has two layers of dough — top and bottom — whereas its European cousin features vanilla and has only one layer of dough at the bottom. Apple pie may not be terribly original as a dessert, but when it melts in your mouth, it holds its place of honor.

FOR THE PIECRUST

2½ cups all-purpose flour
12 tablespoons cold unsalted butter
½ cup ice water
3 tablespoons vegetable shortening
pinch of salt

In a food processor, combine and pulse flour, butter, water, shortening, and salt to form a coarse dough. Wrap dough, and refrigerate for an hour. (I often leave my dough overnight.)

FOR THE FILLING

5 Granny Smith apples, peeled, cored, and sliced
juice of ½ lemon
1 tablespoon vanilla extract
½ cup coarsely chopped walnuts
¼ cup sugar
4 tablespoons unsalted butter

Preheat oven to 350°.

Remove dough from refrigerator, roll out onto a floured board, and place in an 8-inch pie plate. Bake 15 minutes, until crust is golden. Remove from oven. Place apple slices in a concentric circle over crust. Drizzle lemon juice and vanilla over apples. Sprinkle walnuts on top. Sprinkle with ¼ cup sugar and dot with butter. Bake 40 minute. Remove from oven. Let cool.

FOR THE GLAZE
    4 tablespoons apricot jam
    ¼ cup sugar
    ¼ cup rum

In a saucepan, melt jam with ¼ cup sugar and rum. Stir until it thickens a little and pour over apples. That's your glaze. SERVES 4–6.

Strawberry Soup with Raspberries

This is another pleasant version of the strawberry soup offered earlier in the book (see page 198).

    1 cup white wine
    ½ cup sugar
    2 pints ripe strawberries, cleaned and hulled
    1 cup raspberries
    juice of ½ lemon
    a few sprigs mint

In a small saucepan, cook the wine and sugar, about 15 or so minutes, until it thickens and forms a light syrup. Cool.

In a blender, purée half the strawberries with the syrup, raspberries, and lemon juice. Transfer to serving bowl and mix in remaining strawberries. Refrigerate until serving time. Sprinkle with mint. SERVES 4–6.

Note: When out of season, use frozen strawberries.

Panna Cotta With Sliced Peaches and Blackberry Coulis

This Italian dessert is light, silky, and delicious. Its three simple preparation steps — making the *panna cotta,* poaching the peaches, and finally making the coulis — can easily be done a day ahead. The next day, all that remains to be done is assembling before serving.

> 2 tablespoons unflavored gelatin
> 1 tablespoon Amaretto liqueur
> 1 tablespoon vanilla extract
> 4 cups heavy cream
> ½ cup sugar
> 1 cup buttermilk
> zest of 1 lemon

In a bowl, soften gelatin in Amaretto and vanilla. In a small saucepan, over low heat, cook 3 cups heavy cream and the sugar 10–15 minutes, until mixture has reduced to 2 cups. Stir gelatin into the reduced cream and cook a few more seconds. Remove from heat. Stir buttermilk into the mixture and toss in lemon zest. Continue to cool completely.

In a bowl, whip remaining heavy cream until it becomes stiff. Fold into cool cream/buttermilk mixture.

Pour into individual ramekins, cover with plastic wrap, and refrigerate overnight.

FOR THE POACHED PEACHES

This is an exquisite dessert by itself. Served alongside panna cotta it reaches a whole new level.

> 1 cup sugar
> 2 tablespoons vanilla extract
> 6 peaches, whole and unpeeled

In a kettle, bring 2 cups water and sugar to a boil. Reduce heat and cook 15 minutes, until mixture becomes syrupy. Stir in vanilla. Add peaches and simmer 5 minutes. Remove peaches from liquid, peel, and slice. Pour syrup into a bowl, add peaches to syrup, and refrigerate 4 hours or more.

FOR THE BLACKBERRY COULIS
> 2 cups blackberries
> ½ cup sugar
> peach syrup from poaching peaches (recipe above)
> juice of ½ lemon

In a blender, purée blackberries. Strain in a sieve or a colander lined with cheese-cloth placed over a bowl. Discard seeds. In a bowl, mix blackberry juice with sugar. Add 1 ladle peach syrup from the poached peaches, and the lemon juice. Refrigerate.

ASSEMBLING THE DESSERT
Unmold panna cotta onto individual dessert plates by running a knife inside ramekin sides. Place a dessert plate over top, flip, and remove the mold. Garnish with sliced peaches. Top with blackberry coulis. SERVES 4–6.

Orange Slices in a Red Wine

This easy-to-make and most refreshing dessert gives a lovely final touch to any rich or spicy meal.

> 2 cups red wine
> 1 cup sugar
> ¼ teaspoon ground cloves
> ¼ teaspoon ground cinnamon
> 4 navel oranges, peeled, white membrane and pith removed, and
>   sliced
> ½ cup pitted dates, chopped

In a saucepan, over medium heat, heat wine, sugar, cloves, and cinnamon. Simmer 15–20 minutes, until syrupy. Cool and refrigerate. Five minutes before serving, remove syrup from refrigerator, add orange slices to syrup, and toss dates with the oranges. SERVES 4-6.

Plum Tatin

The tatin tart, more known in its original recipe with apples, also lends itself nicely to plums.

> 8 tablespoons butter, plus extra for buttering pie plate
> 1 cup sugar
> 15 little plums, washed, halved, stones removed
> 1 sheet frozen puff pastry
> ½ cup slivered almonds, toasted

Preheat oven to 400°. Butter a glass or ceramic pie plate.

Defrost the frozen sheet of puff pastry as package label directs.

In a skillet, heat butter and sugar over medium heat. Stir well 5 minutes or more, making sure mixture turns amber color and doesn't burn. Add plums, stir, and cook 5 more minutes. Turn heat off. Transfer mixture into the buttered glass or ceramic pie plate. Lay defrosted puff sheet carefully over plums, sealing puff pastry to edges of mold with your fingers. Bake 20 minutes. Cool. When cool, set a serving platter over dish, and flip. The caramel will run on the platter — that's the way it should be. Sprinkle with almonds. SERVES 4–6.

Lemon Cake with Amaretto Cream and Strawberries and Raspberries

Fresh berries are always a welcome conclusion to *any* meal. Your artistic eye can be put to the test in arranging and presenting the fruit. The combination of fresh fruit and lemon cake always works well.

FOR THE LEMON CAKE
3 cups unbleached, sifted flour
½ teaspoon baking powder
½ teaspoon baking soda
½ cup grated lemon zest
1 teaspoon salt
½ cup plain yogurt
½ cup buttermilk
1 tablespoon vanilla
1 cup lemon juice
2 sticks unsalted butter, softened at room temperature, plus extra for buttering pan
2½ cups sugar
6 eggs

FOR THE AMARETTO CREAM
1 cup heavy cream, whipped
½ cup confectioners' sugar
2 tablespoons Amaretto

Preheat oven to 350°.

Butter and flour a 10–12 cup Bundt pan.

In a bowl, mix flour, baking powder, baking soda, lemon zest, and salt. In another bowl, combine yogurt, buttermilk, vanilla, and ½ cup lemon juice. Beat butter with 2 cups sugar until creamy. Add eggs, one by one. Combine with yogurt mixture and dry ingredients. Pour into cake pan. Bake 1 hour. Cool.

In a saucepan, over medium heat, cook remaining lemon juice with remaining sugar until syrupy. Cool. Pour syrup over cooled cake. It will be like a sponge, soaking in the syrup, which will make the cake nice and moist.

Fold confectioners' sugar and Amaretto into whipped cream. Serve a wedge of cake with fruit and a dollop of Amaretto cream. SERVES 4–6.

Poached Pears in Wine Sauce
with Pear Wafers Dipped in Chocolate

This classic dessert becomes extremely elegant with the addition of these unusual "cookies" that consist of pear wafers — made of dried pear slices — dipped in bittersweet chocolate.

>2 cups red wine
>1 cup sugar
>½ teaspoon ground cloves
>½ teaspoon freshly grated nutmeg
>2 strips of lemon zest
>4–6 pears, peeled, cored, and halved

In a kettle, bring wine, 1 cup water, sugar, cloves, nutmeg, and lemon zest to a boil. Reduce heat to low and cook 15–20 minutes, until mixture thickens to syrup consistency. Add pears, cover, and continue cooking another 15 minutes. Turn heat off. Cool. Transfer to serving bowl. Refrigerate.

FOR THE PEAR WAFERS DIPPED IN CHOCOLATE
>3 pears, whole, peeled, cored, and cut into paper-thin slices
>juice of 1 chopped lemon

Preheat oven to 250°.

Place pear slices in a bowl, cover with lemon juice, and let stand for 10 minutes. Remove from bowl and dry with paper towel. Arrange slices side by side in an ovenproof dish. Bake 45 minutes, until slices are crisp and brittle. Remove from oven. Cool.

FOR THE CHOCOLATE
>1 cup chopped bittersweet chocolate
>3 tablespoons heavy cream

In a saucepan, over low heat, melt chocolate and stir in cream. Stir well until it is melted and shiny.

FOR THE WAFERS

Carefully lift 1 pear slice at a time with your fingers and dip in chocolate. (I say carefully, because they will be fragile and brittle.) Set on wire rack to cool. The chocolate coating will harden as it cools and the dried pear slices will look like wafers. Arrange chocolate pear wafers on serving platter.

Remove poached pears from refrigerator and serve with pear wafers. SERVES 4–6.

Napoleon of Almond Wafers with Raspberries

½ cup whole blanched almonds, ground
zest of 1 orange
3 tablespoons butter
2 tablespoons flour
2 tablespoons orange juice
2 teaspoons Grand Marnier or Cointreau

Preheat oven to 475°.

In a bowl, combine all ingredients and stir well to mix. Refrigerate 2 hours or more. Remove mixture from refrigerator and form into little balls of dough the size of ping-pong balls. Place 1 inch apart on a baking sheet and bake 3 minutes. (They will spread into wafers.) Remove pan from oven. Let wafers cool a few minutes before lifting them off the baking sheet with a spatula. Repeat the process until all dough is used up.

FOR THE FILLING AND TOPPING

2 tablespoons confectioners' sugar, plus extra for sprinkling
1 tablespoon vanilla extract
½ cup heavy cream, whipped
½ cup sliced strawberries
1 cup raspberries
½ blackberries

In a bowl, fold confectioners' sugar and vanilla into whipped cream.

Arrange 1 wafer on each individual dessert plate. Spread a layer of whipped cream, add a layer of fruit, add another wafer, repeat the same process, and top with a third wafer. Sprinkle with some confectioners' sugar. SERVES 4–6.

raspberry tart

Raspberry Tart

This crunchy crust made with almonds goes particularly well with the raspberries.

> 1 cup all-purpose flour, plus extra for rolling out dough
> 1 cup ground almonds
> 2 tablespoons shortening
> 8 tablespoons unsalted butter
> ¼ cup ice water
> pinch of salt

FOR THE FILLING
> 1 pint raspberries
> ¼ cup raspberry jam
> 3 tablespoons rum

In a food processor, mix 1 cup flour, almonds, butter, shortening, ice water, and salt. Pulse until dough comes together. Wrap pie dough in plastic film and refrigerate 2 hours or more.

Preheat oven to 350°.

Remove dough from refrigerator. On a floured board, roll out dough into a thin layer and line pie plate with dough. Prick little holes in dough with a fork and bake 15–20 minutes, until golden brown. Remove from oven and let cool. When cool, arrange raspberries to fill pie crust.

In a small pan, over low flame, cook jam with rum until mixture thickens. Pour over fruit. SERVES 4–6.

Plum Compote and Plum Sorbet

I remember trying this dessert in a restaurant in Provence — I had no idea what plum sorbet would look or taste like — and found it surprisingly delicious. I was inspired to replicate it as soon as I got home. This dessert recipe is in 2 parts. First the compote then the sorbet which is made from cooked plums.

FOR THE COMPOTE
        1 cup sugar
        20 plums, stones removed and halved
        ½ lemon, cut into wedges
        1 tablespoon vanilla extract

In a large saucepan, heat 2 cups water and the sugar. Over moderate heat, cook 15 minutes, until it becomes syrupy. Add plums and lemon wedges and continue cooking 10 minutes. Add vanilla. Discard lemon. Cool. Refrigerate.

FOR THE PLUM SORBET
        1 cup syrup from the compote
        8 cooked plums from the compote, puréed in a food processor
        juice of 1 lemon

In a small saucepan, over medium heat, cook syrup a good 10 minutes, until it has reduced by half. In a bowl, combine puréed plums, syrup, and lemon juice. Pour into ice-cream maker and turn machine on 30 minutes. Freeze.

ASSEMBLING THE DESSERT
Remove compote from refrigerator. Place 2 plum halves on each dessert plate, ladle some syrup over them, and top with a dollop or 2 of sorbet. SERVES 6–8.

Lemon Tart

Everyone has a different recipe for this dessert. Many years ago, a chef friend of mine, Pat Korten, suggested I try putting a whole lemon in the processor. "It will impart a better lemon fragrance, and you will not have to squeeze the juice nor grate the zest separately," she said. I followed her suggestion, indeed found it much easier, and have adopted her method every time lemon is required in a dessert.

This piecrust is a bit richer than others offered in this book. But it does melt in your mouth and goes well with the lemon topping.

2 cups all-purpose flour, plus extra for rolling out dough
1 cup unsalted butter
½ cup sugar
½ cup whole blanched almonds, ground
1 egg
2 egg yolks
zest of 1 lemon
3 tablespoons rum
½ teaspoon salt

In a food processor, combine above ingredients and pulse until they form a dough. Cover with plastic wrap and refrigerate 1 hour. Remove from refrigerator. On a floured board, roll out dough and line a 9-inch pie plate. Return to the refrigerator for 15 minutes.

Preheat oven to 350°.

Remove from refrigerator and bake 15–20 minutes, until crust looks blond and dry. Keep oven on.

FOR THE FILLING
- 1 lemon, washed, seeds removed, and quartered
- 4 tablespoons unsalted butter
- 1 cup sugar
- 1 egg
- 2 egg yolks
- 4 tablespoons heavy cream

In a food processor, purée lemon — zest and all — with sugar, butter, cream, egg, and egg yolks. Process until smooth. Pour into pre-baked pie crust and bake 30 minutes, until filling becomes like a custard. Remove from oven. Cool. SERVES 6–8.

Optional: Slice ½ lemon, make a sugar syrup with ½ cup water and ¼ cup sugar (15 minutes). Over low heat, cook the slices 15 minutes in the syrup and let them cool in the syrup. When the pie is cooked and removed from the oven, decorate with syrupy lemon slices.

Tip: Line the bottom of your oven with some foil — the filling has a tendency to overflow. This way, the foil can be removed and discarded with no harm to your oven.

Grapefruit Sorbet

This refreshing dessert can be made without the help of an ice cream maker. It can be served alone or with almond lace cookies.

> 1 cup squeezed grapefruit juice
> ¾ cup sugar
> 2 tablespoons rum
> 2 large grapefruit, cut into halves and sectioned
> 1 egg white
> Almond Lace Cookies, recipe follows

In a saucepan, combine grapefruit juice, sugar, and rum. Bring to a boil, reduce heat, and cook 15 minutes. You may need a minute or 2 more for the syrup to form. Cool.

   In a food processor, purée grapefruit sections. Combine juice-sugar-rum syrup with grapefruit purée. Test for sweetness, since some grapefruits are sweeter than others. Adjust and add a little sugar, if needed. Pour mixture into a small baking dish and freeze until firm (1 hour or so). Remove from freezer and, once again, purée in food processor with the egg white for a few seconds. Spoon into individual custard cups. Place back in the freezer. Five minutes before dessert time, remove from freezer. Serve with Almond Lace Cookies. SERVES 4.

Note: You'll probably have more than needed for four. Don't worry: it keeps well in the freezer.

Almond Lace Cookies

> 2 cups brown sugar
> 2 cups whole blanched ground almonds
> 1 cup butter, melted
> 1 tablespoon vanilla extract

Preheat oven to 375°.

In a bowl, combine all ingredients. On a baking sheet, drop a spoonful of dough every 2 inches. The dough needs space because it will spread into flat cookies. Bake 7 minutes. Remove from oven. Cool a few minutes, and with a spatula, lift cookies onto serving platter. MAKES ABOUT 40 COOKIES.

Rhubarb Tart

FOR THE CRUST
    2 cups all-purpose flour, plus extra for rolling out dough
    4 ounces cream cheese
    12 tablespoons butter

FOR THE FILLING
    1 pound rhubarb, washed, trimmed, and cut into 1-inch pieces
    1 cup sugar
    2 cinnamon sticks
    grated zest of 1 orange
    grated zest of 1 lemon
    6 eggs
    2 cups milk
    1 tablespoon vanilla extract
    confectioners' sugar for sprinkling

Preheat oven to 350°.

In the food processor, combine flour, cream cheese, and butter. Pulse until ingredients form a dough. Wrap dough in plastic wrap and refrigerate 30 minutes.

Meanwhile, in a kettle over medium heat, cook rhubarb, ½ cup sugar, cinnamon, orange zest, and lemon zest 15 minutes. Set aside.

Remove dough from refrigerator. On a floured board, roll out dough and line an 8-inch pie plate. Poke little holes with the tip of a fork or knife in the dough. Bake 15 minutes.

In a bowl, beat eggs with remaining ½ cup sugar until creamy. In a saucepan, heat milk to scalding point and gradually incorporate into eggs. Transfer mixture back into saucepan, turn heat to low, and continue whisking until mixture thickens a little and becomes a custard cream. Turn off heat. Whisk in vanilla.

Spread rhubarb onto pre-baked pie crust. Pour custard over rhubarb and bake 20 minutes, until custard becomes firm. Remove from oven and sprinkle sugar on top of custard. Bake 3 more minutes. Cool. SERVES 6.

Vacherin of Meringue with Raspberries

Vacherin is the name French gastronomy has given to a dessert consisting of 1 or 2 meringues layered with some whipped cream and fruit.

⅓ cup sugar, plus extra for sprinkling
4 egg whites, beaten very stiff
1 tablespoon vanilla extract
⅓ cup confectioners' sugar
½ cup heavy cream, whipped
1 pint vanilla ice cream
4 cups raspberries

Preheat oven to 200°.

Fold ⅓ cup sugar into beaten egg whites. On a baking sheet, drop large spoonfuls of meringue preparation. With a rubber spatula, evenly flatten top of meringues. Sprinkle some sugar on top and bake 2 hours. Cool. Transfer meringues onto a platter. Cover with alminum foil. (If you've made the meringues well ahead of time, store in a covered tin in the refrigerator. Otherwise, they can remain, covered, on your counter until serving time.)

Fold vanilla extract and confectioners' sugar into whipped cream.

Remove ice cream from freezer a little ahead so it becomes slightly soft and can be spread easily.

Place a meringue on each dessert plate. On each meringue, spread layer of ice cream and a layer of whipped cream. Top with raspberries. SERVES 4–6.

Cold Lime Soufflés

This dessert is as elegant as it is simple to prepare. Unlike hot soufflés, which can sometimes be capricious and don't always rise as expected, the cold or frozen variety is foolproof. It is best to prepare this ahead of time, even the day before. It keeps well in the refrigerator.

> 4 egg yolks
> 1 cup sugar
> 2 cups milk
> juice and grated zest of 3 limes
> 1 tablespoon cornstarch
> 1 cup heavy cream, whipped
> 4 egg whites, beaten stiff

Beat egg yolks with sugar until creamy in a bowl. Heat milk to scalding. In a saucepan, combine lime juice and zest, eggs yolks, sugar, cornstarch, and milk over very low heat. Stir with a wooden spoon until mixture thickens — about 15 minutes. Turn heat off. Cool a couple of hours. Fold in whipped cream and beaten egg whites. Pour into individual soufflé dishes. Refrigerate. SERVES 4–6.

Fruit Salad

This once popular — and oft forgotten — dessert returns to the table with a big welcome. Fresh fruit — in whatever combination — is always appreciated, no matter what precedes it. There are dozens of variations to the fruit combination, of course, depending on the season. Here is one that works well in any season.

1 apple, washed, cored and finely cubed
1 pear, washed, cored and finely cubed
1 banana, peeled and sliced
1 plum, washed, pitted, and cut into small pieces
1 peach, washed, pitted and quartered
1 cup seedless grapes, washed, cut into halves
1 cup raspberries
6 dates, pitted and diced
juice of 1 lemon
½ cup orange juice

Combine fruit and juices. Refrigerate. SERVES 6.

Bleu, Blanc, Rouge Tart

This blue, white, and red tart sings of summer, when the berries are ripe and abundant.

2 sheets frozen puff pastry
flour for rolling pastry
8 ounces cream cheese
¼ cup sugar, plus 1 tablespoon for syrup
⅓ cup crystallized ginger, chopped
1 pint raspberries
1 pint blueberries
½ cup strawberry jam
1 egg, beaten and mixed with 2 tablespoons water (egg wash)

Preheat oven to 450°.

Defrost frozen pastry sheets according to package directions.

On a floured board, roll 1 sheet into a rectangle. Roll out second sheet and cut into 4 strips. Place strips and rectangle on a board and freeze 10 minutes.

Remove pastry from freezer. With wet fingers, seal one strip to each side of the rectangle, forming a kind of box.

Bake 20 minutes, until pastry puffs and looks golden brown. Remove from oven and let cool.

In a food processor, combine cream cheese, ¼ cup sugar, and the ginger. Pulse until smooth. Spread cream-cheese mixture evenly onto bottom of pastry "box." Alternate a row of raspberries with a row of blueberries until all fruit is used.

In a small saucepan, heat jam and 1 tablespoon sugar until mixture bubbles and thickens. Pour evenly over fruit. SERVES 8–10.

Sour Cherry Compote

A perfect end to a rich or spicy meal, this compote is delicious served chilled.

> 1 cup sugar
> 1 pound sour cherries, pitted
> 1 tablespoon vanilla extract

In a saucepan, bring 2 cups water and the sugar to a boil.
good 15 minutes, until it becomes thick and syrupy. Add cherries and continue simmering 10 minutes. Cool, stir in vanilla, and refrigerate. SERVES 4–6.

Note: If sour cherries are unavailable, black sweet cherries — though less tart — are fine.

Tip: In Istanbul, this dessert was served to me over a slice of French toast. It was indeed delicious, though unnecessary really after a rich meal. Your call.

Gratin of Baked Raspberries

Bringing a fragrant, warm dessert out of the oven always seems to elevate the end of a dinner into something special, as the tempting aroma winds its way to the dining-room table a step ahead of the dessert itself. This fruit in a baked custard is one of my favorites.

> 4 cups raspberries
> 2 eggs beaten with 2 additional yolks
> 4 tablespoons brown sugar, plus extra for sprinkling
> 1 cup half-and-half
> 1 cup heavy cream
> 1 tablespoon brandy or rum

Preheat oven to 400°.

Divide and arrange raspberries into 4 individual ovenproof dishes. In a bowl, beat eggs and yolks with 4 tablespoons sugar until creamy.

In a saucepan, combine creams, bring to scalding point, and integrate into egg mixture. Return mixture to saucepan and whisk over low heat 8–10 minutes, until it thickens. Turn off heat. Add brandy or rum. Cover raspberries with the custard. Sprinkle with a little sugar. Bake 15 minutes, until tops are light brown and looks firm. Serves 6–8.

Platter of Sliced Fresh Fruit with a Chocolate Sauce

Again, an attractive, uncomplicated and friendly conclusion to any meal, this welcomed array of fresh fruit is my shortcut to the chocolate fondue.

> 1 apple, washed, cored, not peeled and sliced
> 1 pear, washed, peeled, cored and sliced
> 1 kiwi, quartered
> 1 cup strawberries
> ½ cup blueberries

1 few slices pineapple
1 cup semisweet chocolate
½ cup heavy cream

On a serving platter, arrange fruit according to your taste.

In a small saucepan, heat chocolate and cream 2 minutes, stirring until well integrated. Reduce heat and stir 1 more minute, until sauce becomes thick. Turn heat off and pour sauce into a small pitcher. Pass chocolate sauce along with the fruit platter. SERVES 4–6.

Gratin of Peaches

8 tablespoons butter, softened, plus extra for buttering ovenproof dish
4 cups peeled sliced peaches
¾ cup sugar
1 cup all-purpose flour
1 teaspoon baking powder
pinch of salt
½ cup milk
1 tablespoon vanilla extract

FOR THE TOPPING
½ cup sugar
½ cup chopped walnuts
⅓ cup flour
4 tablespoons butter
1 tablespoon ground cinnamon

Preheat oven to 375°. Butter an ovenproof dish

Place peaches in a buttered ovenproof dish.

In a bowl beat 8 tablespoons butter with sugar until creamy. Add flour, baking soda, and salt. Pour milk and vanilla. When batter is well combined, pour over peaches.

For the topping, in a bowl, mix the remaining half cup sugar, walnuts, flour, butter, and cinnamon. Sprinkle over batter. Bake 50 minutes. SERVES 4–6.

"Petits Pots" of Chocolate-Mocha Mousse

1½ cups semisweet chocolate chips or eating chocolate cut into
  small pieces
2 tablespoons decaffeinated instant espresso, powdered or
  granules
4 eggs, separated
1 cup heavy cream, whipped
a few decaffeinated coffee beans, coarsely ground, mixed with 1
  ounce eating chocolate, shaved

In a bowl in the microwave, melt chocolate a few seconds. Mix with coffee.

In a bowl, beat egg whites until stiff.

In a large bowl, fold chocolate-coffee into yolks. Fold in whipped cream. Last, fold in beaten egg whites. Fill little dessert bowls or cups with mousse. Refrigerate 4 hours, or even overnight. Sprinkle a dusting of ground coffee beans and chocolate shavings. SERVES 4–6.

Broiled Fresh Figs with Honey

Figs abound in the Mediterranean for several months of the year. Nothing could be simpler to make than this dessert featuring that tasty fruit.

1 tablespoon butter, plus extra for buttering casserole dish
8 fresh figs, split in half
½ cup honey
1 cup vanilla yogurt, optional

Preheat oven to 400°. Butter a casserole dish

Place figs side by side in buttered casserole dish. Spread honey on top of figs. Dot with butter and bake 10 minutes. Serve with a dollop of vanilla yogurt. SERVES 4.

An Italian Pear Tart

This tart is richer than most. Again, I recommend serving it after a light meal, or after small portions.

FOR THE DOUGH
1½ cups all-purpose flour, plus extra for rolling out dough
8 tablespoons butter
3 ounces cream cheese

Preheat oven to 375°.

In a food processor, make your dough with the flour, the butter, and cream cheese, wrap in plastic wrap, and refrigerate 2 hours. Remove from refrigerator, roll out onto floured board. Line pie plate with dough. Bake 15 minutes. Remove from oven. Keep oven on.

FOR THE FILLING
1 cup whole blanched almonds
½ cup sugar
6 tablespoons butter
3 egg whites
6 pears, peeled, cored, and halved
1 tablespoon vanilla extract

In a food processor, purée almonds, sugar, butter, and egg whites.

Place pears cut side down on pre-baked pie crust. Sprinkle with vanilla. With a spatula, evenly cover pear with almond paste. Bake 40 minutes. A golden crust should have formed on top of the fruit. Remove from oven. Cool. SERVES 8–10.

Grape *Clafoutis* (Custard with Grapes)

Clafoutis, as noted — a baked custard with fruit — is one of France's oldest desserts. It usually comes with cherries, but over the years other fruits have been used as well. Grapes are a nice option.

1 cup milk
½ cup heavy cream
2 tablespoons vanilla extract
4 eggs
¾ cup sugar
½ cup all-purpose flour
24 seedless grapes
butter

Preheat oven to 400°.

In a saucepan, bring milk, cream, and vanilla to a boil. Turn off heat and cool 5 minutes. In a bowl, beat eggs and sugar at high speed until creamy. Add flour.

Gradually pour milk mixture into egg mixture.

Butter 4 individual ramekins or soufflé dishes. Pour egg-milk mixture into ramekins and divide grapes among the ramekins. Bake 12 minutes. Clafoutis is best served warm. SERVES 4.

Plum Compote with a Meringue Topping

2 cups milk
4 yolks
4 egg whites, beaten stiff
1¾ cup, plus ⅓ cup sugar
2 tablespoons vanilla extract
2 pounds plums, quartered and stone removed

In a saucepan, heat milk to scalding. Turn off heat. In a bowl, beat egg yolks with ¼ cup sugar until creamy. Pour hot milk gradually into egg mixture. Transfer back into saucepan, and, over low heat, stir until it thickens. It should have the consistency of a runny cream — not a custard. If for some reason your cream becomes too thick, stir in some milk and turn off heat. Cool. Transfer to a small pitcher. Refrigerate.

In a kettle, bring 1 cup water and ½ cup sugar to a boil. Reduce heat, add 1 tablespoon vanilla, and cook 15 minutes, until mixture becomes syrupy and a little thick. Add plums. Cook 5 minutes. Turn off heat.

Transfer plums and liquid to ovenproof dish. Fold ⅓ cup sugar and remaining 1 tablespoon vanilla into beaten whites. Spread evenly over compote. Bake 15 minutes. The top will become the meringue. Cool.

Serve a portion of meringue and plum compote on each dessert plate and pour vanilla cream around each portion. SERVES 4–6.

Apples in a Hood

4 tablespoons butter, plus extra or buttering ovenproof dish
2 sheets frozen puff pastry
4 Granny Smith apples, peeled, whole, and cored
2 tablespoons rum
¼ cup brown sugar
1 teaspoon ground cinnamon
1 egg beaten with 2 tablespoons water
½ cup slivered, toasted almonds

Defrost frozen pastry sheets according to package directions.

Preheat oven to 350°.

Put apples side by side in buttered ovenproof dish. Insert a dot of butter in the center with 1 teaspoonful of rum. Sprinkle with a layer of brown sugar and a little cinnamon and add small dots butter. Bake 40 minutes. Remove from oven and cool.

Raise oven temperature to 400°.

Roll out puff-pastry sheets. Divide each sheet in half and roll into a square.

Place baked apple in center of each pastry square. Bring sides of pastry up and seal with egg wash. Brush surface with more egg wash and poke tiny holes in pastry with a fork. Place pastries in freezer for 15 minutes.

Remove from freezer and bake 20 minutes, until puff pastry has "puffed," and is golden brown. Remove from oven, cool a little and serve warm. SERVES 4.

Blackberry Tart

FOR THE PIECRUST

    2 cups all-purpose flour
    ½ teaspoon salt
    8 tablespoons butter
    ⅓ cup vegetable shortening
    3 tablespoons ice water

In a food processor, combine flour, salt, butter, and shortening, turn processor on, pulse, and add water gradually as mixture becomes a dough. Wrap dough in plastic wrap and refrigerate 1 hour.

FOR THE FILLING

    5 cups blackberries
    2 tablespoons butter
    ½ cup brown sugar
    ¼ cup granulated sugar, plus 1 teaspoon for sprinkling
    3 tablespoons cornstarch
    2 tablespoons brandy

In a saucepan, cook half the blackberries 10 minutes. Over a sieve, strain over a fine colander and discard seeds. Combine remaining blackberries and blackberry syrup, butter, both sugars, and cornstarch. Cook over medium heat 5 minutes. Stir in brandy. Set aside.

Preheat oven to 350°.

Remove dough from refrigerator, roll out, reserve a third of dough, and line a pie plate. Bake 15 minutes.

Remove piecrust from oven and fill with blackberry mixture. Roll out remaining dough and cut into strips. Arrange strips, lattice fashion, across top of pie. Sprinkle with 1 teaspoon sugar. Bake 50 minutes. Serve hot or cold. SERVES 4–6.

Soufflé Omelette with Grand Marnier

Literally made in minutes — as opposed to its classic cousin, the soufflé, that takes a good half hour to rise and cook — this version tastes as good as, if not better than, its noble relative. This fast version of the Soufflé Grand Marnier also has the added virtue of being foolproof.

I remember as a young girl in Paris admiring my best friend's mother who would often produce this delectable and fluffy dessert for us while telling an animated story, as though the preparation were automatic. At the time it seemed a true miracle to me.

All that is required, I soon learned, is mixing the yolks with some sugar, and a spoonful or more of Grand Marnier (my friend's mother used blackberry jam instead for us girls), and folding it into beaten-stiff egg whites. Cooking it over a medium flame a few minutes — only one side, folding it over, and serving it. *Voilà!*

4 egg yolks
4 tablespoons sugar, plus extra for sprinkling
1 teaspoon flour
2 ounces Grand Marnier
4 egg whites, beaten stiff
2 tablespoons butter

In a bowl, beat yolks with sugar until creamy. Add flour and Grand Marnier. Fold in egg whites.

In a frying pan, over medium heat, melt butter. Pour in batter and reduce heat to low. Cook 8 minutes without disturbing it, on one side only. With a spatula, lift a corner to make sure bottom has slightly caramelized and formed a kind of light crust. It should remain wet and fluffy on top. Turn off heat. With the spatula, fold omelette over in half. Don't worry if it seems to be running. That's the way it should be, and that is what makes it taste so good. Slide omelette onto serving platter. Sprinkle with sugar. Serves 4–6.

Poached Peaches with Lemon Verbena

Not everyone has access to fresh lemon verbena. If you do, however, this preparation is truly worthwhile.

> 6 peaches, peeled and quartered
> 1 cup white wine
> ½ cup sugar
> 2 tablespoons vanilla extract
> ½ cup lemon verbena leaves

Put quartered peaches in a dessert bowl.

In a small kettle, bring wine, sugar, and vanilla to a boil. Add verbena leaves. (Keep one or two leaves for decoration.) Reduce heat and simmer 15-20 minutes until mixture turns syrupy. Drop peaches into verbena syrup, cover, and let stand until cool. Remove verbena leaves and refrigerate.

Serve chilled, decorated with remaining verbena leaves.

Tip: You can also add 3 tablespoons of jam of your choice in the middle of the omelette, before you fold it over.

Dacquoise

This sumptuous meringue-almond layered cake goes back in time to the royal tables of Europe. The caramelized almonds — the *pralin* — contribute greatly to elevating this exquisite confection into a very special dessert. I make my *dacquoise* rarely, but each time I do, I am reminded how gratifying it is to prepare this festive pastry.

FOR THE CARAMELIZED ALMONDS
> ⅔ cup sugar
> 2 cups whole blanched almonds, finely ground in the
> food processor

In a skillet, over medium heat, melt ⅔ cup sugar and add ground almonds. Stir until mixture becomes amber color. Keep stirring as it cools so it doesn't harden into one solid sheet. Set aside.

FOR THE MERINGUE
> 5 egg whites, beaten stiff
> ½ cup sugar

Preheat oven to 200°.

Fold 5 tablespoons caramelized almonds into beaten egg whites.

Cover 2 baking sheets with parchment paper and trace 2 8-inch circles on each sheet. (If you have egg whites left over, put some parchment paper on an additional sheet and fill in same manner.) With a spatula, fill each circle with beaten egg/almond, flattening each top to form 4 even-sized rounds. Bake 1½ hours. Cool.

FOR THE FROSTING
> 4 egg yolks
> 5 tablespoons sugar
> 1 cup unsalted butter, softened at room temperature
> remaining caramelized almonds, reserving 2 tablespoons
> 1 tablespoon vanilla extract
> 1 tablespoon coffee

In a bowl, whisk yolks with 5 tablespoons sugar until creamy. Transfer to saucepan, and, over low heat, continue whisking until it forms a custard. Cool. Stir in vanilla and coffee.

Stir softened butter into cooled egg custard along with half of the remaining caramelized almonds and combine well to form a smooth frosting.

Carefully lift meringue rounds off parchment paper and place first round on cake platter. With a spatula, spread frosting on meringue round and proceed in the same manner for each round until layered cake is complete. Cover top of last round and sides with remaining frosting. Sprinkle remaining caramelized almonds over and on sides of cake. SERVES 8–10.

Note: If you are serving your dacquoise the same day, there is no need to refrigerate it — the frosting should remain soft. If you prepare it ahead, refrigerate, but remove from refrigerator several hours prior to serving dessert.

MENU

The following pages contain a few sample menus to help you plan your dinners with dishes and elements I feel go well together. All are menus I have served over the years, but I stress they are only suggestions. Mixing and matching your own favorite dishes will provide their own rewards.

1

Basket of Young Fresh Vegetables with
an Anchovy Cream (Anchoiade)

Gigot of Monkfish

Carrots Provençal

Apricot Tart

2

Artichoke Hearts Braised
in White Wine

Roast Chicken
with 40 Caramelized Garlic Cloves

Watercress Salad

Strawberry Soup with Raspberries

3

Beet Gazpacho

Salmon on a Bed of Smoked-Eggplant

Caviar with a Julienne of Cucumber

Endive Salad

Chocolate and Strawberry Napoleon

4

Cream of Artichokes, Cold

Greek Roasted Lamb Stuffed with Baby
Spinach, Dill, and Feta Cheese

Boston Lettuce with Lemon Vinaigrette
and Chives

Broiled Pineapple Slices with Brown Sugar

5

Grand Pot-au-Feu
with Warm Marrow Brioches

Cold Little Grapefruit Soufflés

6

Slowly Roasted Tomatoes

Daube of Venison

Arugula Salad with Orange Slices and
Red Onion in a Lemon Vinaigrette

Bananas Flambées

7

Gwen's Caviar Soup

Rack of Lamb

Zucchini Alfredo Topped
with Onion Rings

Watercress Salad

Lemon Tart

8

Cream of Watercress Soup, Cold,
with Caviar

Marinated Grilled Rabbit
in a Mustard Sauce

Boston Lettuce with Lemon Vinaigrette
and Chives

Raspberry Tart

9

Zucchini Carpaccio

Roast Squab with Olives

Baby Spinach Salad with Croutons

Cantaloupe with Beaume de Venise
or Any Other Dessert Wine
of Your Choice

10

Dandelion Salad
with New Potatoes and Bacon

Spanish Tiger Shrimp with Cream,
Lemon, Chili, and Pappardelle

Poached Pears in Wine Sauce with
Pear Wafers Dipped in Chocolate

II

Scallop Kabob with Beet Hummus

Trout with Sorrel

Nathalie's Mint and Dill Salad
with Mesclun

Fruit Salad

I2

Le Grand Aioli

Grilled Sea Bass with Fennel and Herbs

Apricot Crumble

I3

Broiled Asparagus
with Shiitake Mushrooms

Turkish Lamb Dumplings
with a Yogurt Sauce

Almond Tart with Strawberries

I4

Black-Olive Tart

Roasted Cornish Game Hens
with Fresh Figs

Chicory Salad
"Petits Pots" of
Chocolate-Mocha Mousse

I5

Shrimp and White Beans
in a Rosemary and Thyme Vinaigrette
with Lemon and Shallot Gremolata

Eggplant Cutlets Milanese
with a Yogurt Sauce

Arugula with Orange Slices and Red Onion
in a Lemon Vinaigrette

Rhubarb Tart

Use these pages to create your own menus and jot them down here so that you can remember them when planning your own meals. As I mentioned earlier, mixing and matching your own favorite dishes will provide their own rewards.

1

_____
_____
_____
_____
_____

2

_____
_____
_____
_____
_____

3

_____
_____
_____
_____

4

_____
_____
_____
_____

5

6

7

8

9

10

INDEX

A

Almonds
  Almond Lace Cookies, 222
  Almond Tart with Strawberries, 200
  Dacquoise, 236–37
  Floating Islands, 206–7
  Italian Pear Tart, An 231
  Moroccan Lamb Meat Balls with Prunes and Almonds, 120–21
  Napoleon of Almond Wafers with Raspberries, 217
  Sicilian Salad of Lemon and Artichoke, 67
  Sinful, Flourless, Almond Chocolate Cake, 204–5
  White Gazpacho with Almonds and Grapes, 20–21
Amazing Lemon Macaroon Torte, 202–3
Anchovies
  Antipasto of Red Peppers and Anchovies, 17
  Basket of Young Fresh Vegetables with an Anchovy Cream (Anchoiade), 2–3
  Casserole of Red Peppers Stuffed with Anchovies, 180
  Gratin of Fresh Cod with Spinach and Anchovies, 86–87
  Green Sauce, 14–15
  Purée of White Beans with Anchovies, 177
Angel Hair with Trout Caviar, 101
Antipasto, 78
Antipasto of Red Peppers and Anchovies, 17
Appetizers. See First courses
Apples
  Apple Tart, 210–11
  Apples in a Hood, 233
  Chutney, 26–27
  Fruit Salad, 226
  Platter of Sliced Fresh Fruit with a Chocolate Sauce, 228–29
Apricots
  Apricot Crumble, 195

Apricot Tart, 201
Artichokes
  Artichoke Hearts Braised in White Wine, 44
  Baked, Stuffed Artichokes, 45
  Cream of Artichokes, Cold, 33
  Lamb Stew, Avignon Style, 151
  Lemon and Artichoke Risotto, 119
  Moussaka of Artichoke and Veal, 137–38
  Provençal Gâteau of Vegetables and Eggs, 38–39
  Ragout of Artichokes, 42
  Sicilian Salad of Lemon and Artichoke, 67
  Terrine of Artichoke with Tarragon and Chives, 52–53
Arugula
  Arugula with Orange Slices and Red Onion, in a Lemon Vinaigrette, 188
  Pear, Arugula, Blue Cheese, and Walnut Vinaigrette, 59
  Zucchini Carpaccio, 53
Asparagus
  Broiled Asparagus with Shiitake Mushrooms, 54
  Gratin of Swiss Chard and Asparagus, 178–79
  Roasted Mediterranean Vegetables, 171
  Very Green Plate of French Green Beans and Asparagus with Fresh Herbs, A, 54–55
Avocadoes
  Carpaccio of Beets, 56–57
  Tuna Tartare with a Différence, 16

B

Baby Bell Peppers Stuffed with Feta and Olives, 50–51
Baby Spinach Salad with Croutons, 186–87
Bacon
  Chicory with Warm Goat Cheese and Bacon, 63
  Dandelion Salad with New Potatoes and Bacon, 47
Baked, Stuffed Artichokes, 45

Bananas
    Bananas Flambées, 193
    Fruit Salad, 226
Basket of Young Fresh Vegetables with an Anchovy Cream
        (Anchoiade), 2–3
Beans
    Cassoulet, 126–29
    Greek Purée of Lima Beans with Garlic and Olive Oil, 39
    Purée of White Beans with Anchovies, 177
    Shrimp and White Beans in a Rosemary and Thyme
        Vinaigrette, with Lemon and Shallot Gremolata, 4–5
    Soupe au Pistou, 112–13
    Very Green Plate of French Green Beans and Asparagus with
        Fresh Herbs, A, 54–55
Beef
    Grand Pot-au-Feu with Warm Marrow Brioches, 141–43
    Individual Beef Wellingtons, 162–63
Beets
    Beet and Orange Salad, 50
    Beet Gazpacho, 21
    Beet Tartare, 62
    Carpaccio of Beets, 56–57
    Endive, Watercress, and Beet Salad, 189
    Red Beet and Leek Mimosa, 48
    Scallop Kabob with Beet Hummus, 12–13
Beggar's Purses of Stuffed Chicken, 140–41
Black-Olive Tart, 46–47
Blackberries
    Blackberry Tart, 234
    Bleu, Blanc, Rouge Tart, 226–27
    Panna Cotta with Sliced Peaches and Blackberry Coulis,
        212–13
Bleu, Blanc, Rouge Tart, 226–27
Blue cheese. *See* Cheese
Blueberries
    Blueberry Crumble, 203

Platter of Sliced Fresh Fruit with a Chocolate Sauce,
        228–29
Boston Lettuce with Lemon Vinaigrette and Chives, 188
Bouillabaisse, 104–7
Braised Endives, 167
Braised Fennel, 179
Broccoli rabe
    Polenta Squares with Sautéed Swiss Chard, Broccoli Rabe,
        and Pancetta, 156–57
Broccoli with a Zing, 172
Broiled Asparagus with Shiitake Mushrooms, 54
Broiled Chicken with Rosemary and Lemon, 156
Broiled Duck Breasts with Grilled Peaches, 131
Broiled Fresh Figs with Honey, 230
Broiled Pineapple Slices with Brown Sugar, 193
Broiled Trout, 87
Butters, herbed, 69

C

Cabbage
    Salmon in Cabbage Purses on a Bed of Roasted Vegetables,
        98–99
Cakes
    Amazing Lemon Macaroon Torte, 202–3
    Dacquoise, 236–37
    Lemon Cake with Amaretto Cream and Strawberries and
        Raspberries, 215
    Sinful, Flourless, Almond Chocolate Cake, 204–5
    Tarte Tropézienne, 198–99
Cantaloupe
    Cantaloupe with Beaume de Venise or any Other Dessert
        Wine of Your Choice, 196
    Watermelon, Cantaloupe, and Honeydew with Ginger, 206
Cappuccino of Squash and Porcini, 22

Carp roe
    Taramasalata, 12
Carpaccio of Beets, 56–57
Carrots
    Carrots Provençal, 173
    Ragout of Baby Carrot, Green Peas, Snap Peas, Leek, and
        Tiny Potato, 43
Casserole of Eggplant, Tomato, and Chickpeas, Tunisian Style,
    181
Casserole of Red Peppers Stuffed with Anchovies, 180
Casserole of Zucchini and Tomatoes, 172–73
Cassoulet, 126–29
Cauliflower
    French-Greek Cold Dumplings of Cauliflower Mousse in a
        Feta Cheese and Herb Sauce, 58–59
Caviar
    Angel Hair with Trout Caviar, 101
    Cream of Watercress Soup, Cold, with Caviar, 30
    Eggplant Caviar, 37
    Gwen's Caviar Soup, 23
    Nathalie's Salmon on a Bed of Smoked-Eggplant Caviar with
        a Julienne of Cucumber, 81–83
Celeriac
    Fabulous *Purée Blanche* (Mashed Celeriac, Turnip, Garlic,
        Onion, and Potato), The, 175
Cèpes, Mushroom, and Potato Ragout, 185
Cheese
    Antipasto, 78
    Baby Bell Peppers Stuffed with Feta and Olives, 50–51
    Chicory with Warm Goat Cheese and Bacon, 63
    Endive, Toasted Walnuts, and Roquefort Salad, 61
    Fennel Soup with Goat-Cheese Toasts, 34–35
    French-Greek Cold Dumplings of Cauliflower Mousse in a
        Feta Cheese and Herb Sauce, 58–59
    Greek Roasted Lamb Stuffed with Baby Spinach, Dill, and
        Feta Cheese, 138–39

Middle Eastern Salad of Tomato, Black Olives, Cucumber,
        and Feta Cheese, 68
    Pear, Arugula, Blue Cheese, and Walnut Vinaigrette, 59
Cherries
    Cherry *Clafoutis,* 209
    Sour Cherry Compote, 227
Chervil
    Cream of Chervil, Cold, 34
Chicken
    Broiled Chicken with Rosemary and Lemon, 156
    Chicken Bouillabaisse, 124–25
    Chicken Tagine with Preserved Lemons and Olives, 122
    Coq au Vin, 166–67
    Couscous of Lamb and Chicken, 145
    Gâteau of Marinated Chicken in Aspic, 74–75
    Molded Egyptian Baked Rice Stuffed with Chicken and
        Mushrooms with a Turkish Walnut Sauce, 148–49
    Beggar's Purses of Stuffed Chicken, 140–41
    Roast Chicken in "Mourning Clothes"—with Truffle,
        134–35
    Roast Chicken with 40 Caramelized Garlic Cloves, 133
    Roast Chicken with 50 Garlic Cloves, 134
Chicken livers
    Mickey's Mousse of Chicken Livers, 72
    Pâté de Campagne, 75–77
Chickpeas
    Casserole of Eggplant, Tomato, and Chickpeas, Tunisian
        Style, 181
Chicory
    Chicory Salad, 187
    Chicory Salad with Roasted Shallots and Walnuts, 190
    Chicory with Two Salmons, Shrimp, and Mussels, 9
    Chicory with Warm Goat Cheese and Bacon, 63
Chilled Cream of Green Pea Soup, 19
Chocolate
    Chocolate and Strawberry Napoleon, 194

"Petit Pots" of Chocolate-Mocha Mousse, 230

Platter of Sliced Fresh Fruit with a Chocolate Sauce, 228–29

Poached Pears in Wine Sauce with Pear Wafers Dipped in Chocolate, 216–17

Sinful, Flourless, Almond Chocolate Cake, 204–5

Chutney, 26–27

Clams

Bouillabaisse, 104–7

Spaghetti with Clams, 81

Cod

Bouillabaisse, 104–7

Cod Purée with Garlic and Truffles, 108–9

Grand Aioli, Le, 102–3

Gratin of Cod with Leek, Olives, and Truffle (optional), 93

Gratin of Fresh Cod with Spinach and Anchovies, 86–87

Cold Greek Cucumber Soup, 32–33

Cold Lime Soufflés, 225

Cold Little Grapefruit Soufflés, 208

Condiments

Chutney, 26–27

Harissa, 146

Cookies, Almond Lace, 222

Coq au Vin, 166–67

Cornish Game Hens with Fresh Figs, Roasted, 150

Couscous of Lamb and Chicken, 145

Cream of Artichokes, Cold, 33

Cream of Chervil, Cold, 34

Cream of Parsnip Soup with Truffles, Hot, 35

Cream of Sorrel Soup, 24

Cream of Watercress Soup, Cold, with Caviar, 30

Cream of Yellow Pepper Soup, Cold, 31

Cucumbers

Cold Greek Cucumber Soup, 32–33

Cucumber in Yogurt, 40

Gazpacho, 18–19

Middle Eastern Salad of Tomato, Black Olives, Cucumber, and Feta Cheese, 68

Nathalie's Salmon on a Bed of Smoked-Eggplant Caviar with a Julienne of Cucumber, 81–83

D

Dacquoise, 236–37

Dandelion Salad with New Potatoes and Bacon, 47

Daube of Venison, 158–59

Desserts

See also Cakes; Tarts

Almond Lace Cookies, 222

Apples in a Hood, 233

Apricot Crumble, 195

Bananas Flambées, 193

Blueberry Crumble, 203

Broiled Fresh Figs with Honey, 230

Broiled Pineapple Slices with Brown Sugar, 193

Cantaloupe with Beaume de Venise or any Other Dessert Wine of Your Choice, 196

Cherry *Clafoutis,* 209

Chocolate and Strawberry Napoleon, 194

Cold Lime Soufflés, 225

Cold Little Grapefruit Soufflés, 208

Floating Islands, 206–7

Fruit Salad, 226

Grape *Clafoutis* (Custard with Grapes), 232

Grapefruit Sorbet, 222

Gratin of Baked Raspberries, 228

Gratin of Peaches, 229

Napoleon of Almond Wafers with Raspberries, 217

Orange Slices in a Red Wine, 213

Panna Cotta with Sliced Peaches and Blackberry Coulis, 212–13

Desserts *(continued)*

"Petit Pots" of Chocolate-Mocha Mousse, 230

Platter of Sliced Fresh Fruit with a Chocolate Sauce, 228–29

Plum Compote and Plum Sorbet, 219

Plum Compote with a Meringue Topping, 232–33

Plum Tatin, 214

Poached Peaches with Lemon Verbena, 236

Poached Pears in Wine Sauce with Pear Wafers Dipped in Chocolate, 216–17

Rhubarb and Strawberry Soup with White Peaches, 198

Roasted Peaches with Verbena, 192

Soufflé Omelette with Grand Marnier, 235

Sour Cherry Compote, 227

Strawberry Soup with Raspberries, 211

Vacherin of Meringue with Raspberries, 224

Watermelon, Cantaloupe, and Honeydew with Ginger, 206

Dill Salad with Mesclun, Nathalie's Mint and, 187

Dinner parties, xxii

Dips

Scallop Kabob with Beet Hummus, 12–13

Taramasalata, 12

Duck

Broiled Duck Breasts with Grilled Peaches, 131

Cassoulet, 126–29

Duck Confit, 164

E

Eggplant

Casserole of Eggplant, Tomato, and Chickpeas, Tunisian Style, 181

Eggplant Caviar, 37

Eggplant Cutlets Milanese with a Yogurt Sauce, 116–17

Eggplant Fritters, 182

Eggplant Roulades, 114–15

Gâteau of Eggplant, 40–41

Halibut in a Crown of Stuffed and Baked Vegetables, 84–85

Moussaka, 136–37

Nathalie's Salmon on a Bed of Smoked-Eggplant Caviar with a Julienne of Cucumber, 81–83

Provençal Gâteau of Vegetables and Eggs, 38–39

Roasted Mediterranean Vegetables, 171

Terrine of Ratatouille, 60–61

Eggs

Provençal Garlic and Sage Consommé with a Float of Poached Egg, 25

Provençal Gâteau of Vegetables and Eggs, 38–39

Soufflé Omelette with Grand Marnier, 235

Tunisian Briks with Salmon, Capers, and Egg, 10–11

Egyptian Green Herb Soup, 32

Endives

Braised Endives, 167

Endive Salad, 189

Endive, Toasted Walnuts, and Roquefort Salad, 61

Endive, Watercress, and Beet Salad, 189

F

Fabulous *Purée Blanche* (Mashed Celeriac, Turnip, Garlic, Onion, and Potato), The 175

Fennel

Braised Fennel, 179

Fennel Salad with Roasted Walnuts in a Lemon Vinaigrette, 70

Fennel Soup with Goat-Cheese Toasts, 34–35

Grilled Sea Bass with Fennel and Herbs, 103

Feta Cheese. *See* Cheese

Figs
    Broiled Fresh Figs with Honey, 230
    Greek Pork Loin in a Dried Figs Sauce, 123
    Roasted Cornish Game Hens with Fresh Figs, 150
Fillets of Salmon, à la Bourguignonne, 92
Fillets of Skate in an Oyster Emulsion, on a Bed of Spinach,
    96–97
First courses
    See also Salads; Soups
    Antipasto, 78
    Antipasto of Red Peppers and Anchovies, 17
    Artichoke Hearts Braised in White Wine, 44
    Baby Bell Peppers Stuffed with Feta and Olives, 50–51
    Baked, Stuffed Artichokes, 45
    Basket of Young Fresh Vegetables with an Anchovy Cream
        (*Anchoiade*), 2–3
    Beet Tartare, 62
    Black-Olive Tart, 46–47
    Broiled Asparagus with Shiitake Mushrooms, 54
    Carpaccio of Beets, 56–57
    Chicory with Two Salmons, Shrimp, and Mussels, 9
    Cucumber in Yogurt, 40
    Eggplant Caviar, 37
    French-Greek Cold Dumplings of Cauliflower Mousse in a
        Feta Cheese and Herb Sauce, 58–59
    Gâteau of Eggplant, 40–41
    Gâteau of Marinated Chicken in Aspic, 74–75
    Greek Purée of Lima Beans with Garlic and Olive Oil, 39
    Little Round Zucchini Stuffed with a Tomato-Basil Granita,
        66–67
    Mickey's Mousse of Chicken Livers, 72
    Pâté de Campagne, 75–77
    Pita Crackers, 51
    Provençal Gâteau of Vegetables and Eggs, 38–39
    Quenelles of Pike or Shrimp, 5–8

Radishes Served Mickey's Way, 68–69
Ragout of Artichokes, 42
Ragout of Baby Carrot, Green Peas, Snap Peas, Leek, and
    Tiny Potato, 43
Rillettes, 73
Scallop Kabob with Beet Hummus, 12–13
Shrimp and White Beans in a Rosemary and Thyme
    Vinaigrette, with Lemon and Shallot Gremolata, 4–5
Slowly Roasted Tomatoes, 36–37
Stuffed Zucchini Blossoms with Red-Pepper Coulis, 64–65
Taramasalata, 12
Terrine of Artichoke with Tarragon and Chives, 52–53
Terrine of Monkfish with Green Sauce, 14–15
Terrine of Ratatouille, 60–61
Tuna Tartare with a *Différence,* 16
Tunisian Briks with Salmon, Capers, and Egg, 10–11
Very Green Plate of French Green Beans and Asparagus with
    Fresh Herbs, A, 54–55
Zucchini Carpaccio, 53
Fish
    See also Seafood
    anchovies
        Antipasto of Red Peppers and Anchovies, 17
        Casserole of Red Peppers Stuffed with Anchovies, 180
        Gratin of Fresh Cod with Spinach and Anchovies, 86–87
        Purée of White Beans with Anchovies, 177
    carp roe
        Taramasalata, 12
    caviar
        Angel Hair with Trout Caviar, 101
        Cream of Watercress Soup, Cold, with Caviar, 30
        Gwen's Caviar Soup, 23
    cod
        Cod Purée with Garlic and Truffles, 108–9
        Grand Aioli, Le, 102–3

Fish *(continued)*

Gratin of Cod with Leek, Olives, and Truffle (optional), 93

Gratin of Fresh Cod with Spinach and Anchovies, 86–87

Halibut in a Crown of Stuffed and Baked Vegetables, 84–85

health effects of, xx

monkfish

Gigot of Monkfish, 94

Terrine of Monkfish with Green Sauce, 14–15

pike

Quenelles of Pike or Shrimp, 5–8

salmon

Chicory with Two Salmons, Shrimp, and Mussels, 9

Fillets of Salmon, à la Bourguignonne, 92

Nathalie's Salmon on a Bed of Smoked-Eggplant Caviar with a Julienne of Cucumber, 81–83

Salmon and Olive Tart, 91

Salmon in Cabbage Purses on a Bed of Roasted Vegetables, 98–99

Salmon with Onion Confit, Spanish Style, 95

Tunisian Briks with Salmon, Capers, and Egg, 10–11

Sea Bass with Fennel and Herbs, Grilled, 103

Skate in an Oyster Emulsion, on a Bed of Spinach, Fillets of, 96–97

Snapper with Chili and Garlic, Grilled, 97

trout

Angel Hair with Trout Caviar, 101

Broiled Trout, 87

Trout with Sorrel, 90

Tuna Tartare with a *Différence,* 16

Floating Islands, 206–7

French-Greek Cold Dumplings of Cauliflower Mousse in a Feta Cheese and Herb Sauce, 58–59

Fruits

See also specific types

Fruit Salad, 226

Platter of Sliced Fresh Fruit with a Chocolate Sauce, 228–29

G

Galette of Potatoes and Wild Mushrooms, 111

Garlic

Fabulous *Purée Blanche* (Mashed Celeriac, Turnip, Garlic, Onion, and Potato), The, 175

Garlic and Mint Yoghurt Sauce, 170

Grand Aioli, Le, 102-3

Roast Chicken with 40 Caramelized Garlic Cloves, 133

Roast Chicken with 50 Garlic Cloves, 134

Gâteau of Eggplant, 40–41

Gâteau of Marinated Chicken in Aspic, 74–75

Gazpacho, 18–19

Beet Gazpacho, 21

White Gazpacho with Almonds and Grapes, 20–21

Gigot of Monkfish, 94

Goat cheese. *See* Cheese

Grand Aioli, Le, 102-3

Grand Pot-au-Feu with Warm Marrow Brioches, 141–43

Granita, Tomato-Basil, 66

Grapefruit

Cold Little Grapefruit Soufflés, 208

Grapefruit Sorbet, 222

Grapes

Fruit Salad, 226

Grape *Clafoutis* (Custard with Grapes), 232

White Gazpacho with Almonds and Grapes, 20–21

Gratin of Baked Raspberries, 228

Gratin of Cod with Leek, Olives, and Truffle (optional), 93

Gratin of Fresh Cod with Spinach and Anchovies, 86–87

Gratin of Peaches, 229

Gratin of Swiss Chard and Asparagus, 178–79

Greek Pork Loin in a Dried Figs Sauce, 123

Greek Purée of Lima Beans with Garlic and Olive Oil, 39

Greek Roasted Lamb Stuffed with Baby Spinach, Dill, and Feta Cheese, 138–39

Green beans. *See* Beans

Grilled Sea Bass with Fennel and Herbs, 103

Grilled Snapper with Chili and Garlic, 97

Gwen's Caviar Soup, 23

H

Halibut in a Crown of Stuffed and Baked Vegetables, 84–85

Ham

    Pâté de Campagne, 75–77

Harissa, 146

I

Individual Beef Wellingtons, 162–63

Italian Pear Tart, An, 231

Italian Salad of Chicory, Arugula, Radicchio, Lemon, and Capers, 71

Italian Slow-Roasted Pork Shoulder, An, 160–61

J

Jill's Cold Zucchini Soup with Chutney, 26–27

L

Lamb

    Cassoulet, 126–29

Couscous of Lamb and Chicken, 146–47

Greek Roasted Lamb Stuffed with Baby Spinach, Dill, and Feta Cheese, 138–39

Lamb Stew, Avignon Style, 151

Moroccan Lamb Meat Balls with Prunes and Almonds, 120–21

Moussaka, 136–37

Rack of Lamb, 144

Roast Leg of Lamb Provençal with Pastis-Pernod Flambé, 132–33

Turkish Lamb Dumplings with a Yogurt Sauce, 152–53

Leeks

    Gratin of Cod with Leek, Olives, and Truffle (optional), 93

    Leek and Potato Soup, 28

    Leek Tart, 110

    Ragout of Baby Carrot, Green Peas, Snap Peas, Leek, and Tiny Potato, 43

    Red Beet and Leek Mimosa, 48

Lemons

    Amazing Lemon Macaroon Torte, 202–3

    Lemon and Artichoke Risotto, 119

    Lemon Cake with Amaretto Cream and Strawberries and Raspberries, 215

    Lemon Tart, 220–21

    Poached Peaches with Lemon Verbena, 236

Lima beans. *See* Beans

Lime Soufflés, Cold, 225

Little Round Zucchini Stuffed with a Tomato-Basil Granita, 66–67

M

Main courses

    beef

        Grand Pot-au-Feu with Warm Marrow Brioches, 141–43

Main courses *(continued)*

    Individual Beef Wellingtons, 162–63

chicken

    Broiled Chicken with Rosemary and Lemon, 156

    Chicken Bouillabaisse, 124–25

    Chicken Tagine with Preserved Lemons and Olives, 122

    Coq au Vin, 166–67

    Couscous of Lamb and Chicken, 146–47

    Molded Egyptian Baked Rice Stuffed with Chicken and
        Mushrooms with a Turkish Walnut Sauce, 148–49

    Beggar's Purses of Stuffed Chicken, 140–41

    Roast Chicken in "Mourning Clothes"—with Truffle,
        134–35

    Roast Chicken with 40 Caramelized Garlic Cloves, 133

    Roast Chicken with 50 Garlic Cloves, 134

duck

    Broiled Duck Breasts with Grilled Peaches, 131

    Cassoulet, 126–29

    Duck Confit, 164

lamb

    Couscous of Lamb and Chicken, 146–47

    Greek Roasted Lamb Stuffed with Baby Spinach, Dill,
        and Feta Cheese, 138–39

    Lamb Stew, Avignon Style, 151

    Moroccan Lamb Meat Balls with Prunes and Almonds,
        120–21

    Moussaka, 136–37

    Rack of Lamb, 144

    Roast Leg of Lamb Provençal with Pastis-Pernod Flambé,
        132–33

    Turkish Lamb Dumplings with a Yogurt Sauce, 152–53

meatless

    Eggplant Cutlets Milanese with a Yogurt Sauce, 116–17

    Eggplant Roulades, 114–15

    Galette of Potatoes and Wild Mushrooms, 111

    Leek Tart, 110

    Lemon and Artichoke Risotto, 119

    Morel and Truffle Tart, 118–19

    Polenta Squares with Sautéed Swiss Chard, Broccoli
        Rabe, and Pancetta, 156–57

    Roast Portobello Mushrooms with Gremolata, 112

    Soupe au Pistou, 112–13

pork

    Greek Pork Loin in a Dried Figs Sauce, 123

    Italian Slow-Roasted Pork Shoulder, An, 160–61

    Pork Tonnato, 165

    Stuffed Crown Roast of Pork, 154–55

poultry

    Roast Squab with Olives, 135

    Roasted Cornish Game Hens with Fresh Figs, 150

rabbit

    Marinated Grilled Rabbit in a Mustard Sauce, 130–31

seafood

    Angel Hair with Trout Caviar, 101

    Bouillabaisse, 104–7

    Broiled Trout, 87

    Cod Purée with Garlic and Truffles, 108–9

    Fillets of Salmon, à la Bourguignonne, 92

    Fillets of Skate in an Oyster Emulsion, on a Bed of
        Spinach, 96–97

    Gigot of Monkfish, 94

    Grand Aioli, Le, 102–3

    Gratin of Cod with Leek, Olives, and Truffle (optional),
        93

    Gratin of Fresh Cod with Spinach and Anchovies,
        86–87

    Grilled Sea Bass with Fennel and Herbs, 103

    Grilled Snapper with Chili and Garlic, 97

    Halibut in a Crown of Stuffed and Baked Vegetables,
        84–85

    Nathalie's Salmon on a Bed of Smoked-Eggplant Caviar
        with a Julienne of Cucumber, 81–83

Salmon and Olive Tart, 91

Salmon in Cabbage Purses on a Bed of Roasted
Vegetables, 98–99

Salmon with Onion Confit, Spanish Style, 95

Shrimp in a Piperade Sauce, Basque Style, 80

Shrimp, Spanish Style, on a Griddle, 79

Spaghetti with Clams, 81

Spanish Tiger Shrimp with Cream, Lemon, Chili, and
Pappardelle, 100

Stuffed Squid, 88–89

Tiger Shrimp with Feta and Tomato, 99

Trout with Sorrel, 90

veal

Moussaka of Artichoke and Veal, 137–38

venison

Daube of Venison, 158–59

Marinated Grilled Rabbit in a Mustard Sauce, 130–31

Meals, enjoying, xxi–xxii

Meat. *See* Beef; Lamb; Pork

Mediterranean diet, xvi, xvii–xx

Melons

Cantaloupe with Beaume de Venise or Any Other Dessert
Wine of Your Choice, 196

Watermelon, Cantaloupe, and Honeydew with Ginger, 206

Menus, 239–41

Mickey's Mousse of Chicken Livers, 72

Middle Eastern Salad of Tomato, Black Olives, Cucumber, and
Feta Cheese, 68

Mint and Dill Salad with Mesclun, Nathalie's, 187

Molded Egyptian Baked Rice Stuffed with Chicken and
Mushrooms with a Turkish Walnut Sauce, 148–49

Monkfish

Bouillabaisse, 104–7

Gigot of Monkfish, 94

Terrine of Monkfish with Green Sauce, 14–15

Morel and Truffle Tart, 118–19

Moroccan Lamb Meat Balls with Prunes and Almonds,
120–21

Moussaka, 136–37

Moussaka of Artichoke and Veal, 137–38

Mushrooms

Beggar's Purses of Stuffed Chicken, 140–41

Broiled Asparagus with Shiitake Mushrooms, 54

Cappuccino of Squash and Porcini, 22

Cèpes, Mushroom, and Potato Ragout, 185

Galette of Potatoes and Wild Mushrooms, 111

Individual Beef Wellingtons, 162–63

Molded Egyptian Baked Rice Stuffed with Chicken and
Mushrooms with a Turkish Walnut Sauce, 148–49

Morel and Truffle Tart, 118–19

Mushroom Flan, 183

Roast Portobello Mushrooms with Gremolata, 112

Mussels

Bouillabaisse, 104–7

Chicory with Two Salmons, Shrimp, and Mussels, 9

Nantua sauce, 7

Napoleon of Almond Wafers with Raspberries, 217

Nathalie's Mint and Dill Salad with Mesclun, 187

Nathalie's Salmon on a Bed of Smoked-Eggplant Caviar with a
Julienne of Cucumber, 81–83

Olive oil, xxi

Olives

Baby Bell Peppers Stuffed with Feta and Olives, 50–51

Black-Olive Tart, 46–47

Olives *(continued)*

    Chicken Tagine with Preserved Lemons and Olives, 122

    Gratin of Cod with Leek, Olives, and Truffle (optional), 93

    Middle Eastern Salad of Tomato, Black Olives, Cucumber, and Feta Cheese, 68

    Oranges and Black-Olive Salad, Moroccan Style, 70

    Roast Squab with Olives, 135

    Salmon and Olive Tart, 91

Onions

    Fabulous *Purée Blanche* (Mashed Celeriac, Turnip, Garlic, Onion, and Potato), The, 175

    Salmon with Onion Confit, Spanish Style, 95

    Zucchini Alfredo Topped with Onion Rings, 168–69

Oranges

    Arugula with Orange Slices and Red Onion, in a Lemon Vinaigrette, 188

    Beet and Orange Salad, 50

    Orange Slices in a Red Wine, 213

    Oranges and Black-Olive Salad, Moroccan Style, 70

Oysters

    Fillets of Skate in an Oyster Emulsion, on a Bed of Spinach, 96–97

P

Pancetta

    Polenta Squares with Sautéed Swiss Chard, Broccoli Rabe, and Pancetta, 156–57

Panna Cotta with Sliced Peaches and Blackberry Coulis, 212–13

Parsnips

    Cream of Parsnip Soup with Truffles, Hot, 35

Pasta

    Angel Hair with Trout Caviar, 101

    Spaghetti with Clams, 81

Pâté de Campagne, 75–77

Peaches

    Broiled Duck Breasts with Grilled Peaches, 131

    Fruit Salad, 226

    Gratin of Peaches, 229

    Panna Cotta with Sliced Peaches and Blackberry Coulis, 212–13

    Poached Peaches with Lemon Verbena, 236

    Rhubarb and Strawberry Soup with White Peaches, 198

    Roasted Peaches with Verbena, 192

Pears

    Fruit Salad, 226

    Italian Pear Tart, An, 231

    Pear, Arugula, Blue Cheese, and Walnut Vinaigrette, 59

    Platter of Sliced Fresh Fruit with a Chocolate Sauce, 228–29

    Poached Pears in Wine Sauce with Pear Wafers Dipped in Chocolate, 216–17

Peas

    Chilled Cream of Green Pea Soup, 19

    Ragout of Baby Carrot, Green Peas, Snap Peas, Leek, and Tiny Potato, 43

Peppers

    Antipasto of Red Peppers and Anchovies, 17

    Baby Bell Peppers Stuffed with Feta and Olives, 50–51

    Casserole of Red Peppers Stuffed with Anchovies, 180

    Cream of Yellow Pepper Soup, Cold, 31

    Gazpacho, 18–19

    Provençal Gâteau of Vegetables and Eggs, 38–39

    Roasted Mediterranean Vegetables, 171

    Stuffed Zucchini Blossoms with Red-Pepper Coulis, 64–65

    Terrine of Ratatouille, 60–61

    White Gazpacho with Almonds and Grapes, 20–21

"Petit Pots" of Chocolate-Mocha Mousse, 230

Piecrusts, 46, 110, 197, 210, 220–21, 234

Pike, Quenelles of, 5–8

Pineapples

Broiled Pineapple Slices with Brown Sugar, 193

Platter of Sliced Fresh Fruit with a Chocolate Sauce, 228–29

Pita Crackers, 51

Platter of Sliced Fresh Fruit with a Chocolate Sauce, 228–29

Plums

Fruit Salad, 226

Plum Compote and Plum Sorbet, 219

Plum Compote with a Meringue Topping, 232–33

Plum Tatin, 214

Poached Peaches with Lemon Verbena, 236

Poached Pears in Wine Sauce with Pear Wafers Dipped in Chocolate, 216–17

Polenta Squares with Sautéed Swiss Chard, Broccoli Rabe, and Pancetta, 156–57

Porcini, Cappuccino of Squash and, 22

Pork

Cassoulet, 126–29

Greek Pork Loin in a Dried Figs Sauce, 123

Italian Slow-Roasted Pork Shoulder, An, 160–61

Pâté de Campagne, 75–77

Pork Tonnato, 165

Rillettes, 73

Stuffed Crown Roast of Pork, 154–55

Potatoes

Cèpes, Mushroom, and Potato Ragout, 185

Dandelion Salad with New Potatoes and Bacon, 47

Fabulous Purée Blanche (Mashed Celeriac, Turnip, Garlic, Onion, and Potato), The, 175

Fillets of Salmon, à la Bourguignonne, 92

Galette of Potatoes and Wild Mushrooms, 111

Leek and Potato Soup, 28

Ragout of Baby Carrot, Green Peas, Snap Peas, Leek, and Tiny Potato, 43

Poultry

See also Chicken

Broiled Duck Breasts with Grilled Peaches, 131

Cassoulet, 126–29

Duck Confit, 164

Roast Squab with Olives, 135

Roasted Cornish Game Hens with Fresh Figs, 150

Provençal Garlic and Sage Consommé with a Float of Poached Egg, 25

Provençal Gâteau of Vegetables and Eggs, 38–39

Purée of White Beans with Anchovies, 177

Q

Quenelles of Pike or Shrimp, 5–8

R

Rabbit in a Mustard Sauce, Marinated Grilled, 130–31

Rack of Lamb, 144

Radicchio

Roasted Mediterranean Vegetables, 171

Roasted Radicchio, 176

Radishes

Radish Vinaigrette, 49

Radishes Served Mickey's Way, 68–69

Ragout d'Agneau à la mode d'Avignon, 151

Ragout of Artichokes, 42

Ragout of Baby Carrot, Green Peas, Snap Peas, Leek, and Tiny Potato, 43

Raspberries

Bleu, Blanc, Rouge Tart, 226–27

Floating Islands, 206–7

Fruit Salad, 226

Raspberries *(continued)*

    Gratin of Baked Raspberries, 228

    Lemon Cake with Amaretto Cream and Strawberries and Raspberries, 215

    Napoleon of Almond Wafers with Raspberries, 217

    Raspberry Tart, 218

    Raspberry Tart with Vanilla Custard, 197

    Strawberry Soup with Raspberries, 211

    Vacherin of Meringue with Raspberries, 224

Red Beet and Leek Mimosa, 48

Red peppers

    Antipasto of Red Peppers and Anchovies, 17

    Casserole of Red Peppers Stuffed with Anchovies, 180

    Red-Pepper Coulis, 40–41

    Stuffed Zucchini Blossoms with Red-Pepper Coulis, 64–65

Rhubarb

    Rhubarb and Strawberry Soup with White Peaches, 198

    Rhubarb Tart, 223

Rice

    Lemon and Artichoke Risotto, 119

    Molded Egyptian Baked Rice Stuffed with Chicken and Mushrooms with a Turkish Walnut Sauce, 148–49

Rillettes, 73

Risotto, Lemon and Artichoke, 119

Roast Chicken in "Mourning Clothes"—with Truffle, 134–35

Roast Chicken with 40 Caramelized Garlic Cloves, 133

Roast Chicken with 50 Garlic Cloves, 134

Roast Leg of Lamb Provençal with Pastis-Pernod Flambé, 132–33

Roast Portobello Mushrooms with Gremolata, 112

Roast Squab with Olives, 135

Roasted Cornish Game Hens with Fresh Figs, 150

Roasted Mediterranean Vegetables, 171

Roasted Peaches with Verbena, 192

Roasted Radicchio, 176

S

Salads

    Arugula with Orange Slices and Red Onion, in a Lemon Vinaigrette, 188

    Baby Spinach Salad with Croutons, 186–87

    Beet and Orange Salad, 50

    Boston Lettuce with Lemon Vinaigrette and Chives, 188

    Chicory Salad, 187

    Chicory Salad with Roasted Shallots and Walnuts, 190

    Chicory with Warm Goat Cheese and Bacon, 63

    Dandelion Salad with New Potatoes and Bacon, 47

    Endive Salad, 189

    Endive, Toasted Walnuts, and Roquefort Salad, 61

    Endive, Watercress, and Beet Salad, 189

    Fennel Salad with Roasted Walnuts in a Lemon Vinaigrette, 70

    Fruit Salad, 226

    Italian Salad of Chicory, Arugula, Radicchio, Lemon, and Capers, 71

    Middle Eastern Salad of Tomato, Black Olives, Cucumber, and Feta Cheese, 68

    Nathalie's Mint and Dill Salad with Mesclun, 187

    Oranges and Black-Olive Salad, Moroccan Style, 70

    Pear, Arugula, Blue Cheese, and Walnut Vinaigrette, 59

    Radish Vinaigrette, 49

    Red Beet and Leek Mimosa, 48

    Sicilian Salad of Lemon and Artichoke, 67

    Tomato with Cilantro, 49

    Turkish Tomato Tartare, 57

    Watercress Salad, 190

Salmon

    Chicory with Two Salmons, Shrimp, and Mussels, 9

    Fillets of Salmon, à la Bourguignonne, 92

Nathalie's Salmon on a Bed of Smoked-Eggplant Caviar with a Julienne of Cucumber, 81–83
Salmon and Olive Tart, 91
Salmon in Cabbage Purses on a Bed of Roasted Vegetables, 98–99
Salmon with Onion Confit, Spanish Style, 95
Tunisian Briks with Salmon, Capers, and Egg, 10–11
Sauces
    Garlic and Mint Yogurt Sauce, 170
    Green Sauce, 14–15
    Nantua sauce, 7
    Walnut Sauce, 148
Sausages. *See* Pork
Scallop Kabob with Beet Hummus, 12–13
Sea Bass with Fennel and Herbs, Grilled, 103
Seafood
    See also Fish
    Bouillabaisse, 104–7
    Chicory with Two Salmons, Shrimp, and Mussels, 9
    Clams, Spaghetti with, 81
    Scallop Kabob with Beet Hummus, 12–13
    shrimp
        Bouillabaisse, 104–7
        Chicory with Two Salmons, Shrimp, and Mussels, 9
        Quenelles of Pike or Shrimp, 5–8
        Shrimp and White Beans in a Rosemary and Thyme Vinaigrette, with Lemon and Shallot Gremolata, 4–5
        Shrimp in a Piperade Sauce, Basque Style, 80
        Shrimp, Spanish Style, on a Griddle, 79
        Spanish Tiger Shrimp with Cream, Lemon, Chili, and Pappardelle, 100
        Tiger Shrimp with Feta and Tomato, 99
    Squid, Stuffed, 88–89
Shrimp
    Bouillabaisse, 104–7
    Chicory with Two Salmons, Shrimp, and Mussels, 9

Quenelles of Pike or Shrimp, 5–8
Shrimp and White Beans in a Rosemary and Thyme Vinaigrette, with Lemon and Shallot Gremolata, 4–5
Shrimp in a Piperade Sauce, Basque Style, 80
Shrimp, Spanish Style, on a Griddle, 79
Spanish Tiger Shrimp with Cream, Lemon, Chili, and Pappardelle, 100
Tiger Shrimp with Feta and Tomato, 99
Sicilian Salad of Lemon and Artichoke, 67
Side dishes
    Braised Endives, 167
    Braised Fennel, 179
    Broccoli with a Zing, 172
    Carrots Provençal, 173
    Casserole of Eggplant, Tomato, and Chickpeas, Tunisian Style, 181
    Casserole of Red Peppers Stuffed with Anchovies, 180
    Casserole of Zucchini and Tomatoes, 172–73
    Cèpes, Mushroom, and Potato Ragout, 185
    Eggplant Fritters, 182
    Fabulous *Purée Blanche* (Mashed Celeriac, Turnip, Garlic, Onion, and Potato), The, 175
    Gratin of Swiss Chard and Asparagus, 178–79
    Mushroom Flan, 183
    Purée of White Beans with Anchovies, 177
    Roasted Mediterranean Vegetables, 171
    Roasted Radicchio, 176
    Spinach Dumplings, 184–85
    Spinach, Mediterranean Style, 169
    Swiss Chard Cakes, 174
    Tomato Tart, 178
    Zucchini Alfredo Topped with Onion Rings, 168–69
    Zucchini Cakes, Greek Style, 170
Sinful, Flourless, Almond Chocolate Cake, 204–5
Skate in an Oyster Emulsion, on a Bed of Spinach, Fillets of, 96–97

Slowly Roasted Tomatoes, 36–37
Snapper with Chili and Garlic, Grilled, 97
Sorbet
    Grapefruit Sorbet, 222
    Plum Compote and Plum Sorbet, 219
Sorrel Soup, Cream of, 24
Soufflés
    Cold Lime Soufflés, 225
    Cold Little Grapefruit Soufflés, 208
    Soufflé Omelette with Grand Marnier, 235
Soupe au Pistou, 112–13
Soups
    Beet Gazpacho, 21
    Bouillabaisse, 104–7
    Cappuccino of Squash and Porcini, 22
    Chicken Bouillabaisse, 124–25
    Chilled Cream of Green Pea Soup, 19
    Cold Greek Cucumber Soup, 32–33
    Cream of Artichokes, Cold, 33
    Cream of Chervil, Cold, 34
    Cream of Parsnip Soup with Truffles, Hot, 35
    Cream of Sorrel Soup, 24
    Cream of Watercress Soup, Cold, with Caviar, 30
    Cream of Yellow Pepper Soup, Cold, 31
    Egyptian Green Herb Soup, 32
    Fennel Soup with Goat-Cheese Toasts, 34–35
    Gazpacho, 18–19
    Gwen's Caviar Soup, 23
    Jill's Cold Zucchini Soup with Chutney, 26–27
    Leek and Potato Soup, 28
    Provençal Garlic and Sage Consommé with a Float of
        Poached Egg, 25
    Rhubarb and Strawberry Soup with White Peaches,
        198
    Soupe au Pistou, 112–13

Strawberry Soup with Raspberries, 211
Tomato Soup with Puff Pastry, 29
White Gazpacho with Almonds and Grapes, 20–21
Sour Cherry Compote, 227
Spaghetti with Clams, 81
Spanish Tiger Shrimp with Cream, Lemon, Chili, and
        Pappardelle, 100
Spinach
    Baby Spinach Salad with Croutons, 186–87
    Egyptian Green Herb Soup, 32
    Fillets of Skate in an Oyster Emulsion, on a Bed of Spinach,
        96–97
    Gratin of Fresh Cod with Spinach and Anchovies,
        86–87
    Greek Roasted Lamb Stuffed with Baby Spinach, Dill, and
        Feta Cheese, 138–39
    Green Sauce, 14–15
    Spinach Dumplings, 184–85
    Spinach, Mediterranean Style, 169
Squab with Olives, Roast, 135
Squash
    Cappuccino of Squash and Porcini, 22
    Zucchini Carpaccio, 53
Squid, Stuffed, 88–89
Strawberries
    Almond Tart with Strawberries, 200
    Chocolate and Strawberry Napoleon, 194
    Lemon Cake with Amaretto Cream and Strawberries and
        Raspberries, 215
    Platter of Sliced Fresh Fruit with a Chocolate Sauce,
        228–29
    Rhubarb and Strawberry Soup with White Peaches, 198
    Strawberry Soup with Raspberries, 211
Stuffed Crown Roast of Pork, 154–55
Stuffed Squid, 88–89

Stuffed Zucchini Blossoms with Red-Pepper Coulis, 64–65
Swiss chard
    Gratin of Swiss Chard and Asparagus, 178–79
    Swiss Chard Cakes, 174

T

Taramasalata, 12
Tarts
    Almond Tart with Strawberries, 200
    Apple Tart, 210–11
    Apricot Tart, 201
    Black-Olive Tart, 46–47
    Blackberry Tart, 234
    Bleu, Blanc, Rouge Tart, 226–27
    Italian Pear Tart, An, 231
    Leek Tart, 110
    Lemon Tart, 220–21
    Morel and Truffle Tart, 118–19
    Raspberry Tart, 218
    Raspberry Tart with Vanilla Custard, 197
    Rhubarb Tart, 223
    Salmon and Olive Tart, 91
    Tomato Tart, 178
Terrine of Artichoke with Tarragon and Chives, 52–53
Terrine of Monkfish with Green Sauce, 14–15
Terrine of Ratatouille, 60–61
Tiger Shrimp with Feta and Tomato, 99
Tomatoes
    Casserole of Eggplant, Tomato, and Chickpeas, Tunisian
        Style, 181
    Casserole of Zucchini and Tomatoes, 172–73
    Gazpacho, 18–19
    Little Round Zucchini Stuffed with a Tomato-Basil Granita,
        66–67

    Middle Eastern Salad of Tomato, Black Olives, Cucumber,
        and Feta Cheese, 68
    Roasted Mediterranean Vegetables, 171
    Slowly Roasted Tomatoes, 36–37
    Terrine of Ratatouille, 60–61
    Tiger Shrimp with Feta and Tomato, 99
    Tomato-Basil Granita, 66
    Tomato Soup with Puff Pastry, 29
    Tomato Tart, 178
    Tomato with Cilantro, 49
    Turkish Tomato Tartare, 57
    White Gazpacho with Almonds and Grapes, 20–21
Torte, Amazing Lemon Macaroon, 202
Trout
    Angel Hair with Trout Caviar, 101
    Broiled Trout, 87
    Trout with Sorrel, 90
Truffles
    Cod Purée with Garlic and Truffles, 108–9
    Cream of Parsnip Soup with Truffles, Hot, 35
    Gratin of Cod with Leek, Olives, and Truffle (optional), 93
    Morel and Truffle Tart, 118–19
    Roast Chicken in "Mourning Clothes"—with Truffle, 134–35
Tuna Tartare with a *Différence,* 16
Tunisian Briks with Salmon, Capers, and Egg, 10–11
Turkish Lamb Dumplings with a Yogurt Sauce, 152–53
Turkish Tomato Tartare, 57
Turnip
    Fabulous *Purée Blanche* (Mashed Celeriac, Turnip, Garlic,
        Onion, and Potato), The, 175

V

Vacherin of Meringue with Raspberries, 224
Veal, Moussaka of Artichoke and, 137–38

Vegetables
See also specific types
Basket of Young Fresh Vegetables with an Anchovy Cream (*Anchoiade*), 2–3
Fabulous *Purée Blanche* (Mashed Celeriac, Turnip, Garlic, Onion, and Potato), The, 175
Grand Aioli, Le, 102–3
Grand Pot-au-Feu with Warm Marrow Brioches, 141–43
Halibut in a Crown of Stuffed and Baked Vegetables, 84–85
Provençal Gâteau of Vegetables and Eggs, 38–39
Ragout of Baby Carrot, Green Peas, Snap Peas, Leek, and Tiny Potato, 43
Roasted Mediterranean Vegetables, 171
Salmon in Cabbage Purses on a Bed of Roasted Vegetables, 98–99
Soupe au Pistou, 112–13
Venison, Daube of, 158–59
Very Green Plate of French Green Beans and Asparagus with Fresh Herbs, A, 54–55

W

Walnuts
Chicory Salad with Roasted Shallots and Walnuts, 190
Endive, Toasted Walnuts, and Roquefort Salad, 61
Fennel Salad with Roasted Walnuts in a Lemon Vinaigrette, 70
Molded Egyptian Baked Rice Stuffed with Chicken and Mushrooms with a Turkish Walnut Sauce, 148–49
Pear, Arugula, Blue Cheese, and Walnut Vinaigrette, 59
Watercress
Cream of Watercress Soup, Cold, with Caviar, 30
Endive, Watercress, and Beet Salad, 189
Watercress Salad, 190

Watermelon, Cantaloupe, and Honeydew with Ginger, 206
White beans. *See* Beans
White Gazpacho with Almonds and Grapes, 20–21
Wine consumption, xxi

Y

Yogurt
Cold Greek Cucumber Soup, 32–33
Cucumber in Yogurt, 40
Eggplant Cutlets Milanese with a Yogurt Sauce, 116–17
Garlic and Mint Yogurt Sauce, 170
Turkish Lamb Dumplings with a Yogurt Sauce, 152–53

Z

Zucchini
Casserole of Zucchini and Tomatoes, 172–73
Halibut in a Crown of Stuffed and Baked Vegetables, 84–85
Jill's Cold Zucchini Soup with Chutney, 26–27
Little Round Zucchini Stuffed with a Tomato-Basil Granita, 66–67
Roasted Mediterranean Vegetables, 171
Stuffed Zucchini Blossoms with Red-Pepper Coulis, 64–65
Terrine of Ratatouille, 60–61
Zucchini Alfredo Topped with Onion Rings, 168–69
Zucchini Cakes, Greek Style, 170
Zucchini Carpaccio, 53

raspberry tart

Chutney Chutney

Olive Oil

herbes de provence